San Juan County, Utah:

People, Resources, and History

Edited and with an introduction by
Allan Kent Powell

Utah State Historical Society
1983

Contents

Preface

    This volume on San Juan County history is published for the benefit of four groups: the residents of the county with the hope they might come to know their heritage and themselves better through these pages; the visitor to the county who wishes not only to enjoy the magnificient scenic wonders of southeastern Utah but also to learn of the people and their struggles to gain and maintain a foothold in this vast land; those whose interest in Utah and western history draws them to seek an understanding of the development of the Four Corners region and its relationship to other areas; and San Juan County's schoolchildren, that they might have a supplemental volume on their own region for use as they study Utah and American history.

    This volume grew out of the efforts of a number of people. In 1981 a proposal was submitted to the Utah Endowment for the Humanities for a lecture series similiar to previously held series in Emery and Carbon counties. The Utah Endowment for the Humanities awarded funds for an eight-part lecture series by historians and comments by local residents. Under the able and enthusiastic direction of project director Janet Wilcox, lectures were held in Blanding, Monticello, White Mesa, and Montezuma Creek during the spring and fall of 1982. The local response was warm and encouraging, so she and Sunny Redd approached the San Juan County Commission about providing funds for publication of the lectures and comments. Convinced that the book would be of great value to the citizens of the county, the commissioners encouraged the Utah State Historical Society to proceed with editorial work and in December 1982 allocated funds in the county's 1983 budget for publication costs.

Introduction

For several centuries Utah sat on the fringe of penetration by Spanish explorers and traders pushing north out of New Mexico. In the sixteenth century Cortes, Coronado, and other Spanish conquistadores heard Indian accounts of the fabulous lands of Lake Copala and El Gran Teguayo to the north, which historians identify as in the vicinity of Utah Lake and the Great Salt Lake. During the sixteenth and seventeenth centuries plans were formulated and expeditions launched to find these "mysterious kingdoms of the north." Apparently, some came close to their objective. Brigham Young University history professor Ted J. Warner writes that documents in the Spanish archives of New Mexico, National Archives in Mexico City, and the archives in Seville, Spain, contain ". . . numerous suggestions . . . that Spaniards on authorized as well as unauthorized expeditions penetrated southern Utah before 1776."[1]

One of these expeditions about which information has recently come to light is the 1765 trip of Juan Maria Antonio Rivera and four others who, according to historian Donald C. Cutter, ". . . became the first known white men to enter Utah when they crossed the line somewhere northeast of Monticello [in San Juan County] probably on October 6, 1765."[2] Passing through Dry Valley, across the base of the La Sal Mountains, and traveling down Spanish Valley, the group left San Juan County and traveled on a few miles past present Moab to the Colorado River, their intended goal. Here, before returning to New Mexico, they left a large cross on the meadow of the river, establishing Spain's claim to the region.

Eleven years later, in 1776, the Dominguez-Escalante expedition left Santa Fe to make contact with the natives to the

1

northwest and to open an overland route from Santa Fe to the Spanish settlements in California. On the first leg of its journey, the small group led by the Franciscan fathers skirted to the east of San Juan County as it passed by present Dove Creek, Colorado. Later, after abandoning the westward journey to California in favor of returning to New Mexico, the group crossed the Colorado River at the Crossing of the Fathers, touching the extreme southwest corner of San Juan County before entering present Arizona.

After the Spanish Trail was opened between Santa Fe and Los Angeles, the 1,200-mile route became the main corridor through the Southwest between 1830 and 1848. This famous trail, as it left Santa Fe, entered Utah and San Juan County near Ucolo, two miles south of Piute Spring, an often used campsite. Following a northwesterly course toward the Colorado River crossing at Moab, the route passed through Dry Valley paralleling present Highway 163 past Looking Glass Rock, thence to La Sal Junction, and on to Cane Springs Canyon which, with its bounteous supply of water, made it an important stopping place on the trail. Following a steep narrow trail out of Cane Springs Canyon to the top of Blue Hill, the trail gradually descended through Spanish Valley toward the Colorado River.

The Spanish explorers, missionaries, traders, trappers, and horse dealers, whose ephemeral tracks of a hundred and fifty years ago have long since disappeared, were followed by Anglo explorers beginning with the William Huntington expedition in 1854. Huntington took wagons from the Mormon settlements across the Spanish Trail as far as the head of Spanish Valley in San Juan County. After abandoning the wagons the group continued south, reaching the Hovenweep ruins near the present Colorado border before returning home. The following year saw the establishment of the Elk Mountain Mission at the strategic crossing of the Colorado River which Rivera had visited many years earlier. Though the mission lasted only three months because of Indian hostilities, the mission leader, Alfred Billings, took a few men and explored south across Dry Valley and around the eastern side of the Blue Mountains to Comb Wash which they followed to the San Juan River. From this point they pushed forty miles further south to a settlement of Navajos with whom they traded. They then returned to the newly constructed rock fort near the Colorado River, which they abandoned a few days later.

Further Mormon exploring ventures in San Juan County were marked by an interlude of twenty-five years until 1879 when Silas S. Smith led an expedition to locate a route and settlement site for the San Juan Mission. This Mormon exploring hiatus in southeastern Utah did not mean the region was forgotten. Between 1859 and 1880 a number of federal government explorers penetrated the area.

The first of these was Captain John N. Macomb of the United States Army Corps of Topographical Engineers. As chief topographical engineer in New Mexico, Macomb was instructed to find the best route between Santa Fe and the Mormon settlements in southern Utah, determine the course of the San Juan River, and locate the confluence of the Green and Colorado rivers. Accompanied by John Strong Newberry, considered America's foremost geologist, Macomb and his men followed the Spanish Trail into San Juan County where their explorations took them near the La Sal Mountains, to the overlook of the confluence of the Green and Colorado rivers, then back across Peter's Hill and the east slope of the Blue Mountains to the San Juan River.

The Civil War interrupted further exploring activities for a decade until John Wesley Powell made his historic voyages down the Green and Colorado rivers in 1869 and 1871. Members of the Ferdinand V. Hayden Survey made a reconnaissance trip into San Juan County in 1875. Led by James L. Gardner and Henry Gannett, the group surveyed the La Sal Mountains before crossing Dry Valley to conduct a similiar reconnaissance of the Blue Mountains. Their plans were cut short when an Indian attack forced them to abandon their records and scientific equipment as they fled eastward into

Colorado. In the following year, 1876, parties from the Hayden survey returned to San Juan County to make a cursory examination of the Blue Mountains and the San Juan River drainage.

The line between exploration and settlement of the San Juan region was crossed in 1879 as Mormons launched a major colonizing effort under the direction of Silas S. Smith to gain control of southeastern Utah. The San Juan Mission came in the twilight of a far-reaching and ambitious western colonization effort launched by the Mormon church following their exodus from Nauvoo, Illinois, in 1846 and the establishment of Salt Lake City in 1847. A brief review of the settlement of Utah communities reveals several interesting patterns and offers a context for understanding the significance of the San Juan settlement achievement.

By the end of 1847, two communities, Bountiful and Farmington, were established a few miles north of Salt Lake City, and in 1848, following the purchase of Fort Buenaventura from Miles Goodyear, Mormons moved into Weber Valley with the establishment of Ogden. The following year, 1849, witnessed the move west to adjoining Tooele Valley and south to Utah Valley with the establishment of Provo and, at the end of 1849, further south into Sanpete Valley with the establishment of an outpost at Manti 120 miles from Salt Lake City. The year 1850 saw further activity in Utah Valley with settlements at Lehi, Springville, and Payson. In Weber Valley, Harrisville was settled north of Ogden. The years from 1851 to 1856 witnessed the greatest activity as the settlements of Nephi, Fillmore, Beaver, Parowan, and Washington were established in southern Utah as part of a Mormon corridor to the Pacific Ocean. To the north, Brigham City was settled in 1851 and a foothold in Cache Valley made at Wellsville in 1856. The settlement of Sanpete Valley was strengthened with the founding of Ephraim and Mount Pleasant in 1852, while an abortive attempt was made in 1855 by Elk Mountain missionaries to push east from the Sanpete Valley to the Colorado River.

The Utah War brought an interlude in the settlement process from 1857 until 1859 when the only new areas opened were in the valleys just east of Salt Lake City and Ogden at Heber City, Coalville, Morgan, and Huntsville. New settlements were also made at Logan and Providence in Cache Valley and Moroni and Gunnison in Sanpete Valley. In 1860 Deseret was established in Millard County in west central Utah, and the promise and need of a western cotton industry led to the founding of St. George in 1861 near Washington in southwestern Utah.

The Sevier Valley, south of Sanpete Valley, was settled in 1863 as the pressure for land by the older communities of Manti, Ephraim, and Mount Pleasant led to the new settlements of Salina, Richfield, and Monroe. Further south from Sevier Valley, along present-day U.S. Highway 89, the settlements of Panguitch and Kanab were made in 1864.

For the next thirteen years there was relatively little activity in Utah's colonization saga. In northern Utah, Lewiston was established at the north end of Cache Valley in 1870 and the same year Randolph in Rich County near the Wyoming border. Escalante, which was the last settlement the San Juan pioneers passed as they pushed toward the east, was founded in 1875. Seventy miles east of Panguitch, Escalante marked the direction Mormon settlement efforts would take during the next decade.

The death of Brigham Young in 1877 briefly delayed the march eastward, but the period from 1876 to 1880 saw the Mormon occupation of the vast Colorado Plateau. Perhaps in no other time since the pioneer arrival in 1847 had so much territory come under Mormon domination. This occupation stretched from the Uinta Mountains on the north to the Little Colorado River in Arizona on the south and from the rim of the Great Basin eastward toward the Rocky Mountains. It included the present-day areas of the Uinta Basin with Vernal established in 1878; Castle Valley with Price, Huntington, Castle Dale, and Ferron settled in 1877; the Moab area resettled in 1880; San Juan County with the settlement of Bluff in

1880; Bicknell in Wayne County in 1882; and the area around Snowflake, Arizona, beginning in 1876. Other areas would be settled later, but none on a scale or with the same sense of mission as that of the Colorado Plateau and specifically San Juan County.

The Mormon foothold at Bluff was very tenuous, especially as Indian relations bordered on open hostility, the San Juan River proved unmanageable for irrigation purposes, the shortage of good farm land limited the size of the community, and Texas cattlemen saw the Hole-in-the-Rockers as a distinct challenge to their use of the extensive and lush range land in the county. Suggestions were made that Mormon church authorities release the Bluff settlers from their mission call and allow them to settle in a more favorable locality. After a visit by President Joseph F. Smith and Apostle Erastus Snow, those who wanted to leave were permitted to do so; however, for those willing to remain in the face of dire circumstances, the church leaders promised they would be "doubly blessed of the Lord."[3]

Fortunes did take a turn for the better after the arrival of Francis Hammond in 1885 to assume duties as San Juan Stake president. Under Hammond, the Mormons abandoned their futile farming efforts and gave their full energies to raising livestock. In time the Mormon cattlemen, in an unusual alliance with drought and low market prices, wore down the non-Mormon cattlemen and by the early 1890s controlled San Juan County's livestock industry. At the same time a new opportunity opened with sheep, and most San Juan County livestock men acquired large herds of them. This change from agriculture to livestock meant the abandonment — for San Juan County at least — of Brigham Young's home industry-self-sufficiency economic philosophy in favor of an export economy dependent on national markets.

The Mormon entry into the San Juan livestock industry on a large scale was coupled by a successful effort to establish communities at strategic locations along the access routes to the mountain grazing lands. Consequently, Monticello was established on North Montezuma Creek and Verdure on South Montezuma Creek in 1887. A third settlement on White Mesa was also planned for 1887. However, since the anticipated influx of Mormons into San Juan County did not materialize, the plan was delayed until the establishment of Blanding in 1905 under the direction of Walter C. Lyman, a member of the original San Juan Mission who became stake president in 1902.

Since the 1900 census, when San Juan County registered a population of 1,023, the growth rate has been fairly even at about a thousand new people each decade, except for the 1920s when the population remained at 3,500 and the 1950s when the population nearly doubled from 5,300 to over 9,000 people. Another significant growth was registered between 1970 and 1980 when the number zoomed from 9,600 to 13,000.

Both periods of unprecedented growth, the 1950s and 1970s, were the result of uranium and oil booms. It is expected that in the future the county will continue to roller coaster its way through the boom-bust national and international cycles, while tourism and recreation will continue to become more and more important in the county's economy. Blessed with an array of national parks, national monuments, national recreation areas, national forests, primitive areas, and state parks, San Juan County draws a large number of in-state and national tourists as well as an ever-increasing number of international visitors.

The essays and comments that follow focus on specific themes and subjects in San Juan County's history. Though not a comprehensive history of the county, they offer many new insights and bring together in one volume a sense of San Juan County's heritage through an examination of the major forces and issues that have molded and shaped the promising, but challenging, destiny of southeastern Utah.

In the first section on the prehistoric peoples of the San Juan area, Winston Hurst, a native of San Juan County and an expert on southwestern archaeology with special emphasis on early ceramics, outlines, in terms of time span, the first 98 percent of the region's history. He reviews the three major prehistoric groups who made their homes in the San Juan region: the Paleo-Indians, the Archaic cultures, and the Anasazi — all of whom predate the historic Indians. He observes that although archaeologists have been able to sketch in the broad outlines of these prehistoric cultures, the study has just begun. Unfortunately, some of the answers to the important questions about these early people may have been lost already because of inept past archaeological efforts or unscientific collecting and looting of significant sites. Robert Hosler, speaking for many of the San Juan County citizens who have developed a keen interest in the area's prehistoric residents, calls for the establishment of a local depository for reports, artifacts, and information about the early inhabitants. Convinced that interested local amateurs and outside professional archaeologists have for too long been jealous and suspicious of each other, although they share common interests and concerns, Hosler summons a new alliance among those interested in San Juan County's prehistory.

Part two reviews the historic Indian groups of San Juan County. Gregory C. Thompson, assistant director of libraries and head of special collections for the University of Utah's Marriott Library, outlines the history of the Utes, Paiutes, and Navajos from 1700 to the present. He finds that each group had a highly developed economic system and that they demonstrated strong resistance to the non-Indian intruders into the area between 1870 and 1923. The Indians of San Juan County are somewhat unique in American history because they have remained in their homeland without being forced to move to another location as was the fate of so many American Indian tribes. In the early 1890s San Juan County's Indians and their supporters were nearly successful in having the entire county declared an Indian reservation. Clyde J. Benally, in his review of the Navajo experience in the Southwest, gives us an insider's glimpse into Navajo history and life as he touches on the communal concept of property; the

Navajo family; Navajo government; chants, rites, mythical figures, ceremonies, and medicine men; sheep raising; silversmithing; weaving; hogans; the importance of the trading post; and other facets of his people and culture.

By 1880 San Juan County's native inhabitants faced an important challenge as Mormon settlers, blasting and hacking their way over the Hole-in-the-Rock trail, came from the settlements of southwestern Utah to control and Christianize the Indians while snatching the San Juan region from non-Mormons who had begun to view the area with keen interest. The third essay looks at the uniqueness of the Hole-in-the-Rock trail, as it stretches nearly two hundred miles from Escalante in Garfield County to Bluff. The trail, listed in the National Register of Historic Places, is remarkable because of the conviction and struggle that marked the effort to construct a road across one of the most rugged and isolated sections of the United States. The essay, "The Hole-in-the-Rock a Century Later," documents how much of this unique resource still remains and recalls the story of the 250 individuals who made the memorable trek during the winter and early spring of 1879-80. The essay is followed by comments from Lynn Lyman, a son of Walter C. Lyman — one of the original members of the Hole-in-the-Rock expedition. He (Lynn) was a member of the first party to retrace the route of the Hole-in-the-Rock expedition in 1940. Since then he has carefully examined and studied the trail and guided numerous expeditions over it in a heroic and successful effort to locate the trail and increase understanding and awareness of its historical importance.

Once the difficult Hole-in-the-Rock journey was completed, San Juan pioneers set about building the community of Bluff and in time looked to the establishment of new communities. Gary Shumway, professor of history at California State University at Fullerton, in a paper presented at the Twenty-seventh Annual Meeting of the Utah State Historical Society in September 1979, recounts the making of Blanding. In this excellent portrait of his home town, Dr. Shumway

sketches the individuals, groups, forces, traditions, myths, obstacles, and accomplishments which shaped the community.
Clarence Rogers, a life-long resident of San Juan County, follows with recollections about the settlement of Blanding, the
construction of the tunnel to bring irrigation water to White
Mesa, adobe making, and several dramatic events in the
county's history.

Part five examines the livestock and agricultural history
of San Juan County. Charles S. Peterson, professor of history
at Utah State University and author of numerous articles and
books on southeastern Utah, sees San Juan County as different
— different because of its unusual geology, large size, remoteness, unique experiences, and heavy emphasis on ranching. In
his essay he tells the story of San Juan's cowboys, cattle barons, sheepherders, and dry farmers, pointing out the conflicts
and adjustments that have colored the agricultural experience
in the county. His review is highlighted by character sketches
of Texas-trained cattlemen, Mormon cowboys, Mexican
sheepherders, and hopeful dry farmers. Most of these men
displayed a spartan-like commitment to their employers or
their own undertakings — a necessary quality as the county's
agricultural fortunes bounced along the narrow tightrope between success and failure. Peterson's observations are given
careful scrutiny by Hardy Redd, a San Juan County rancher
whose family has been involved in livestock since the first
days of the county. Redd emphasizes the staying power of the
Mormon cattlemen in the establishment of a viable agricultural base for San Juan's economy. Preston G. Nielson, also a
San Juan cattleman, provides a perspective on San Juan's agriculture and livestock industry since 1959. He observes that
the expenses of operating a farm or ranch continue to rise
without accompanying increases for goods produced. Nielson
also outlines the significant advances that have been made
during the past twenty-five years with better fertilizer; sprays
for insects, noxious weeds, and plant diseases; methods of irrigation with sprinklers; development of new water sources;
more selective animal breeding; and range rehabilitation.

The development of San Juan roads and the management of county resources is examined in part six. Jay M. Haymond, coordinator for collections and research at the Utah State Historical Society, outlines the development of the San Juan road system from the Hole-in-the-Rock trail to the upgrading of old roads and new road construction during the 1960s. He finds that roads were almost always built or upgraded because of the demand for natural resource development and that federal funds for roads were usually essential to the success of these undertakings. Calvin Black, San Juan County commissioner, follows this essay with a review of his experience with roads and road construction in the county. He then rehearses the difficulties for the county as the assessed valuation of property during the past thirty years has fluctuated radically because of instability in the uranium and oil industry. Commissioner Black outlines the county's push for state legislation to implement a county tax stability program to provide a reserve or trust fund, thereby allowing the county to maintain adequate funding levels without raising the mill levy when the total valuation level drops. Kenneth Bailey, also a member of the San Juan County Commission, follows with a statement of similar concerns and a demonstration of the extent, in terms of dollars, of the fluctuation in assessed valuation. He then traces the tremendous growth in county expenditures for roads.

Part seven looks at San Juan County's uranium industry. Gary L. Shumway, a long-time student of the Colorado Plateau's uranium industry, traces the development of uranium mining in southeastern Utah from the first decade of the twentieth century to the present. Mining was usually unprofitable, often dominated by large companies, and colored by a cadre of impoverished but dedicated prospectors and miners. However, with the development in the early 1950s of the cold war with Russia and the setting of lucrative prices and long-range planning by the Atomic Energy Commission, a uranium boom swept the Colorado Plateau and brought previously unknown wealth to San Juan County. Though the uranium market has fluctuated since the 1950s, Professor Shumway projects a bright long-range outlook as America turns more and more to nuclear power plants. Hanson L. Bayles, in his comments, describes the changes in uranium mining since the boom of the early 1950s, and Don Kemner follows with an account of the changes which the oil boom brought to Montezuma Creek in the late 1950s and early 1960s.

The last section of this volume focuses on education in San Juan County. Jessie L. Embry, director of the Charles Redd Center oral history program at Brigham Young University, draws extensively from an excellent collection of interviews to sketch the difficulty that plagued administrators in finding teachers for San Juan County and to explain how these low-paid, young, and usually unmarried ladies handled their primitive and remote one-room schools. Following this essay Reta Bartell recalls her experiences as a teacher and supervisor. She was responsible for implementing curricula in the public schools during the early 1960s for Indian children who spoke little or no English. The section concludes with comments by Zenos Black, a native of San Juan County, who graduated from the University of Utah in 1930. Black taught school in Idaho for twelve years before he was appointed superintendent of the San Juan School District in 1943, a position he held until 1967. From his perspective as an administrator for twenty-four years, he recounts the problems of teacher recruitment, scarce funding, caring for the widely scattered one-room schools, and supervising teachers with unusual styles and methods; the implementation of an Indian education program; the traditional resistance to consolidation proposals; and the special challenges in meeting the demands of an exploding school population.

Allan Kent Powell

Introduction

NOTES

¹ Richard D. Poll et al., eds., *Utah's History* (Provo, Utah: Brigham Young University Press, 1978), p. 36.

² Donald C. Cutter, "Prelude to Pageant in the Wilderness," *Western Historical Quarterly* 8 (January 1971): 4.

³ Cornelia Adams Perkins, Marian Gardner Nielson, and Lenora Butt Jones, *Saga of San Juan*, 2d ed., (San Juan County: Daughters of Utah Pioneers, 1968), p. 76.

PART ONE

Prehistory

Hovenweep Ruin, Hovenweep National Monument, 1940s. Utah State Historical Society Collections.

The Prehistoric Peoples of San Juan County, Utah

Winston Hurst

There is good reason to believe that San Juan County has been inhabited by humans for at least 11,000 or 12,000 years. Unfortunately, the written history of the area covers only the last 130 years (perhaps 250, if vague references in Spanish and Mexican documents are included), and that represents less than 2 percent of man's sojourn here. The remaining 98 to 99 percent of the human experience in San Juan County is the vast and fascinating domain of prehistory, whose only record consists of the material remains that the prehistoric peoples left behind. This record is accessible through the young science of archaeology.

Archaeology can be defined as the endeavor to understand past human behavior through the study of man's patterned material remains (dwellings, tools, garbage, etc.). Like any science, it seeks first to describe, then to explain. Both stages are absolutely dependent upon detailed and precise documentation — in notes, maps, stratigraphic drawings, photographs, etc. — of the most minute details of the locations and layouts of archaeological sites and the arrangement of artifacts, soil deposits, and features such as fireplaces and storage bins within them. It is this emphasis on documentation, reflecting the primary emphasis on knowledge and understanding, that makes archaeology very different from simple digging for artifacts. Digging solely for artifacts results in a collection of handsome antiques that can be displayed and admired, while causing irreparable disturbance to the depositional structure of the sites being dug. Archaeology does the

17

same but endeavors to preserve the site structure in the form of maps, notes, diagrams, and photos in public archives and published reports, so that the artifacts can be made more meaningful by assignment to a time, a place, and a role in an identified culture. Thus, archaeology does not apply to any

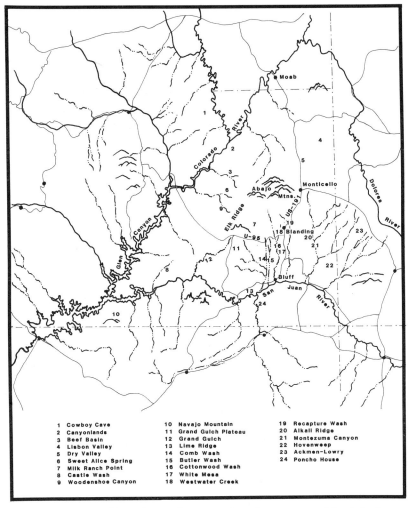

1	Cowboy Cave	10	Navajo Mountain	19	Recapture Wash
2	Canyonlands	11	Grand Gulch Plateau	20	Alkali Ridge
3	Beef Basin	12	Grand Gulch	21	Montezuma Canyon
4	Lisbon Valley	13	Lime Ridge	22	Hovenweep
5	Dry Valley	14	Comb Wash	23	Ackmen-Lowry
6	Sweet Alice Spring	15	Butler Wash	24	Poncho House
7	Milk Ranch Point	16	Cottonwood Wash		
8	Castle Wash	17	White Mesa		
9	Woodenshoe Canyon	18	Westwater Creek		

Figure 1. Map of San Juan County showing geographical features and archaeological sites referred to in the text.

and all overt interest in man's material leavings but rather is restricted in its scope to include only that which has as its primary objective the accumulation of documented information.

In 1879, when the Indians apprehensively watched the Mormons blast through the Hole-in-the-Rock en route to settlement at Bluff, there was little knowledge of the area's earlier cultures. There were no books describing the peoples who had built and abandoned the thousands of ruined stone houses in the country, or the origins of the Utes, Paiutes, and Navajos who still occupied the area. Now, after a century of archaeological research, we have pushed the frontiers of our knowledge back beyond 11,000 years ago and are able to sketch in the bold outlines and many of the details of man's sojourn here prior to his first recorded history.

The following discussion is intended to provide only a basic outline of San Juan County's prehistory. Those interested in pursuing the subject in greater depth and detail would find a convenient starting point in two recent Bureau of Land Management publications: Lloyd M. Pierson's *Cultural Resource Summary of the East Central Portion of Moab District*[1] and Paul R. Nickens's *Contributions to the Prehistory of Southeastern Utah.*[2] Together they provide a useful summary of the history and prehistory of most of San Juan County north of the San Juan River. This presentation is drawn largely from those syntheses.

After decades of careful study of their languages, their ancient settlements, and their cultures, it has become clear that the ancestors of the Utes and Paiutes spread northeastward out of the southwestern Great Basin within the last 1,000 years and likely arrived in southeastern Utah sometime after A.D. 1200 or 1300. Linguistic and archaeological evidence indicates that the Navajos are also relative latecomers. Their earliest well-dated remains are localized in the Gobernador area east of Farmington, New Mexico, dating to the early 1500s.

But who preceeded the Utes/Paiutes and Navajos? Was

the land abandoned and desolate, or was it occupied by another people? When the Utes and Navajos, and later the Euro-Americans, arrived, they found the land covered with the remains of thousands of crumbled stone houses. Neither the Indians nor the whites could tell who had built and lived in these houses, though all groups developed folklore stories, myths, and legends to account for them. Certain features in Navajo and Ute/Paiute stories hint that some of the houses were still inhabited when their people first arrived. By 1880, however, the ruins lay desolate, abandoned, reduced to rubble, their inhabitants forgotten. Who were these people, whom the Utahns call the "Moki" (after the Ute word "Mokwitz" for Hopi) and the archaeologists call the "Anasazi" (after the Navajo word "Anaasazi," meaning alien or enemy ancestor)?

Years of study have revealed that these people were ancestors of the modern Pueblos and that they practiced a farming, village lifeway from the early centuries A.D. until they abandoned the Four Corners area abruptly in the late 1200s. But where did they come from? Did the earliest Anasazi move into the area from another place or evolve locally out of an earlier culture? Recent research traces their roots to the "Archaic" peoples, who practiced a wandering, hunting, and food-gathering life-style in the southeast from about 6000 B.C. until some of them developed into the distinctive Anasazi culture in the first centuries A.D.

But the Archaic peoples were not the first in the area either. They were preceded by a series of hunting and gathering cultures during and immediately following the dying gasps of the last glacial period of the Ice Age. There are also hints of even earlier people in the American West — perhaps many thousands of years earlier — but the evidence for them is weak, spotty, and controversial.

The early big game hunters (Figure 2) have come to be known as "Paleo-Indians," and virtually everything known about them has been learned somewhere outside of San Juan County (mostly in deeply buried campsites and big-game kill

Figure 2. Typical big game species hunted by the Paleo-Indians with human figures for scale. Lower to upper: woolly mammoth, associated with Clovis subculture; giant bison, associated with Folsom subculture; and modern bison, associated with Plains subcultures.

sites in the High Plains east of the Rockies and in the basin and range country of southern Arizona). Like all cultures, that of the Paleo-Indians changed slowly through time. After careful examination of numerous sites, it has become possible to identify a series of Paleo-Indian cultures, each recognizable by its distinctive artifact styles. The remains of each of these cultures tend to be associated with the remains of certain species of game animals, many of them now extinct.

By the tenth millennium B.C. the Paleo-Indians were specializing in the hunting of the woolly mammoth, a hairy form of elephant which stood as high as twelve feet at the shoulder. Their primary hunting implement was a spear, tipped with a distinctive type of stone point whose style is called "Clovis." A thousand years later the mammoth had passed into extinction, and the Paleo-Indians were focusing their efforts on a giant, now extinct, form of bison and using a very handsome style of spear point known as "Folsom." During the eighth and seventh millennia B.C. a series of characteristic spear point styles succeeded one another in popularity, together forming part of what is known as the "Plano complex." Plano complex points, very handsomely flaked and of styles unlike those of later groups, are often found in association with modern large-game species, including the bison.

Although no definite Paleo-Indian sites have been identified in San Juan County, there have been occasional isolated finds of the distinctive Paleo-Indian spear points. Fortunately, several of these finds have been documented and recorded,

Hovenweep Ruin, 1979. Photograph by G. B. Peterson, Photogeographics, Bountiful, Utah, © 1983.

thus making the knowledge of Paleo-Indian occupation here something other than folklore or rumor. Clovis points have been found in the Montezuma Canyon drainage, in Lisbon Valley, and just across the Arizona line on the Navajo Reservation. Folsom points have been found in the Montezuma Canyon drainage, on Lime Ridge near Mexican Hat, at Sweet Alice Spring west of North Elk Ridge, and in the Moab area. Plano complex points have been found in the Moab area, the Hovenweep area, and Comb Wash. Additional Paleo-Indian artifacts have been reported from areas surrounding San Juan County in all directions, and remains of the big game animals hunted by the Paleo-Indian have been reported from San Juan and adjacent counties. A notable example of the latter is a mammoth bone found in Butler Wash, now on display in the Blanding library. It is thus very likely that Paleo-Indian groups were present in what is now San Juan County, and it is probably simply a matter of time before a Paleo-Indian camp or kill site is recognized and, let us hope, properly excavated.

It is difficult to recognize a Paleo-Indian site once the distinctive spear points have been removed. Since the points tend to be relatively large and attractive, it is likely that few have escaped the keen eyes of arrowhead hunters. Perhaps a number of sites now visible only as nondescript chipping debris and generalized stone tools are Paleo-Indian sites whose diagnostic points have been removed to a place of honor in someone's arrowhead display or cigar box.

By 6000 B.C. the moist, cool conditions typical of the late Pleistocene, or Ice Age, had given way to a drier, hotter climate in the Southwest, and many of the large mammal species that had roamed America had passed into extinction. As the Ice Age and its large animals vanished, so also did the Paleo-Indian cultures. By 5000 B.C. the Archaic way of life (Figure 3), with a more generalized tool kit and subsistence base, had entirely replaced the Paleo-Indian cultures. Although the relationship between the two cultural complexes is not clear, there is mounting evidence that an Archaic lifestyle was established in the Great Basin and Far West before

7000 B.C. and that it displaced the Paleo-Indian life-style in the Four Corners states as the Paleo-Indians followed the surviving large herds of big game eastward onto the Great Plains.[3]

For over five millennia, the southwestern cultures evolved slowly within the generalized Archaic lifeway. Much like the Utah Paiutes and Goshutes of the 1800s, the Archaic peoples subsisted on wild foods, migrating from place to place through the course of the year as necessary to take advantage of the shifting availability of different wild foods. Grinding stones ("mano": handstone, and "metate": millingstone) became a basic part of the survival equipment in Archaic times as the people made increasing use of grasses and other small seed foods. Excellent basketry, cordage, and

Figure 3. Artist's conception of an archaic temporary camp.

nets of hair and vegetable fiber assumed an important role. Point styles continued to evolve slowly through time, and it is possible to assign them and their associated sites to gross time periods.[4]

Little is known of Archaic houses, possibly because they were insubstantial brush huts much like Paiute wickiups and similar shelters used by desert, foraging people in other parts of the world. Numerous Archaic sites have been recorded and mapped in San Juan County, and typical Archaic points are commonly represented in private "arrowhead" collections. Very few sites with Archaic components have been excavated in the county, however. The most significant ones that have been excavated are Sand Dune and Dust Devil Caves near Navajo Mountain, excavated by the Museum of Northern Arizona as part of the Glen Canyon Dam project.[5] The University of Utah has excavated another important Archaic site, Cowboy Cave, in Wayne County a few miles outside San Juan County northwest of the confluence of the Green and Colorado rivers.[6]

In late Archaic times, during the last centuries B.C., the people began to supplement their wild food gathering with maize horticulture. By A.D. 200 horticulture had assumed a significant role in the economy, and the late Archaic peoples of San Juan County were settling into the Anasazi lifeway.

The Anasazi inhabited the Four Corners country for the next fifteen centuries, leaving a heavy accumulation of house remains and debris. Because their culture changed continually (and not always gradually) during that time, it is possible to slice up their 1,500-year occupation into periods, each with its characteristic complex of settlement and artifact styles. Since 1927 the most widely accepted nomenclature for the Anasazi sequence has been the "Pecos Classification," which is generally applicable to the whole Anasazi Southwest (northern Arizona, southern Utah, southeastern Colorado, and northwestern New Mexico). Although originally intended to represent a series of developmental stages, rather than periods, the Pecos Classification has come to be used as this period sequence:

Basketmaker I:	pre-A.D. 1 (an obsolete synonym for Archaic)
Basketmaker II:	approx. A.D. 1 to 450
Basketmaker III:	approx. A.D. 450 to 750
Pueblo I:	approx. A.D. 750 to 900
Pueblo II:	approx. A.D. 900 to 1100
Pueblo III:	approx. A.D. 1100 to 1300
Pueblo IV:	approx. A.D. 1300 to 1600
Pueblo V:	approx. A.D. 1600 to present

Pueblo IV and V are absent in the Four Corners country, which was abandoned by the Anasazi at the end of the Pueblo III period. The other periods, as represented in San Juan County, will be described below, following a brief over-view of Anasazi geography.

As the Anasazi settled into their village farming life-style, there emerged a series of recognizable subcultures, each with its own territory. These are outlined in the accompanying map (Figure 4). Note that San Juan County lies largely within the area occupied by the Mesa Verde Anasazi (a misnomer — the cultural heartland seems to be the mesa-canyon country between the foot of the Mesa Verde and Comb Wash), with the southern (south of the San Juan River) and extreme west-ern part of the county joining northern Arizona to form the Kayenta Anasazi culture area. West of the Colorado River, the Kayenta culture grades gradually and imperceptibly into the Virgin Anasazi subculture of southwestern Utah and north-western Arizona. To the north of the Anasazi peoples — north of the Colorado and Escalante rivers — Utah was the home of a heterogeneous group of small-village dwellers known collectively as the Fremont. Since neither the Virgin Anasazi nor the Fremont played a significant role in the pre-history of San Juan County, they will not be discussed here. The following discussion pertains primarily to the Mesa Verde and secondarily to the Kayenta Anasazi.

Although they continued to move around in pursuit of

seasonally available foods, the earliest Anasazi concentrated increasing amounts of effort on the growing of crops and the storage of surpluses. They made exquisite baskets and sandals, for which reason they have come to be known as "Basket-

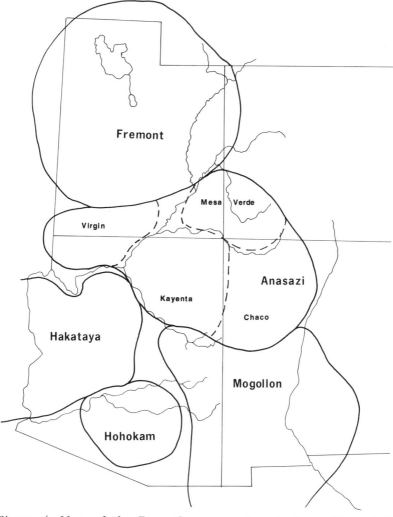

Figure 4. Map of the Four Corners region during mid to late Anasazi times (A.D. 500-1300) showing approximate distribution of cultures and subcultures mentioned in the text.

makers." They stored their goods (and often their dead) in circular cists — small pits often lined with upright stone slabs and roofed over with a platform of poles, twigs, grass, slabs of rock, and mud. Basketmaker II houses were apparently somewhat more sturdy than those of the Archaic, rather like a Paiute winter wickiup or a Navajo hogan. Very few have been excavated. At a very important site near Durango, Colorado, however, a Basketmaker II village was excavated during the 1940s.[7] Houses there were found to consist of a dome of cribbed large sticks or small logs positioned over a shallow dish-shaped floor with a central heating pit and diverse storage pits. The heating pit was not a fireplace but rather a repository for hot rocks heated in a fire outside the house. Other shallow pithouses that may date to early Basketmaker times have been identified around the head of Grand Gulch, in Castle Wash to the west of Grand Gulch, and in the Hovenweep area.[8] Sites of this time period have been excavated in Glen Canyon, near Navajo Mountain, in the Kayenta area in Arizona, and on Castle Wash.[9] Numerous major sites of this period in dry caves were ransacked by collectors in Grand Gulch and Butler Wash during the 1890s, but none was adequately reported.

By A.D. 500 the early Anasazi peoples had settled into the well-developed farming village cultural stage that we know as Basketmaker III (Figure 5). Although they probably practiced some seasonal moving and continued to make considerable use of wild resources, they had become primarily farmers living in small villages. Their houses were well-constructed pithouses, consisting of a hogan-like superstructure built over a shallow pit, often with a small second room or antechamber on the south or southeast side.

Settlements of this time period are scattered widely over the canyons and mesas of San Juan County, in small hamlets of one to three houses, and occasionally in villages of a dozen or more. By about A.D. 700 evidence of the development of politico-religious mechanisms of village organization and integration appears in the form of large, communal pitrooms.

Figure 5. Artist's conception of a typical Basketmaker III pithouse hamlet in the Alkali Ridge area about A.D. 700, looking northward toward the Abajo Mountains and Bears Ears.

One such structure, with a diameter of forty feet, has recently been excavated next to the old highway in Recapture Creek by archaeologists from Brigham Young University.[10]

Three other important changes took place before A.D. 750: the old atlatl, or spear thrower that had been used to propel darts (small spears) from time immemorial, was replaced by the bow and arrow; the bean was added to corn and squash to form a major supplement to the diet; and the people began to make pottery. By A.D. 600 the Anasazi were producing quantities of pottery of two wares: gray utility ware and black-on-white painted ware.

Late Basketmaker settlements have been excavated and described from Milk Ranch Point on Elk Ridge, the Highway U-95 right-of-way west of Comb Wash, the Highway U-191 right-of-way west of Bluff, the Energy Fuels excavations on White Mesa, in the Recapture Reservoir location northeast of Blanding, and from Alkali Ridge and Montezuma Canyon east of Blanding.[11] Others have been identified and documented in surveys for government inventories and in advance of chaining projects, mineral exploration activities, and construction projects. Much of the information on this period in San Juan County derives from conservation-motivated projects mandated by law in advance of public developments.

By A.D. 750 these farming, pottery-making people in their stable villages were on the threshold of the life-style that we think of as being typically Puebloan. From this time on we call them Pueblos.

The period from about A.D. 750 to 900 is called Pueblo I by archaeologists. During this period the Anasazi settled even more comfortably into a village farming life-style. Although the population continued to be scattered widely in small hamlets over the landscape, some very large villages developed. One such village, excavated by Dr. Brew of Harvard University in the 1930s, is located on Alkali Ridge and has over 160 known rooms (Figure 6). Still larger villages of this period are presently being excavated near Dolores, Colorado, in advance of construction of the McPhee Dam and reservoir.

Perhaps the most significant developments in Pueblo I times were: 1) the replacement of pithouse habitations with large living rooms on the surface; 2) the development of a sophisticated ventilator-deflector system for ventilating pitrooms; 3) the growth of the San Juan redware pottery complex; and 4) some major shifts in settlement distribution. Whereas the pithouses had been the dwelling places in Basketmaker times and surface rooms consisted only of relatively small storage cists, some of the surface rooms began to be used for habitation during part or all of the year. The pithouses were excavated deeper, and where the Basketmaker houses had had a secondary small room known as an antechamber, there was later only a chimney-like ventilator shaft. As the heat from the central fireplace rose through a smokehole in the pithouse roof, it drew fresh air through this ventilator shaft into the room where a large deflector slab caused the draft to disperse throughout the room. This system became a standard feature of pit structures in this and

Figure 6. Artist's conception of a large Pueblo village on Alkali Ridge about A.D. 825, looking northwest toward the Bears Ears and the Abajo Mountains.

all later periods of Anasazi culture.

In late Basketmaker times a new pottery technology had appeared in San Juan County, producing very fine, thin-walled, orange-fired pottery with black or red designs, of fine workmanship. During Pueblo I times this pottery was in great demand throughout the Anasazi country and was being exported for hundreds of miles. There is good reason to believe that most, if not all, of this pottery was manufactured in central San Juan County, perhaps between (south) Cottonwood Wash and Montezuma Canyon.[12] The previously mentioned large site on Alkali Ridge appears to have been a manufacturing center for Abajo red-on-orange, a distinctive type of pottery with red designs on an orange background, during early Pueblo I times. The black-on-white decorated pottery became more refined in finish and design during this period, and the culinary grayware jars were frequently embellished by leaving several coils unobliterated just below the mouth.

Some interesting shifts in the distribution of Anasazi settlements occurred during Pueblo I times. Large areas appear to have been abandoned, while others experienced dense populations. In San Juan County the Grand Gulch Plateau had been inhabited by a significant population of Basketmaker peoples but seems to have been abandoned during Pueblo I.[13] At the same time, in the brushy points and foothills of Elk Ridge between 7,000 and 8,000 feet elevation, there is a remarkable density of small Pueblo I sites.[14] It is not yet known whether these small sites were seasonal settlements of specialized function or more permanent base settlements, though they were likely the former. Nor is it known what resources the people were exploiting. It is interesting to note that the sites are concentrated in the transition zone, which is a major ecotone between the Upper Sonoran pinyon-juniper-sage ecological zone and the tall forests of the Canadian zone. Such environments are characterized by a diversity of wild plants and animals, and it may be that the density of Pueblo I sites there reflects a resurgent emphasis on the gathering of wild species.

Figure 7. Artist's conception of a late Pueblo II or early Pueblo III unit-type pueblo about A.D. 1100 on the Grand Gulch Plateau near Comb Wash, looking northeast toward the Abajo Mountains. The structure at the far right is a circular tower.

Pueblo I sites have been located and documented over much of southern San Juan County, with the exception of the area west of Comb Wash as noted previously and the Dry Valley country north of the Blue Mountains.[15] Excavations of Pueblo I sites in the county have been conducted on Milk Ranch Point, at the Energy Fuels mill site and city sewage lagoon locations on White Mesa south of Blanding, at Alkali Ridge east of Blanding, and in Montezuma Canyon southeast of Blanding.[16] Other important excavations have been conducted in Pueblo I sites near the Utah-Colorado border in the Ackman-Lowry area, at Mesa Verde National Park, in the Dolores area, and in the La Plata Valley southeast of Mesa Verde.[17]

The two-hundred-year period subsequent to A.D. 900 is known as Pueblo II. The tendency toward aggregation evidenced in Pueblo I sites reversed itself in this period, as the people dispersed themselves widely over the land in thousands of small stone houses. With the exception of some of the more arid areas north of the Abajo Mountains and west of Grand Gulch, Pueblo II is represented in almost every canyon and mesa in the county below 8,000 feet.

During Pueblo II, stone masonry replaced the pole and mud architecture of Pueblo I, the surface rooms became year-round habitations, and the pithouses (now completely subterranean) assumed the largely ceremonial role of the pueblo kiva. It is during this period that the house style known as the unit pueblo (Figure 7) and the ubiquitous small cliff granaries became popular. In the unit pueblo the main house is a block of rectangular masonry living and storage rooms, located immediately north or northwest of an underground kiva, immediately southeast of which is a trash and ash dump, or midden. The fallen masonry buildings comprise the Moki mounds that dot the countryside, and the kivas have slumped and filled until they are visible as mere shallow depressions. The trash middens (sacred to the Pueblo Indians and used by them for burial of the dead) have been almost completely ransacked by artifact hunters, many so long ago that they now look deceptively undisturbed.

The redware pottery industry continued to flourish, as a fine, red-slipped ware with black designs was traded throughout much of the Colorado Plateau. Sometime during the middle of the Pueblo II period, however, the redware tradition ended in the country north of the San Juan River and blossomed in the area south of the river. Virtually all the red or orange pottery found in San Juan County sites postdating A.D. 1000 was made south of the San Juan River in the Kayenta Anasazi country. The reasons for this shift are unknown, and the problem is a fascinating one. Production and refinement of the black-on-white and gray (now decorated by indented corrugation) wares continued uninterrupted in both areas, but the redware tradition migrated across what appears to have been an ethnic boundary. This, together with the almost complete absence of black-on-white pottery in the aforementioned Pueblo I site on Alkali Ridge, suggests that the San Juan County redwares were made by a few specialists who moved *en masse* in the A.D. 1000s.

The styles of stone artifacts also changed somewhat during Pueblo II. The beautiful barbed and tanged "Christmas-tree" style point that had been popular since late Basketmaker III times was replaced by a more utilitarian, often cursorily flaked, style with side notches and square base. By the end of the period, the old trough-shaped metate that had been popular for half a millennium was relaced by a flat slab form with no raised sides. The change in grinding technology appears to have accompanied a change from a hard, shattering, flint corn to a soft, non-shattering flour corn. This permitted use of smaller metates, thus increased efficiency of floor space.[18]

Pueblo II sites are ubiquitous in San Juan County, comprising the majority of the small-house ruins known colloquially as "Moki mounds." Sites of this period have been excavated in Glen Canyon, in the Navajo Mountain area, on Grand Gulch Plateau, in Butler Wash southwest of Blanding, at the Edge of the Cedars pueblo in Blanding, at the White Mesa Energy Fuels mill south of Blanding, in Recapture Wash northeast of Blanding, on Alkali Ridge east of Blanding, in Montezuma Canyon southeast of Blanding, and in Beef Basin, northwest of the Abajo Mountains.[19]

During the 1100s and 1200s the Anasazi population began once again to aggregate into large villages, as it had done during Pueblo I times. This period is known as Pueblo III, and it lasted until the final abandonment of the Four Corners country by the Anasazi during the late 1200s. Numerous small unit pueblos continued to be occupied during this period, but there was a tendency for them to become more massive and to incorporate the kivas into the room block. A number of very large villages developed, of which the "Ten-acre Ruin" on Alkali Ridge and the big mound in Cottonwood Wash are representative examples. It was also during this period that most of the cliff villages such as the famous examples at Mesa Verde National Park and Navajo National Monument, were built. Pueblo III sites have been excavated on Alkali Ridge east of Blanding, in Westwater Creek southwest of Blanding, in Montezuma Canyon southwest of Blanding, at Poncho House on Chinle Wash southwest of Bluff, and in

Poncho House. USHS Collections

Woodenshoe Canyon west of Blanding.[20]

During Pueblo III times the Mesa Verde Anasazi developed the thick-walled, highly polished, incredibly beautiful pottery known as Mesa Verde Black-on-White. They continued to make corrugated gray pottery, different only in detail (notably rim shape) from that produced earlier. Redwares, often with two or three-color designs ("polychromes"), continued to be imported north of the river from the Kayenta country. Arrowheads continued largely as before but were often very small and more finely made.

Starting sometime after A.D. 1250 the Anasazi packed up and moved out of San Juan County, often walking away from their settlements as though intending to return in a few minutes — or so it looks. Why did they leave behind their beautiful cooking pots and baskets? Perhaps because they had no cars, pickup trucks, or horses, and made nearly everything they owned. When forced to migrate a long distance, it was more efficient to leave the bulky items and replace them after they got to their destination.

We know that they moved south. Classic late Mesa Verde style settlements can still be recognized in New Mexico and Arizona, in high, defensible locations in areas where the local Anasazi sites look quite different.[21] By A.D. 1400 almost all the Anasazi from throughout the Southwest had aggregated into large pueblos scattered through the drainages of the Little Colorado and Rio Grande rivers in Arizona and New Mexico. Their descendants are still there in the few surviving pueblos, still very much Anasazi.

Consider the magnitude of the event: a large population of people whose ancestors had been in the area for thousands of years, whose sacred places were here, who were intimate with and very much a part of this land, suddenly abandoned it forever. What tremendous trauma must have accompanied the move. Why did they leave? It is impossible to find a single cause that can explain it, but there appear to be several that contributed. First, the climate during the Pueblo III period was somewhat unstable, at least in parts of the

Water pocket and prehistoric ruins in Bullet Canyon, 1979. Photograph by G. B. Peterson, Photogeographics. © 1983.

Southwest, with erratic rainfall patterns, arroyo cutting, and periods of drought. This weather problem climaxed with a thirty-year drought starting about 1270. Perhaps the people had expanded in population and pressed the limits of the land's capacity to support them so that they were unable to survive the climatic upheavals of the thirteenth century.

Could they have been driven out by nomadic tribes, such as Utes or Navajos? No direct evidence exists of either group, or any other like them, being in the area that early. There is mounting evidence, however, that the Numic-speaking peoples, of whom the Utes and Paiutes are part, had spread northwestward out of southwestern Nevada and were in contact with the Pueblo-like peoples of western Utah by A.D. 1200. It is certainly possible that they were in San Juan County shortly after that, especially since Ute and Paiute sites are very difficult to distinguish from Anasazi campsites, and we may not be recognizing them. Navajos were in northwestern New Mexico by 1500, but we do not know where they were before that. Perhaps the answer lies in a combination of the bad-climate and the arriving-nomads theories.

It is interesting to imagine foraging groups looking with covetous eyes upon the material wealth and bounteous storehouses of the pueblo villages as they came in to trade skins or wild products for produce or woven cloth. They may have been inclined to help themselves to the storehouses to the extent that they became a nuisance. Demographic pressures from nomadic hunting-foraging groups may well have combined with the thirteenth-century climatic disturbances to create an environment not amenable to the continuation of the Anasazi cultural system.

Although we do not yet know the answers to these questions, there is good reason to believe that we will some day if archaeologists are able to excavate enough of the right sites before the relic collectors do.

Virtually nothing is known of San Juan County archaeology between A.D. 1300 and 1700. There are hints of light Hopi usage of the western part of the county, but their presence appears to have been intermittent and limited to short visits. As stated previously, evidence of the Ute/Paiute peoples is lacking, perhaps due to the ephemeral and hard-to-recognize character of their sites. Navajos were definitely inhabiting the county as far north as Elk Ridge by the late 1700s and possibly as early as 1620.[22] Later Navajo sites are known from the Canyonlands and Lisbon Valley country dating to the late 1800s or early 1900s.

In conclusion, a century of archaeological study permits us to adumbrate the basic outlines of a succession of San Juan County's inhabitants since the end of the Ice Age. The Anasazi, or Moki, culture whose ruins dominate our perception of San Juan prehistory, was a relatively late development, appearing nearly 10,000 years after the arrival of the first known inhabitants. By the time the Anasazi departed about A.D. 1300, however, their ancestors had been in the area for thousands of years. The Navajos and Ute/Paiutes are relative newcomers to the Four Corners, with a tenure measured only in centuries. In a very real sense, the western Mesa Verde and northwestern Kayenta Anasazi are the only true natives of San

Juan County, their culture having evolved out of ancestral Archaic groups in this area over hundreds of generations. Clearly, then, to love the San Juan country is to love the Anasazi, whose remains are as essential a part of the country as are the canyons, sage flats, and juniper woodlands.

Although we are able now to broadly outline the lost ninety-eight percent of San Juan County's cultural history, we have only just begun. Disappointingly little is known about the details of the cultures and lifeways of our predecessors, and the science of archaeology is only just beginning to mature into a discipline capable of pursuing these problems. For every question that has been answered, there are a thousand significant questions that remain unanswered. How dense was the population at different periods of prehistory? How was the population distributed over the landscape at different periods? Were all the Anasazi house sites occupied year round, or were some used seasonally? If some were used seasonally, which ones were the primary, home-base winter villages? How were the people organized socially, politically, and economically? Is it possible to recognize communities among the thousands of Anasazi house sites? How specialized were the Anasazi artisans (potters, weavers, builders, hide workers, flint knappers, etc.), and what systems and mechanisms operated by which local artisans interacted in local, regional, or even continental trade networks? What details can be learned of Anasazi farming methods and their relationship to the natural environment? What changes in social organization, economic systems, settlement location distribution, and technology took place from period to period? Why did those changes take place?

An endless series of such questions could be asked about the Anasazi, and we know much more about them than we do of their Archaic and Paleo-Indian predecessors. The more one begins to ask these kinds of questions, the more interesting they become, and every question inspires several more. After a century of sometimes arrogant, sometimes hesitant, always experimental, sometimes sadly inept, and sometimes

Prehistoric Anasazi basket from Westwater Ruin, 1977. USHS Collections.

very good archaeology, the outline of that ninety-eight per cent of our prehistory that was once forgotten is again discernible. But all of that is merely preliminary to the important work. Now comes the challenge, the real intellectual excitement, as we move on to the questions whose answers will breathe life and color into our understanding of San Juan County's prehistory.

Answers to a great many of these questions were once preserved in prehistoric remains. Unfortunately, so much of that patterning has been disturbed, blurred, or completely obliterated by relic collectors, chaining projects, and inept archaeology, that answers to some questions may be permanently lost. Our ability to answer others will be determined by the attitude of San Juan County's citizens during the next two decades.

NOTES

[1]Lloyd M. Pierson, *Cultural Resource Summary of the East Central Portion of*

Moab District. Cultural Resource Series No. 10, Bureau of Land Management, Utah State Office, Salt Lake City, 1980.

[2]Paul R. Nickens, A Summary of the Prehistory of Southeastern Utah, *Contributions to the Prehistory of Southeastern Utah*, Cultural Resource Series No. 13, BLM, Utah, 1982.

[3]Cynthia Irwin-Williams, "Post-Pleistocene Archeology, 7,000-2,000 B.C.," in *Handbook of North American Indians*, vol. 9, *Southwest*, ed. Alfonso Ortiz, (Washington, D.C.: Smithsonian Institution, 1979), pp. 31-42.

[4]Cynthia Irwin-Williams, The Oshara Tradition: Origins of Anasazi Culture, *Eastern New Mexico University Contributions in Anthropology (1)*, Portales, 1973.

[5]Alexandar J. Lindsay et al., *Survey and Excavations North and East of Navajo Mountain, Utah, 1959-1962*, Museum of Northern Arizona Bulletin No. 45, Flagstaff, 1969.

[6]Jesse D. Jennings, Cowboy Cave, *University of Utah Anthropological Papers No. 104*, Salt Lake City, 1980.

[7]Earl H. Morris and Robert F. Burgh, Basketmaker II Sites Near Durango, Colorado, *The Carnegie Institution of Washington Publication 604*, Washington, D.C., 1954.

[8]William D. Lipe, "Anasazi Communities on the Red Rock Plateau, Southeastern Utah," in *Reconstructing Prehistoric Pueblo Societies*, ed. W. A. Longacre (Albuquerque: University of New Mexico Press, 1970), pp. 84-139; and Joseph C. Winter, Hovenweep 1974, *Archaeological Report No. 1*, San Jose State University, San Jose, Calif., 1975.

[9]Floyd W. Sharrock et al., Excavations, Glen Canyon Area, *University of Utah Anthropological Papers No. 73*, Salt Lake City, 1962, 1964; Lindsay et al., *Survey and Excavations North and East of Navajo Mountain, Utah, 1959-1962*; S. J. Guernsey and A. V. Kidder, Basketmaker Caves of Northeastern Arizona, *Peabody Museum Papers 8 (2)*, Harvard University, Cambridge, Mass., 1921; and Lipe, "Anasazi Communities on the Red Rock Plateau."

[10]Marian Jacklin, Recapture Wash, Report on BYU Excavation of 42Sa8895, in preparation.

[11]Winston Hurst, BYU Excavations at Milk Ranch Point, FS158, Bruce Louthan, assembler, MS on file with USDA Forest Service, Intermountain Region, Ogden, Utah, 1974; Gardiner F. Dalley, Highway U-95: Comb Wash to Grand Flat, Special Report, MS on file, Department of Anthropology, University of Utah, Salt Lake City, 1973; Curtis J. Wilson, assembler and editor, Highway U-95 Archaeology: Comb Wash to Grand Flat, vol. II, Special Report, MS on file, Department of Anthropology, University of Utah, Salt Lake City, 1974; Robert B. Neilly, Basketmaker Settlement and Subsistence along the San Juan River, Utah: The U.S. 163 Archaeological Project, MS on file, Utah Division of State History, Salt Lake City, 1982; William E. Davis, 1981 Excavations on White Mesa, San Juan County, Utah, MS submitted to Energy Fuels Nuclear, Inc., by Plano Archaeological Consultants and Abajo Archaeology, 1983; Asa S. Nielsen, in preparation; Report on BYU Excavations at Site on Recapture Dam and Reservoir; John Otis Brew, The Archaeology of Alkali Ridge, Southeastern Utah, *Papers of the Peabody Museum of American Archaeology and Ethnology No. 12*, Cambridge, Mass., 1946; and Diana Christensen, "Excavations at Cave Canyon, 1978, Montezuma Canyon, Utah" (M.A. thesis, Department of Archaeology and Anthropology, Brigham Young University, 1980).

[12]William A. Lucius and David A. Breternitz, "The Current Status of Redwares on the Mesa Verde Region," in Collected Papers in Honor of Erik Kellerman Reed, ed. by A. H. Schroeder, *Papers of the Archaeological Society of New Mexico No. 6*, 1981, pp. 99-111.

[13]William D. Lipe and R. G. Matson, "Human Settlement and Resources in the

Cedar Mesa Area, Southeastern Utah," in The Distribution of Prehistoric Population Aggregates, ed. George J. Gumerman, *Prescott College Anthropological Reports No. 1*, Prescott, Ariz., 1971, pp. 126-51.

[14]Evan I. DeBloois, The Elk Ridge Archaeological Project: A Test of Random Sampling in Archaeological Surveying, *Archaeological Report No. 2*, USDA Forest Service, Intermountain Region, Ogden, Utah, 1975.

[15]Richard A. Thompson, *A Stratified Random Sample of the Cultural Resources in the Canyonlands Section of the Moab District*, Cultural Resources Series No. 1, BLM, Utah, 1979.

[16]Davis, 1981 Excavations on White Mesa, San Juan County, Utah; Richard Talbot, Allison Bingham, and Asa S. Nielsen, Archaeological Excavations at 42Sa9937 (Aeromatic Village) in San Juan County, Utah, MS on file, Cultural Resource Management Services, Department of Anthropology, Brigham Young University, Provo, Utah, 1982; John Otis Brew, The Archaeology of Alkali Ridge, Southeastern Utah, *Papers of the Peabody Museum of American Archaeology and Ethnology No. 12*, Cambridge, Mass., 1946; Gregory R. Patterson, "A Preliminary Study of an Anasazi Settlement (42Sa971) Prior to A.D. 900 in Montezuma Canyon, San Juan County, Southeastern Utah" (M.A. thesis, Department of Anthropology, Brigham Young University, Provo, Utah, 1975); and Blaine A. Miller, "A Study of a Prudden Unit Site (42Sa971-N) in Monteuzma Canyon, San Juan County, Utah" (M.A. thesis, Department of Anthropology and Archaeology, Brigham Young University, Provo, Utah, 1976).

[17]Paul S. Martin, Archaeological Work in the Ackmen-Lowry Area, Southwestern Colorado, 1937, *Field Museum of Natural History, Anthropological Series*, vol. 23, no. 2, Chicago, 1939; Alden C. Hayes and James A. Lancaster, Badger House Community, Mesa Verde National Park, *Publications in Archaeology*, 7E, Wetherill Mesa Studies, U.S., Department of Interior, National Park Service, Washington, D.C., 1975; William Lipe and Cory Breternitz, Approaches to Analyzing Variability among Dolores Area Structures, A.D. 600-950, *Contract Abstracts*, 1(2):21-28; and Earl H. Morris, Archaeological Studies in the LaPlata District, Southwestern Colorado and Northwestern New Mexico, *The Carnegie Institution of Washington, Publication No. 19*, Washington, D.C. 1939. It should be noted that Brew, Martin, and Morris all report good Pueblo I sites as "modified Basketmaker" or "Basketmaker III" sites.

[18]Phillip L. Shelley, personal communication.

[19]Jesse D. Jennings, Glen Canyon: A Summary, *University of Utah Anthropological Papers No. 81*, University of Utah, Salt Lake City, 1966; Lindsay et al., *Survey and Excavations North and East of Navajo Mountain, 1959-1962*; Sharrock et al., Excavations, Glen Canyon Area; Dalley, Highway U-95: Comb Wash to Grand Flat; Wilson, Highway U-95 Archaeology: Comb Wash to Grand Flat, vol. II; Paul R. Nickens, Woodrat Knoll: A Multicomponent Site in Butler Wash, Southeastern Utah, MS on file, Department of Anthropology, University of Denver, Colorado, 1977; Dee F. Green, First Season Excavations of Edge of the Cedars Pueblo, Blanding, Utah, MS on file, Department of Sociology and Anthropology, Weber State College, Ogden, Utah, 1970; Davis, 1981 Excavations on White Mesa, San Juan County, Utah; Nielsen, Report on BYU Excavations at Site on Recapture Dam and Reservoir; Brew, The Archaeology of Alkali Ridge, Southeastern Utah; Craig Harmon, Cave Canyon Village: The Early Pueblo Components, Publications in Archaeology, Department of Anthropology and Archaeology, Brigham Young University, Provo, Utah, 1979; Donald E. Miller, "A Synthesis of Excavations at Site 42Sa863, Three Kiva Pueblo, Montezuma Canyon, San Juan County, Utah" (M.A. thesis, Department of Anthropology, Brigham Young University, 1974); Miller, "A Study of a Prudden Unit Site (42Sa971-N) in Monteuzma Canyon, San Juan County, Utah"; and Jack R. Rudy, Archaeological Excavations in Beef Basin, Utah, *University of Utah Anthropological Papers No. 20*, University of Utah, Salt Lake City, 1955.

[20]Alfred V. Kidder, Explorations in Southeastern Utah in 1908, *American Journal of Archaeology*, 2d ser., vol. 1 , Norwood, Mass., 1910, pp. 337-59; Brew, The Archaeology of Alkali Ridge, Southeastern Utah; La Mar W. Lindsay, Excavations of Westwater Ruin 42Sa14, San Juan County, Utah: First Field Season, MS on file, Utah Navajo Development Council, Blanding, Utah, 1978, and *Big Westwater Ruin, Excavation of Two Anasazi Sites in Southern Utah, 1979-1980*, Cultural Resource Series No. 9, BLM, Utah, 1981; Miller, "A Synthesis of Excavations at Site 42Sa863, Three Kiva Pueblo, Montezuma Canyon, San Juan County, Utah"; Samuel J. Guernsey, Explorations in Northeastern Arizona, *Papers of the Peabody Museum of American Archaeology and Ethnology* (vol. 12, no. 1), Harvard University, Cambridge, Mass., 1931; and J. Terry Walker, "A Description of ML1147, an Undisturbed Archaeological Site, Manti-LaSal National Forest, Utah" (M.A. thesis, Department of Anthropology, Brigham Young University, Provo, Utah, 1977).

[21]E. L. Davis, "Anasazi Mobility and Mesa Verde Migrations" (Ph.D. diss., Department of Anthropology, University of California, Berkeley, 1964).

[22]J. Lee Correll, "Navajo Frontiers in Utah and Troublous Times in Monument Valley," *Utah Historical Quarterly* 39(1971): 145-61; and Clyde Benally, *Dineji Nahee' Naahane'; A Utah Navajo History* (Monticello: San Juan School District, 1982).

Archaeology in
San Juan County

Robert Hosler

After visiting with many of the residents of San Juan County over the last seventeen years, I have been duly impressed with their concern that the archaeological artifacts and, in too many cases, the reports of scientific information gathered were not being returned to or remaining in San Juan County — the place of origin. There is a strong opinion that these materials were being taken from the area to build up big eastern colleges, and even museums of other countries, instead of being used to assist the people of the county. Some people feel that many of these archaeologists were an elitist group who gave no thought to helping build a research center here but were interested only in having residents of San Juan raise funds for them to perform archaeological excavations.

I found a small group of residents who only voiced an opinion against the archaeologists as justification for their own destruction of sites in order to sell the artifacts. Fortunately, ninty-five percent of San Juan County residents want the Anasazi sites, artifacts, and reports of information gathered from excavated sites to become a part of an archaeological research center that future archaeologists can use as a reference center. This research center should have laboratories, a library, and a repository to preserve all materials for future use.

It seems that the residents of San Juan County and the archaeologists have similar views as to how sites, artifacts, and reports should be treated. Now they differ only in how money should be raised to build a research center. Residents feel that the professional archaeologist has a responsibility to assist. He has come to San Juan County for years, excavated Anasazi sites, and, like the common pot-hunter, left nothing but a hole in the ground.

Many uninformed residents feel the archaeologists have only a selfish interest in site preservation. They come into the county, excavate a site very secretively and leave, not reporting what was discovered. They come from large powerful eastern colleges and are interested only in building up collections for their schools of archaeology. Contributing to the problem are the two permit-issuing agencies of the federal government — the Bureau of Land Management and the U.S. Forest Service — which do not inform residents about permits for archaeological work.

Early visitors to prehistoric ruins in White Canyon. Special Collections, Marriott Library, University of Utah.

Local residents recall the University of Sweden coming a few years ago and carrying away valuable materials with the permission of the federal government agencies.

Some amateur archaeologists have taken this local attitude, with which they have been confronted, as a justification for pot-hunting. They misunderstand that the people of San Juan County do not want archaeologists unqualified in Anasazi archaeology coming to San Juan sites without a legal responsibility to leave artifacts and return written reports to our local repository at the Edge of the Cedars Museum. The people want more input into who is given permits — especially as specialists in southeastern Utah Anasazi archaeology. This will help prevent further destruction of sites and artifacts, address the problem of reports not being sent to the county, and provide better policing to protect remaining sites.

Three Fingers Ruin, Hammond Canyon, USHS Collections.

It has been suggested that permit issuance be tied to payment of repository expenses at the local Edge of the Cedars. Both the BLM and Forest Service would have a responsibility to collect and turn over funds charged these specialists who are granted permits to work in San Juan County. Through this program the professional archaeologist could help meet his responsibility for the local repository of artifacts.

The Anasazi sites, artifacts, and scientific reports are of true value to the residents of San Juan County. We have proven our interest by promoting the building of the Edge of the Cedars Center. We ask that the professional archaeologist forget rumors and hearsay as we forget some of the inappropriate sites that have been excavated but not reported in a professional manner. Let us work together for improvement in all areas of archaeological endeavor on all of southeastern Utah Anasazi land.

PART TWO

Indians

Navajo women at hogan in Monument Valley. USHS Collections.

Utah's Indian Country: The American Indian Experience in San Juan County, 1700-1980

Gregory C. Thompson

The history of the Indians of San Juan County, Utah, is most interesting and quite revealing. Limited space greatly narrows the scope of the discussion of the history; still one is able to identify several themes that run throughout it. One theme is physical and cultural survival. A second is the ability to adapt to a new culture and incorporate desired elements into traditional ways and life-styles. A final theme is the success of the adaption and the expansion of influence and land holdings which have accompanied this success.

Our time frame for this discussion stretches from about 1700 to the present. Within this block of time, San Juan's Indian history can be related to three periods of development or change. The first is the traditional period where one Indian group related to others in its region but had almost no lasting contact with non-Indians. The second is identified as the tumultuous period, for it marked the time of intense contact between Indians and non-Indians, often with combative overtones. A third is the expansive period where the Indian groups of San Juan County have recovered from the most negative aspect of contact with whites and have increased their ability to survive successfully in a non-Indian dominated world. While this development has been uneven for the Indians in the county, the pattern is well enough developed to be recognizable. In the final analysis, a look at the history of the Indian groups in the county over a nearly three-hundred-year period indicates that San Juan County was occupied Indian country long before whites came to the area and, despite hardships caused by white contact, still is Utah's Indian county.

The Traditional Period: 1700-1870

If we were to go back to the year 1700 and survey the present San Juan County region, we would find three major Indian groups located in the area. These groups would be the Navajos to the south, the Paiutes to the west and southwest, and the Utes to the east and northeast.

Each of these groups had been in their respective regions for many years. Their understanding of the geography and the ecology of the area was exceptionally well developed. These people knew how to survive in a land where deserts, mountains, valleys, and canyons were the main geological features. Each of these groups had its own highly

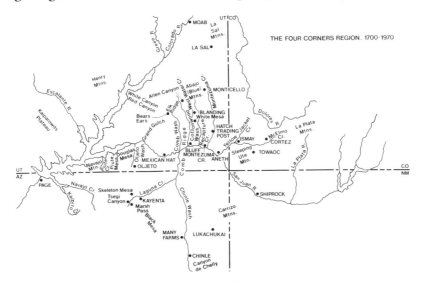

developed economic system which allowed the people to survive in the rigorous terrain in which they lived. To the east were the Utes. They were the mountain people, and they knew how to hunt small game and the larger game located in their domain. Trips were made onto the plains to hunt buffalo. These people also understood the types of food available to them from plants and bushes. According to the season and the location — all well known and very much a part of the life pattern of the Utes — berries and other foods were gathered and prepared for use. The Navajos hunted and gathered in those areas where such activities would help supplement their food supply, but they also herded sheep and goats and used the meat and products from these animals to support their economic system. Good knowledge of the grazing areas by the season was necessary for the Navajos to successfully herd their animals. The Paiutes also were a hunting and gathering people similar to the Utes; however, they tended to hunt smaller game — rabbits, antelope, deer, mountain sheep, and mud-hens — and rely more on their gathering capabilities to collect roots, seeds, berries, and insects. All three groups cultivated crops in a limited horticultural practice. Corn, beans, squash, sunflowers, and later melons were planted and harvested. For the three groups life remained reasonably stable despite the occasional intrusion of non-Indians into their areas.[1]

The groups also traded with each other during this time period. The Utes offered buckskins, native plants, and buffalo robes, among other items. The Navajos were known for their blankets and horses, especially after 1700. And the Paiutes offered mountain sheep horn bows and some foods. After the adoption of the horse and the developed skill in its use, first by the Utes and then by the Navajos, a very brisk trade in slaves developed within the groups. The pattern was usually for the mounted, faster Navajos or Utes to raid the Paiutes for children and women and sell or trade them to the Spanish in New Mexico or California.

As the slave trade experience indicates, the three groups

were not always on friendly terms with one another and did raid each other through periods of conflict. Most notable were the Ute-Navajo raids during the 1700s and 1800s. The newly arrived intruders into the land of the Indians, the Spanish, were able to use these periods of hostility to their advantage as they attempted to gain control over the land and its people. Throughout this time period, until 1848, both Spanish and their successors — the Mexicans — were able to develop and maintain alliances with one group or the other as the need dictated. The result was Ute "guides" leading Spanish expeditions against raiding Navajos or Navajo "scouts" directing other expeditions against Ute groups who had been raiding New Mexico and Spanish settlements.

The main characteristic, however, throughout this traditional period was the continued practice by the three Indian groups of life-styles and economics that had been practiced for years in the past. The Spanish intruders failed to disrupt or drastically alter the existing life-style.

Prior to 1848 both Spanish and Mexican governments had claimed control over the Four Corners region. Their central administrations were controlled from Mexico City, located many miles to the south. This made their control of the Four Corners area very weak. This was especially noted by those observing the actions of the Mexican government. The United States government was one of those that sensed the weakness and that desired control of the whole Southwest region, including the Four Corners area. Change was in the air and the Indian groups were aware of this fact.

War between Mexico and the United States broke out in 1846. It ended with the negotiating of the Treaty of Guadalupe Hidalgo in 1848. Signed by both governments, the treaty gave the United States the rights of sovereignty to the Southwest and the Four Corners, which included San Juan County. This meant the United States had the right of political control over the people located in the Four Corners, but the government did not own the land nor could they lay claim to that land without first negotiating with the people who owned and controlled it: the Navajos, the Utes, and the Paiutes. Despite the changes in outside governments claiming control over the area, the Indian nations had retained their claim to the land they lived on. But that was not to last for long; as the observers had noted earlier, change was in the air. This sense of change was to bring about a new set of circumstances that would greatly affect the people of the Four Corners and San Juan County.

Once the United States claimed sovereignty over New Mexico, Colorado, Utah, and northern Arizona, agents moved quickly to ensure that this sovereignty would be recognized. Treaties of Friendship and Peace were signed with most of the Indian groups in these territories. The government hoped that the past pattern of raids on settlements between Indian groups would end. It did not. To deal with the situation required the government to take more severe action. A large military expedition was sent to quiet the Navajo. The result was the rounding up of Navajos and the removal of more than 6,000 people in the "The Long Walk" to southern New Mexico. For four years — from 1864 to 1868 — the Navajo people were held at Bosque Redondo near Fort Sumner. The event had a dramatic effect on the history of Indian affairs in San Juan County, Utah.[2]

A number of Navajos were able to outmaneuver Colonel Christopher "Kit" Carson and the United States Army troops sent to locate and move the people south. One group was led by a Navajo known as Haashkeneinii. He and some seventeen followers fled north from the Monument Valley area towards the Navajo Mountain region where they crossed the San Juan River.[3]

This was not the first time Haashkeneinii had been into the area nor was it the first time Navajos had crossed the San Juan River and used the area north of the river as an escape region. Maps of the seventeenth and eighteenth centuries show the area north of the river as having been known as Navajo area.[4] In 1823, only two years after the Mexican government had declared its independence from the Spanish,

Francisco Salazar was sent with a detachment of troops after Navajos who had been raiding their settlements. Salazar tracked the Navajos and their livestock herds to the San Juan River where they had crossed the river and headed towards the Bears Ears region just south of Elk Ridge.[5] These Navajos obviously knew the area south and north of the San Juan and were quite willing to use it as an escape region when necessary. In 1823 Mexican records indicate that Utes were reporting the presence of Navajos in the La Plata and Sleeping Ute Mountain region and ranging west into Utah.[6]

At the time Haashkeneinii was leading his people north, he was reported to be only in his thirties and a recognized medicine man who was a leader of Navajos in the Monument Valley-Oljeto area. Others were also using the southeast Utah region as a residence. Kigalia (K'aayelii) was born near the Bears Ears in 1801 and had become one of the principal Navajo headmen north of the San Juan River by the time of the 1864 Carson expedition.[7] His region seemed to stretch from the Bears Ears to the Henry Mountains and from the La Sals south to Montezuma Creek. He lived in this region until 1894 when, after his death, he was buried along Montezuma Creek. A second Navajo individual is also known to have herded livestock in the area at the time of the Bosque Redondo. Born in 1821 in White Canyon west of the Abajos, "Pointed Foot" or Kee Diniihi used much the same region as Kigalia.[8] These Navajos were not the only people to live and use this region in the 1830s, 1840s, and 1850s. So did the Utes and Paiutes. The record indicates each group gave the other great respect, and each responded to the pressure the others put on the region. The result seems to be that while all used the region north of the San Juan River, no one fully controlled the land. Each used their own section and at times may have existed side-by-side.

This observation is supported by the accounts of members of the Church of Jesus Christ of Latter-day Saints, or Mormons, who tried to settle Moab in 1854-55. They noted that a number of Indians were in the area. The main groups were Utes and Navajos. They traded with both and in doing so got caught in the middle of an Indian relations problem when the Sheberetch band of Utes, located near Moab and the La Sal Mountains, was accused by the Navajos of stealing horses. The Mormons acted as negotiators and brought about a settlement of the dispute, but in doing so showed their defensive weaknesses and small numbers. Later, the Mormons were forced to abandon their settlement efforts when Indian pressure against them increased.[9]

This attempted settlement in San Juan County along with the later expedition of Kit Carson indicated to the Indian groups in the area that the more peaceful and traditional times of the past were changing. Of course, they could not foretell the dramatic force with which this change was going to occur nor the tumultuous times it was going to bring to their lives. But they knew change was occurring. The pressure was building on all sides of them, and all three Indian groups felt it.

The Tumultuous Period: 1870-1923

The tumultuous period began about 1870 and continued through 1923 without interruption. It is obvious that the Indian groups, especially the Navajos and the Utes, resisted the intruders and struggled hard to maintain control over their respective regions. Witness the driving of two United States Geological Survey teams from the area in 1875 as evidence. Both parties were part of the surveys under the leadership of F. V. Hayden, with Henry Gannett leading one and James L. Gardner the other. Both were working in the La Sal Mountains region. In their written report they observed:

> The most desperate rascals from each [Paiute and Ute bands] congregate there . . . and acknowledge no authority but their own chieves [*sic*] — murderers and robbers everyone. The bands number respectively from 7-20 about as poor and desperate as mountain brigands usually are . . . . Their regular trading is done with the native tribes from whom they obtain arms, ammunition and horses in exchange for . . . hunting for game or men.[10]

These men were attacked in Dry Valley after leaving the La Sal region by a band of ten Indians and forced to make a run eastward into Colorado. Ouray, a leader among the Colorado Utes, insisted to the Southern Ute agent that the attacking force was not his people but rather "a well-known band of outlaws, formerly Pi-Utes of Utah, now acknowledging no authority, though some disaffected Utes had joined them." Others admitted that the Indians were part of the Weeminuche group that lived in the Sleeping Mountain region.

The same year, the famous western photographer William H. Jackson, also working for the Hayden survey, met a group of Indians in the Montezuma Creek area that forced him to beat a hasty retreat toward Colorado. One year later, two other Hayden survey parties operating in the Abajo Mountains appear to have felt the pressure of Indian people not wanting intruders in their land. Neither group spent long in the area before turning toward Colorado.

Others who felt the pressure of the Indians trying to protect their region were the early prospectors who wandered into the San Juan River region looking for mineral wealth. Some did not wander out. In 1881 James Merrick and Ernest Mitchell were killed in the Monument Valley area by Paiutes. Mitchell was a member of the Mitchell family that had a ranch at the mouth of Montezuma Creek. Earlier, Merrick had stumbled on a mine which might have been the fabled silver mine, the Pishlaki Mine, which was reportedly first located by Haashkeneinii. Returning to the area, Merrick and Mitchell were attacked and killed. Many years later, Haashkeneinii's son, Haashkeneinii Biye, told Charles Kelly that he and other Navajos trailed the two prospectors to the mine site where they found a group of Paiutes robbing the bodies of the two.[11] Other reports indicate that Utes killed the two miners. Regardless, the message continued to be one of "enter the region at very high risk."

That same year, two ranchers were killed in a remote location along the Utah-Colorado border. Originally it was thought that Weeminuche Utes were responsible, but a

Navajo by the name of Little Captain, who was the first to report the killings to the whites, thought they were Paiutes since they fled south to the Butler Wash area below Bluff and then on to Indian Creek after crossing over the Abajos and mixing with a group of Uncompahgre Utes who were crossing Dry Valley. By the time pursuing whites caught up with them, the Indians had made their way to the west side of the La Sal Mountains. Making contact, a fight occurred at a location known as Pinhook Valley. Nine pursuers were killed. The Indians lost from seven to eighteen — the number is not really known — before moving out at night and ending the skirmish.[12]

To see that additional problems did not develop, the army was called from Fort Lewis, the closest military post to the area, located on the La Plata River near Durango, Colorado. This force consisted of the 9th Cavalry under a Captain Carroll and a detachment of the 13th Infantry. It is interesting to note one company of men was made up of black soldiers, a situation of much concern to all residents of San Juan County.[13] Peace was restored.

In the south the Navajos and the Paiutes observed the Mormon Hole-in-the-Rock group make their way to and settle in the Bluff, Utah, area. Charles S. Peterson notes in his book, *Look to the Mountains*, that Jim Mike, a Paiute, in an interview with Lynn Lyman, remembers hearing the dynamite blasting of the group as they made their way to Bluff.[14] The pressure of the whites increased throughout San Juan County with the result being increased conflict between Indians and the intruders. More murders occurred, with troops from Fort Lewis continually being called to Utah to quiet the Indians and settle the disputes.[15]

In the spring of 1884, two prospectors, Samuel Walcott and James McNally were killed near Navajo Mountain. Haashkeneinii Biye was accused of the killing by Dine Ts'osi or "Slender Navajo." Haashkeneinii, his father, was the one actually arrested and taken to Fort Wingate. Haashkeneinii Biye fled and reportedly joined the developing group of Utes and

Paiutes living in the Abajo Mountains region and to the south.[16]

Troops were sent from Fort Wingate but failed to arrest Haashkeneinii Biye. In the meantime, his father had been moved to St. Johns, Arizona, but was later released on bond. Haashkeneinii Biye was never arrested, and, later, a grand jury failed to indict him or anyone else for the killings. The result was that Haashkeneinii spent a total of seven months in jail for a crime he did not commit.[17]

This incident caused considerable concern in the area and was of note in the nation as a whole. Partially because of this incident and other incidents, the Navajo claim to the region south of the San Juan River was recognized in the Executive Order of May 17, 1884.[18] The order was signed by Chester A. Arthur, president of the United States. Later, realizing part of the land belonged to Paiutes, President Benjamin Harrison rescinded the Paiute strip portion of the order in 1892.[19] The strip was given back to the Navajos by legislative act on March 1, 1933.[20] The Executive Order of 1884 began

Navajos riding to annual squaw dance. Photograph by Charles Kelly. USHS Collections.

the formalizing of a long process that helped to establish San Juan County as Utah's Indian county.

A second event supporting this view of southeastern Utah was the 1888-89 attempted removal of the Southern Ute bands to San Juan County and the making of the remaining portion of the county into a large Indian reservation.[21]

Although the effort to make San Juan County into a reservation ultimately failed, it is important to understand the approach and thought that went into the consideration. In March 6, 1880, a Ute agreement with all the bands of Colorado Utes was signed by the United States government. The northern bands were to be moved to the Uinta Basin. The three Southern Ute bands — the Muache, the Capote, and the Weeminuche — were to be moved to a new reservation located along the La Plata River. The new reservation was deemed unfit.[22]

After six years of consideration and debate, the area north of the San Juan River was proposed as a potential reservation. One reason for this consideration was the fact that only 800 whites lived in the county and the Indians would be isolated from white contact. A second reason was that the area was very well known to the Utes, especially the Weeminuche band. They wanted to move to the area and make it their permanent home. The inspectors felt the new reservation, which contained some 2.9 million acres or nearly two million acres more than their Colorado reservation, contained good agriculture land.[23]

The reservation to be created stretched from the San Juan River in the south to the La Sal Mountains in the north, a distance of seventy-five miles. The eastern boundary was to be the Utah-Colorado border with the western edge of the reservation running along the eastern banks of the Colorado River.

The three Southern Ute bands agreed to the proposed reservation in a series of negotiations with a three-man commission established by the United States Congress. By November 1888 the commission had obtained the signatures of three-quarters of the male adults of the Southern Ute bands. On January 11, 1889, this document was presented to Congress for approval. Senate Bill No. 389 passed that body on February 1 but bogged down in the House.[24] A coalition of non-Indians led a successful fight to defeat the legislation. Miners, Mormon settlers, cattle and land company entrepreneurs, and eastern Indian policy reformers all lobbied Congress to defeat the proposed reservation.[25] Each group had its own reasons for wanting the Southern Utes to remain in Colorado.[26]

Had the legislation passed, San Juan County would have been a series of Indian reservations with only a very small segment on the northern tier remaining outside reservation classification. Three separate reservations would have made up the county: the San Juan Paiute reservation in the southwestern corner, the Navajo reservation in the south, and the Southern Ute reservation in the central portion. Although the Southern Ute reservation failed, the important point from the experience was that the federal government as well as the surrounding states and territories all considered San Juan County as prime land for establishing Indian reserves. At the turn of the century, many considered San Juan County as Utah's Indian county, an image that continued to the twentieth century.

Further attempts to move the Southern Utes out of the state of Colorado to Utah, which held only territorial status politically, continued into the 1890s, but the effort in 1889 proved to be the major attempt. After that, congressional attempts to pass the necessary legislation lacked the broad support needed for success. The county was saved from its all-reservation status. However, for the Indian people located in the county, the times remained tumultuous for another quarter of a century.

More specifically, three major events occurred from the turn of the twentieth century to 1923 to give credence to the view that life for the Indian groups located in the county was neither easy nor peaceful.

In 1907 the United States government had been pressuring the Navajos located on the reservation to send their children to school.[27] The Indian agent stated that the children located in the San Juan area were to be gathered together and transported to Shiprock where they would be placed in boarding schools. Because of the remoteness of the region and the lack of money, the Office of Indian Affairs, that administrative agency which was responsible for the welfare of the Indians, had not built a school in San Juan County for the Indian students to attend. The parents of the students did not want the children moved so far away from them.

Ba'ililii, a powerful leader and wealthy medicine man who had been born in Canyon de Chelly but had moved to the Aneth area, led the Navajos' resistance to their children's being sent to boarding schools. Ba'ililii's protest was strong enough to force the agent to call in troops from Fort Wingate. The troops were to arrest Ba'ililii and did so in a surprise raid on his camp. Two Navajos were killed and a number were arrested. It was not until July 1909 that the last two jailed, Ba'ililii and Polly, were released and returned home.[28]

The experience only confirmed to the Indians that their traditional ways of living were being threatened by the United States government and that the constant stream of intruders into their region was forcing the Indians to change their way of living. With each passing year they felt new pressure to abandon old life-styles and adopt the ways of the whites.

The second major incident to occur in the early part of the twentieth century involved the remaining San Juan Paiutes and Weeminuche Utes living in the county. A majority of the group, the Paiutes, had lived in the "Paiute Strip" region and south earlier but had been forced north to Douglas Mesa, Comb Wash, and Allen Canyon by Navajos by about 1900. Leadership at this time seemed to be with a Ute, Mancos Jim, who was related to one of the Paiute leaders, Posey, by marriage. A third leader in the group, Polk, was probably of mixed blood — Ute and Paiute. As Mancos Jim grew older, the power of leadership shifted to Posey and from the Ute to the Paiute group.[29]

As these people were pushed into the Allen Canyon region both population and livestock increased among the Indians, Mormons, and other whites. The increased pressure brought more altercations between the groups and increased tensions. The whites accused the Indians of stealing cattle and disrupting the peace. The Indians countered with charges that the whites were herding cattle on their grazing areas and mixing their cattle with the Indian cattle. The whites wanted the Indians moved out of the area and to either the Ute or Navajo reservations. The settlers felt the federal government had a responsibility to handle what was fast becoming an explosive situation by removing the Indians and protecting the white herds.

Posey.
USHS Collections.

The tensions between the two groups exploded into conflict when Chacon, a Spanish sheepherder for one of the settlers, was killed in 1914. The white residents formed a posse, tracked down, and attempted to arrest Tse-ne-gat, also known as Everett Hatch, who was charged with the killing. Mancos Jim, Polk, and Posey, all members of Tse-ne-gat's band, resisted the arrest of the accused and forced a standoff with the posse. General Hugh L. Scott of the United States Army, who had been involved in the Ba'ililii arrest, was called in again to negotiate a settlement. Tse-ne-gat was arrested and peace was restored to San Juan County. Tse-ne-gat was sent to Denver to stand trial for murder. He was later acquitted.[30]

Because the problem of meeting the needs of the Paiutes and Utes, who became identified as the Allen Canyon Indians in the government literature, was not solved, the restored peace was shaky at best. Trouble broke out again in 1923 when two Indian boys were accused of stealing from a sheep camp.[31] After much discussion the Indian group agreed to turn the boys over to the law. The boys were tried and found guilty of theft.

While the sheriff was holding the boys at his home for the six-hour period required by Utah state law, one of the boys grabbed a gun and attempted to kill the sheriff. The gun misfired and the boy scurried to a group of Indians gathered near the courthouse in Blanding. Posey, a member of the group, and the others then fled. The sheriff and a hastily gathered posse gave chase by car. The posse was able to corner the group, and on the second day the Indians, except for Posey, surrendered. The group was herded back to Blanding and imprisoned in the basement of the Mormon chapel. Posey had escaped from the main group, but in the course of fleeing was shot in the hip. White descriptions of the events indicated Posey died of the wounds. Indian testimony indicated Posey was poisoned by food sent to him by his pursuers who were encouraging him to give up. After agreeing to keep the peace those held in the chapel were released and sent back to their homes in Allen Canyon.[32]

Bullpen in Blanding where Indians were incarcerated during the Posey War, 1923. Photograph Copyright 1979 Steve Lacy Wild Bunch Photos.

The incident again focused considerable national attention on San Juan County and its Indian-white relations. The result highlighted rather dramatically the condition of the Allen Canyon group and the need to provide better for them.

A long-time friend of the Allen Canyon people, E. Z. Black, of Blanding, Utah, was named as a sub-agent, a newly created position for the Allen Canyon group, to see to the schooling of the children, to the well-being of the group, and to an improvement in the general situation for the Indians.[33] He reported administratively to the Indian agent in Towaoc, Colorado, the agency location for Ute Mountain Utes, who earlier were identified as the Weeminuche band of the Southern Utes. As part of his assignment, Agent Black arranged for each Allen Canyon family to receive their own allotments of land in the canyon in 1923.[34]

After the 1923 incident, conflicts of the nature of the Ba'ililii affair, the Tse-ne-gat affair, and the Posey killing ended. So did the tumultuous period in San Juan County Indian history. Although times were not always the best after

66

1923, the conflicts and problems between white citizens and Indian residents did not break out in open warfare. The period from 1870 to 1923 was that time in history when the Indian residents located within the borders of the county met head-on the intruders into their area. The experiences indicated the difficulty two societies had trying to exist together.

The Expansion Period: 1923-1980

While the Allen Canyon people were struggling to maintain a home and land base in San Juan County, the Navajos were expanding the Utah reservation and learning to exploit financially the oil and gas resources located on their land.

In 1905 almost 7,000 acres were added to the Navajo reservation north of the San Juan River in the Aneth area. Additional reservation land was added in 1933 by congressional enactment. Part of this addition included the "Paiute Strip" region that had been granted earlier but then returned to the public domain. Also added at this time was additional land in the Aneth area. This Aneth extension was most important, for it included land rich in oil and gas resources. The final expansion to the Navajo reservation came with the McCracken addition in 1958. This parcel of land was an exchange for land lost to the building of Glen Canyon Dam and the creation of Lake Powell.[35]

These additions to the Navajo reservation brought increased royalties from oil and gas leases and meant the people were better able to determine their own life-styles and economic development than in the past. By the 1960s it was apparent that the Navajos were well on their way to becoming a major economic, social, and political force in San Juan County.

With the help of federal and state governments and the use of the natural resource money, education for tribal members living in Utah was given increased attention. Earlier boarding schools gave way to day schools. Students were bused, usually very long distances, to schools. The schools were located in the northern region of the county, a characteristic that placed unusual burdens on Indian students. To offset bus rides as long as five hours a day, new schools were located closer to the Indian students' homes. By the 1980s a much more satisfactory geographical balance of schools for all grades from kindergarten through high school had been achieved. Two new high schools located within the reservation in the southern part of the county were added to the existing high schools in Blanding and Monticello. Finally, special consideration has been paid to the curriculum taught. Culturally enriched Indian materials have been written and incorporated into the existing curriculum program to educate better both Indian and non-Indian students.

New housing programs have also changed old traditional patterns. Typical non-Indian housing has replaced the traditional housing for many Navajos. In addition more Navajos have chosen to move off the reservation and to Blanding and other communities than ever before.

With more money, better education, and broader political influence, Navajos also began to have more control in local and county politics. Tribal members, especially in the decade of the 1970s, took an active role with the county school board and with other county government agencies. Having more than fifty percent of the county's population by the 1980 United States census, the Navajos increasingly exercised the right to control their own destiny.

The Allen Canyon Indians represented all that was left of the Ute and Paiute groups that had existed in the county at an earlier time. Because it was so hard to get their children to school in Blanding and to transport supplies to their homes in Allen Canyon, people began to move closer to town. Over a period of time the community resettled on White Mesa south of Blanding. Lacking the resources of the Navajos, the Allen Canyon Indians have had a much harder time adjusting to the changes in life-style that occurred during the tumultuous period. In more recent time these people have received federal government recognition through the Ute Mountain Tribal Council in Colorado. The community is governed by a local council of elected members. As a group, the Allen Canyon Indians elect a community member to sit on the Ute Mountain Ute Council and represent their interests. The member is also on the community council.

Summary

When one reviews the full sweep of American Indian history in San Juan County, one is struck by several developments. Unlike so many other areas in Utah and the West, the San Juan County region has had Indian residents living in the area throughout the full time span of our discussions. Navajos, Paiutes, and Utes were using the region long before A.D. 1700 and continue to do so today. Although the initial stage of contact with non-Indians was very costly to traditional lifestyles, these three peoples and their traditions are still represented in the county today. If one listens carefully, all three languages can be heard spoken either at White Mesa or on the Navajo reservation. One can also witness other cultural characteristics from the traditional life-style still being used on a daily basis.

As in the past, San Juan County is Utah's Indian county with its Indian residents contributing much to the cultural, economic, and social diversity of the state. The history indicates this pattern will continue to grow and strengthen in the years to come.

NOTES

[1]For discussions on the cultural life-style of each of the tribes see Isabel T. Kelly, "Southern Paiute Bands," *American Anthropologist 36* (October-December 1934): 548-60; Isabel T. Kelly, "Southern Paiute Ethnography," in *Paiute Indians II* (New York: Garland Publishing Inc., 1976), pp. 1-194; Clyde Benally, *Dine Ji Nakee' Naahane: A Utah Navajo History* (Monticello, Utah: San Juan School District, 1982); H. Baxter Liebler, "The Social and Cultural Patterns of the Navajo Indians," *Utah Historical Quarterly 30* (Fall 1962): 299-325; James Jefferson, Robert W. Delaney, and Gregory C. Thompson, *The Southern Utes: A Tribal History*, ed. by Floyd A. O'Neil (Ignacio, Colorado: Southern Ute Tribe, 1972); and Fred A. Conetah, *A History of the Northern Ute People*, ed. by Kathryn L. MacKay and Floyd A. O'Neil (Salt Lake City: Uintah-Ouray Ute Tribe, 1982).

[2]Lynn R. Bailey, *The Long Walk: A History of the Navajo Wars, 1846-1868* (Los Angeles: Westernlore Press, 1964); Lawrence Kelly, *Navajo Roundup: Selected*

Correspondence of Kit Carson's Expedition Against the Navajo, 1863-1865 (Boulder, Colorado: Pruett Publishing Co., 1970); Gerald F. Thompson, *The Army and the Navajo: The Bosque Redondo Reservation Experiment* (Tucson: University of Arizona Press, 1976); and Clifford Earl Trafzer, *The Kit Carson Campaign: The Last Great Navajo War* (Norman: University of Oklahoma Press, 1982), provide excellent descriptions of this period in Navajo history.

[3]J. Lee Correll, "Navajo Frontiers in Utah and Troublous Times in Monument Valley," *Utah Historical Quarterly* 39 (Spring 1971): 149-51; and Benally, *Dine Ji Nakee' Naahane*, pp. 136-38.

[4]Correll, "Navajo Frontiers In Utah," p. 146.

[5]Ibid.

[6]Ibid.

[7]Ibid., pp. 146-47.

[8]Ibid., p. 147.

[9]Charles S. Peterson, *Look to the Mountains: Southeastern Utah and the La Sal National Forest* (Provo, Utah: Brigham Young University Press, 1975), pp. 11-15. See also Faun McConkie Tanner, *The Far Country: A Regional History of Moab and La Sal, Utah* (Salt Lake City: Olympus Publishing Company, 1976), pp. 45-61.

[10]Quoted in Peterson, *Look to the Mountains*, p. 64. See also *New York Times*, September 9, 1875.

[11]Peterson, *Look to the Mountains*, p. 66, and Correll, "Navajo Frontiers in Utah," pp. 151-52.

[12]Tanner, *The Far Country*, pp. 115-46.

[13]The best discussions of the military history of Fort Lewis in these years is by Robert W. Delaney, *Blue Coats, Red Skins, and Black Gowns: 100 Years of Fort Lewis* (Durango, Colorado: Durango Herald, 1977). The Indians also greatly disliked the black soldiers.

[14]Peterson, *Look to the Mountains*, p. 58. For a full discussion see David E. Miller, *Hole-In-The-Rock: An Epic in the Colonization of the Great American West* (Salt Lake City: University of Utah Press, 1966).

[15]Delaney, *Blue Coats, Red Skins, and Black Gowns*, pp. 1-22.

[16]Benally, *Dine Ji Nakee' Naahane*, pp. 151-58.

[17]Ibid.

[18]Ibid.

[19]Ibid.

[20]Ibid.

[21]Gregory C. Thompson, "The Unwanted Indians: The Southern Utes in Southeastern Utah," *Utah Historical Quarterly* 49 (Spring 1981): 189-203. See also Gregory C. Thompson, *Southern Ute Lands, 1848-1899: The Creation of a Reservation*, Occasional Paper No. 1, Center of Southwest Studies (Durango, Colorado: Fort Lewis College, 1972), pp. 31-49, for a discussion of how these events contributed to the establishing of the present-day Southern Ute and Ute Mountain Ute reservations in southwestern Colorado.

[22]Thompson, *Southern Ute Lands*, pp. 22-23.

[23]Thompson, "The Unwanted Indians," p. 198.

[24]U.S., Congress, Senate, "Bills Introduced," *Congressional Record*, vol. 2, part 2, 50th Cong., 2d sess., February 1, 1889, p. 1390.

[25]Thompson, "The Unwanted Indians," pp. 199-202.

[26]Thompson, *Southern Ute Lands*, pp. 43-47.

[27]Benally, *Dine Ji Nakee' Naahane*, pp. 170-73.

[28]Ibid.

[29]Floyd A. O'Neil and Gregory C. Thompson, "White Mesa Ute History Project," MS prepared for Utah Division of State History, Salt Lake City, and for Energy Fuels

Nuclear, Inc., Blanding, Utah 1980, p. 7. See also Forbes Parkhill, *The Last of the Indian Wars* (New York: Collier Books, 1961), pp. 54-63.

[30]Parkhill, *The Last of the Indian Wars*, pp. 94-99, 110-14.

[31]O'Neil and Thompson, "White Mesa Ute History Project," pp. 10-11.

[32]Ibid.

[33]Ibid.

[34]Ibid.

[35]Benally, *Dine Ji Nakee' Naahane*, pp. 142, 160. See also *The Navajo Yearbook: 1951-1961, A Decade of Progress*, Report No. 8 (Window Rock, Arizona: Navajo Agency, 1961), pp. 259-62.

The Navajos*

Clyde J. Benally

> In beauty (happily) I walk.
> With beauty before me I walk.
> With beauty behind me I walk.
> With beauty below me I walk.
> With beauty above me I walk.
> It is finished (again) in beauty.
> It is finished in beauty.

It is generally agreed that the Navajos, the largest Indian tribe in the United States, came into the Southwest sometime after A.D. 1300, even though the Dine' (the "People") themselves do not attest to this. The Dine' mention their strong relationship to the Anasazi, the Ancient Ones, in their mythology and ceremonies. This relationship justifies to them permanent ties and absolute use rights to the native land that is bounded by four sacred mountains: the Blanca Peaks in New Mexico on the east, Mount Taylor in New Mexico on the south, the San Francisco Peaks in Arizona on the west, and the Hesperus Peaks in Colorado on the north. The Navajos live "in severely eroded plateau country . . . colorful, beautiful to look at, but hard to make a living from."[1]

In this red earth country of monoliths, buttes, and bridges of rock made by erosion of time, the Dine' had no concept of real ownership of land but instead one of communal property. Use rights were established by anyone who used and needed the land. The Dine' philosophy embodied

*This chapter was published in *The Peoples of Utah*, Helen Zeese Papanikolas, ed. (Salt Lake City: Utah State Historical Society, 1976).

Father Sky and Mother Earth as the parents of all and gave no individual absolute title to a piece of the sky or the earth. Also, they asked, who in his right mind would hold absolute ownership when his existence on this earth is but brief?

Father Sky is sacred as are his offerings: air, wind, thunder, lightning, and rain. Mother Earth is also sacred and all that she offers the Navajos is therefore sacred: mountains, vegetation, animals, and water. Many prayers for blessings are addressed to Mother Earth, Father Sky, the Four Winds, and White Dawn, to name a few.

Food and shelter are more than utilitarian objects for the Navajos who are always conscious that these are Mother Earth's gifts. Their food is simple and easily prepared. Mutton is commonly eaten; other meats are small game like rabbits and prairie dogs and large game such as deer and antelope. Infrequently a horse is butchered and all of the animal is used: the meat and entrails are eaten fresh or dried for later needs and the hide is made into footwear, belts, and articles of clothing. Corn is used not only for food but for offerings to the gods and for the mundane yet useful repair of leaky baskets. A large portion of Navajo myth is centered around corn, telling how Changing Woman (Nature), who created the ancestors of the Dine', gave instructions on how it should be raised. The dependability of corn for food is emphasized; cornmeal mush, cakes, and bread are some of the corn foods.

When wheat flour was stocked by trading posts, the Navajos conceived their well known fried bread, made from flour, baking powder, salt, and water (sugar and milk may be added), formed into flat rounds, and fried in lard or animal fat. Every cook has her own special recipe. For baking loaf bread, an outdoor earth oven is used.

The hogan, like corn, has deep religious importance. A similar structure, the Navajos believe, was used by the gods when they first laid down the ceremonies for the people. Every ceremony ends with a sacred hogan chant and everyone inside the hogan must be awake when it is sung.

There are two types of hogan, both built according

to religious dictates that require four main support posts: one each in the east, west, south, and north for the different gods in these directions. The hogan always faces east and the space inside is organized around the centrally placed fireplace.

The conical type of hogan is the original kind and is made by leaning cedar logs together to form a smoke hole and doorway. The domed-roof, or round hogan, is larger and has support posts arranged in a circle with logs laid horizontally from post to post. The logs are intersticed one upon the other until a small smoke hole is left at the top of the dome. The support poles are usually in multiples of four. A typical domed hogan usually has eight supports, but there could be as many as twelve. The logs are covered with brush, bark, and dirt.

Chants for the purification and blessing of the hogan belong to a multitude of rituals that are the fabric of the complex Navajo religion. Religious rites and the conduct of daily life are centered in the Navajo ideal: to live in sacred harmony, in beauty, and in blessedness. A vast knowledge of Navajo myths, history, and folk tales is needed to understand the repetitive, seemingly meaningless chants — often called "sings" or "dances."

Some rites are short, like the diagnostic ritual in which the hand trembler (diviner) observes a sick person to determine the nature of his illness and the appropriate healing ceremony. A significant short rite is the morning prayer to White Dawn to welcome a new day. Pollen from corn tassels is used and is richly symbolic of purity as well as of peace, happiness, and prosperity. Pollen-sprinkling along with specific chants consecrate and sanctify hogans, patients, prayer sticks, dry (sand) paintings, and cornmeal mush that is eaten ceremonially. Navajos call the haze in the air, pollen of morning sky and pollen of evening sky.[2]

The complex and lengthy rituals include, among many, the various three-day sings, five-day sings, and the nine-day sings. Some of these are often referred to as the Squaw Dance (Enemyway or Enemy chant), the Yei bi chai (Night chantway), and the Fire Dance (Mountain chantway).[3]

The roster of mythical figures in these sings appears to be endless; each has an important role in the history of the Dine', and their names instantly relate the Navajos to certain periods of time in their past. A few of these names are Rock Crystal Talking God, Happiness Boy, White Shell Woman, White Corn Boy, Yellow Corn Girl, First Man, Big Snake, Pollen Boy, and Cornbeetle Girl. While the lengthy sings go on, the medicine man performs an extremely complicated ritual with his bundle of herbs, prayer sticks, pollen, emetics (at times), and sand and sandstone for the dry paintings. The following, taken from a Beautyway ceremony, sung to the medicine man's ministrations, has only perplexity for the uninitiated:

> Dusty Body [Rattler], youth chief, I have made
> you an offering . . . Dusty Body maiden
> chief an offering . . .
> Pollen Body [Bull Snake], youth chief . . .
> Pollen Body maiden chief . . . Arrowsnake,
> youth chief . . .
> Arrowsnake, maiden chief . . . . [4]

For the Navajos, however, every line of a sing is important.

Under the two categories of ceremonies, Blessingway and Evilway, there are far too many ceremonies for any one medicine man (singer) to know all of them. Most medicine men specialize in one to six or seven ceremonies, and rarely will a medicine man specialize in more than eight. Everything has to be learned by memory. It takes years to learn the songs or chants, the myths and origins of each song, each ceremonial ritual, and the design and interpretation of sand paintings — if they are used. Learning is accomplished through apprenticeship to noted medicine men. After their education, medicine men have to be ceremonially ordained for each ceremony they perform.

During his training, each medicine man must acquire his own medicine bundle. This can be done by the ritualistic gathering of a bundle from an aging medicine man or by making up a new bundle. The type of ceremony that the medicine man knows will determine the kind and size of the medicine bundle. Collection of a new medicine bundle is time-consuming and includes herbs, pollens, feathers, sacred mountain dirt, stones, scrub oak branches, juniper bark, cattail flags, wild rice grass, rock sage, bear grass, plants with pods, and many other grasses and tree branches.

The medicine man, further, must be able to identify exactly every herb, plant, and other necessary object required in particular ceremonies. Like a medical doctor, he is on call at all times but goes to the patient's hogan to perform the necessary ceremony. The Navajo people usually know which medicine man in their area specializes in each ceremony. The chants are followed by serving food to the spectators, and, with the medicine man's fee, can be expensive.

Navajo society is close-knit; families are organized around the mother, grandmother, and sometimes, older sisters. A man usually lives with his wife in her mother's community. (Marriages are exogamous, outside the parents'

Navajo woman spinning wool, 1973. Photograph by Ken Hochfeld, USHS Collections.

clans.) The children inherit the mother's clan, and the cousins of the clan are referred to as brothers and sisters. Because of these strong ties, a Navajo has deep obligations in helping and in participating in functions involving his kin. If a ceremony is to be performed, the patient's kin are expected to assist in it. Males are obligated to their maternal clans and it is not unusual for a husband to leave his family to help his mother's kin.

Present Navajo society has had a long evolution. The first contact with foreigners occurred in the sixteenth century. From the Spanish the Dine' adopted practices that changed them from food hunters to sheep raisers. Besides acquiring sheep and horses from the Spanish, they discarded their buckskin clothing for the wool of the white men and learned silversmithing and the use of money (beso) as a medium of exchange. Intermarriage with the Spaniards produced the Nakai-di-nee clan.

From the time of this Spanish intrusion, the Dine' had to adapt to an ever-changing environment. The Navajos believe that almost all cultural practices originated within the tribe, but that weaving, farming, livestock raising, and some legends were learned from the Spanish and other southwestern Indian tribes. The Navajos are known as the most innovative of tribes, taking from other cultures what could be useful, discarding what could not, and being self-supporting under the poorest economy. Their flocks of sheep that must graze on vegetation so sparse that hogans are miles from each other attest to the great adaptability of the Navajos. In 1871 Willy Arny, a trader, persuaded a few Navajos to sell their wool at Fort Defiance, Arizona. The animals were spindly

> and gave no more than a pound or two of wool, hacked off with a homemade knife shaped from a tin can. But when the Navajos saw an economic advantage they took it. By 1886, they had a million pounds of wool to trade, and by 1890, two million.[5]

By crossing their Merino ewes with Rambouillet rams, the Navajos produced a hardy sheep with thick wool. Today sheep, the wealth of the Navajos, move through all of Navajo-

Navajo woman displaying rug, 1973. Photograph by Ken Hoch-feld, USHS Collections.

land, watched over by excellent male and female herders of all ages.

In both silversmithing — using bold, simple designs often with embedded turquoise — and in weaving, the Navajos became superb craftsmen.[6] Weaving with cotton was learned from the agricultural Pueblo Indians. Later when the Spanish drove sheep north into Arizona and New Mexico in 1540, wool was used. Mastering wool dyeing by using native roots, berries, and bark, the Navajos are credited with creating the first native tapestries in the United States. The predilection for red to traders, like Don Lorenzo Hubbell, and tourists coming into the land of the Dine' on Fred Harvey buses, together with new analine dyes in bright colors, threatened the craft for a while. Navajo weavers were given pictures to reproduce and in their experimentation with the analine dyes and their hurry to sell more of their work, a period of poor-quality rugs came off the looms. The market for Navajo rugs never waned, and weavers gave all their time to this source of income, always steady while drought and floods regularly ruined their crops. Blankets for their own use were no longer made; instead the softer wool blankets from Pendleton, Oregon, were bought at trading posts.

The Southwest Museum in Los Angeles displays many rugs in traditional designs that were original to the Navajos. The principal Utah Navajo weaving district is part of Monument Valley in the Four Corners area and is called Teec Nos Pos. The designs from this area are the most complex, "the least Indian and the most like oriental. . . . "[7] Outstanding weavers from this area are Alice Nelson, Hilda Begay, Emma Yabeney, Mrs. Saltwater, and Ester Williams.[8]

After the Spanish, who changed Navajo life with horses, sheep, and silver works, the next contacts with white men were the English-speaking Bilagaana ("white man"). This major event in the lives of the Navajos began when Mexico gave the responsibilities for the Dine' to the United States under the Treaty of Guadalupe Hidalgo in 1848. The preceding eight decades and the following two were the bloodiest in Navajo history, with wars against the Apaches, Utes, Spanish, Pueblos, and Comanches over slave raiding. Until the treaty, the Navajos governed themselves in clan units with the eldest or medicine man acting as head or chief. There was no head chief over all the Navajos, and trouble arose when a few chiefs signed treaties with white men who thought the clan leaders were representing the whole tribe. The treaty, for example, of November 22, 1846, signed by Narbona and other leaders was not accepted by Manuelito and other younger Navajos. Raiding continued, despite the treaty, until 1864 when large forces under Kit Carson conquered the Navajos. About eighty-five hundred Navajos were forced to take the "Long Walk" to Bosque Redondo in New Mexico. For four terrible years they were confined in a concentration camp, their self-sufficiency and independence destroyed. The captive Dine' began their homeward journey after the Treaty of 1868, and those who endured and survived regarded themselves with high esteem.

Navajos, living in the western part of the Navajo country, who had escaped from the United States militia into the rugged steep canyons of the San Juan and Colorado rivers of Arizona and Utah and were able to survive untouched, also thought of themselves as heroes because of their cunning and ability to elude capture.

The Treaty of 1868 ended the intense suffering of the Navajos and made them amenable to trading with whites. By 1877 six trading posts were established on the Navajo Reservation; by 1943, the peak in trading, ninety-five traders were licensed. The reservation trader was far different from the early itinerant trader who brought guns, liquor, and trinkets to Indian camps in return for furs. The reservation trader lived among confined Indians in his trading post with a reliable water supply nearby.[9] Because the Navajos lived far off in inaccessible terrain, the trader was often the only white man they ever saw. This isolation insured the Navajos' keeping their culture free from the white man's influence; it also, until the 1930s, gave traders great authority that was often misused, resulting in exploitation of the Dine' when selling their wool, rugs, and silver jewelry. Although 25 percent profit was the federally set limit, the isolation of the trading post gave dishonest traders the opportunity to buy and sell at their prices.

The trading post was the central meeting point for the widely scattered Navajos. For trading information, advice from the trader in business, personal, and government matters, medical help, the fearful burial of the dead, Indians rode hundreds of miles, first on horseback and later in pickup trucks. The trader continued in this role until the federal relief programs, begun in 1933, brought an increase in white personnel and diminished somewhat his status. A poignant novel of this period is Oliver La Farge's *Laughing Boy*, the story of a young Indian who was demoralized by his first contact with whites.

Navajo women wearing full orange, purple, and green sateen skirts and velveteen tops, their wealth in necklaces of silver, coral, and turquoise around their necks and silver bracelets on their arms, haggled with the trader over their rugs. Silver bracelets, bridles, squash necklaces, and buttons — often made of United States dimes and quarters — were pawned for supplies. The pawn could remain hanging in the trading post for years. Wool and rugs were sold to cut down the price of the pawn ticket. A sample pawn ticket on a silver bracelet:

Woman-Who-Doesn't-Smoke[10]

flour and coffee	$1.45	2/19/30
sateen	1.80	3/15/30
	3.25	
rug pd.	2.00	4/ 3/30
	1.25	
velveteen	2.50	5/20/30
	3.25 [*sic*]	
coffee, sugar	1.10	6/ 5/30
	4.35	
wool	4.35	6/10/30
plus $2 to trade out	$0.00	

82

Navajos near the Utah border traded at Oljato, Gouldings, Gap (for many years run by Joe Lee, son of John D. Lee who was held responsible for the Mountain Meadows Massacre), Hatch's, Aneth, and trading posts in Bluff and Blanding.

It has been a long and slow progress from the trader representing the Indians to the present tribal government begun by United States agents. The policy of the government in education and in tribal affairs was to transform Navajos into white men.

The United States directed social and cultural change at every level of tribal society. Although Navajos were given livestock and farm implements, they also were forced, in many cases, to cut their conjos (long hair tied in a bun) before receiving wagons; and children, frightened by separation from their families and far from their hogans, had their hair cut as soon as they arrived at school. The proud tradition of wearing conjos was destroyed with severe loss of self-esteem.

At the beginning the tribal government was merely administrative in nature and carried out the programs of the Bureau of Indian Affairs. Since then the Navajos have learned the intricacies of laws and bureaucracy and are now on the verge of total self-government. The various branches of the Navajo tribal government plan, control, and administer their own programs. The overriding theme is self-determination in conducting their own affairs. To accomplish these goals, there is a big push by the tribe toward education while keeping its Navajoness.

No longer working only with the Bureau of Indian Affairs, Navajos today run for local school boards, county commissions, and state legislatures. The tribe communicates and works directly with the state and national governments. All in all, the Navajo, a great learner, has mastered the white man's politics.

Since the Treaty of 1868, Navajoland has been expanded many times. Westward expansion was initiated by unilateral executive order of May 17, 1884, and took in northeastern Airzona and southeastern Utah below the San Juan River.

Father Harold Baxter Liebler, Episcopalian missionary to the Indians, 1973. Photograph by Ken Hochfeld, USHS Collections.

The order of March 10, 1905, added the Aneth area north of the San Juan. The Paiute Strip had been classified in various ways until it was added to the reservation along the Aneth Extension by act of March 1, 1933. The Land Exchange Act of September 2, 1958, added McCracken Mesa and other lands north of the Aneth Extension area. This exchange was for land presently covered by the water of Lake Powell.

The United States Indian policy is slowly changing, giving Indians a voice in the policies and programs that affect them. This makes education more meaningful and develops expertise in the handling of tribal affairs.

While the future looks bright, a tremendous amount of effort is needed to improve Navajo education and to introduce industrial development to create jobs on the reservation, even though more Navajos are moving into the cities for work.

In Navajoland today adults in both Indian and "American" dress and little girls wearing cotton dresses, boys in jeans still travel the dusty road to trading posts where cases of the ubiquitous soda pop bottles are stacked. Some of the Navajos attend Father Baxter Liebler's Saint Christopher Episcopal Mission church or Catholic and Mormon services. For medical services they have, besides their medicine men, the Seventh Day Adventist Hospital near Goulding's Trading Post. Their children ride hours on yellow school buses for their education and when of high school age attend boarding schools as far away as the Indian school in Brigham City, Utah, where they meet students from other tribes. Many never return to live on the reservation where mothers still admonish children not to kill spiders because they are friends. It was Mrs. Spider, they say, who taught Navajo women how to spin fine threads from leaf fibers, cotton, and wool into useful articles.[11]

Great-grandfathers still explain the beginning of time through folk tales and how the First People were led out of the pitch in the center of the earth to the outside by Coyote and Badger. Coyote (usually the epitome of irresponsibility) told them, "Our tunnel is straight and will lead you to the dry land of the new world, but if you follow the crooked tunnels of the blind mole you will always live in the earth."[12]

The First People followed Coyote and Badger and emerged into Navajoland where on its red earth they lived close to nature and where they survive to this day in their hogans, looms nearby, and flocks of sheep spread out, grazing on the sparse life-nurturing plants.

NOTES

[1]Leland C. Wyman, ed., *Beautyway: A Navaho Ceremonial* (New York, 1957), p. 5.

[2]Gladys A. Reichard, *Navajo Religion: A Study of Symbolism*, 2d ed. (New York, 1963), pp. 251-52.

[3]See Wyman, *Beautyway*, and Leland C. Wyman, *Blessingway* (Tucson, 1970). A discussion of Enemyway is found in the latter.

[4]Wyman, *Beautyway*, p. 105.

[5]Ruth M. Underhill, *The Navajos* (Norman, Okla., 1956), p. 181.

[6]See Elizabeth Compton Hegemann, "Pioneer Silversmiths," *The Masterkey* 36-37 (1962): 44-59, 102-13; David L. Newmann, "Navajo Silversmithing," *El Palacio* 77 (1971): 13-32; and *Arizona Highways*, July 1974.

[7]See Carl Schaefer Dentzel, "Native American Tapestries of the Navajo," *Arizona Highways*, July 1974.

[8]Ibid., p. 6.

[9]See Elizabeth Compton Hegemann, *Navaho Trading Days* (Albuquerque, 1963) and Frank McNitt, *The Indian Traders* (Norman, Okla., 1962).

[10]Hegemann, *Navaho Trading Days*, p. 341.

[11]Franc Johnson Newcomb, *Navajo Folk Tales* (Santa Fe, 1967), p. xiii.

[12]Ibid., p. 53.

PART THREE

The Hole-in-the-Rock Trail

Looking down the Hole-in-the-Rock. USHS Collections.

The Hole-in-the-Rock Trail a Century Later

Allan Kent Powell

Because historic sites and places reverenced by a people tell much about their culture, development, and values, the Hole-in-the-Rock trail is of immense importance as a symbol of the pioneering effort throughout the Intermountain West from 1847 until into the twentieth century. There remains much of the original 180-mile road, opened in 1879 and 1880 through one of the most isolated, desolate, and difficult areas of the United States, to inspire, illuminate, and challenge us. Familiarity with the trail raises questions of why and how this unique relic of the pioneer experience came to be and how it can be best used and preserved for the benefit and enrichment of the people of this county, this country, and the world. For just as shrines like Jamestown, Plymouth, Independence Hall, the Alamo, and Gettysburg speak of freedom and the birth and survival of this nation, the Hole-in-the-Rock trail rings of commitment, dedication, and accomplishment in the settlement of the West.

While there were many factors and forces in the pioneer process, no other single trail experience more vividly and forcefully etches the nature of the pioneer experience on one's consciousness. The Hole-in-the-Rock trail is a unique inheritance from our western pioneers. Unlike other treasured heirlooms from these people — such as a Bible, gun, stick of furniture, or piece of jewelry which conjure up memories of our predecessors in the comfort of our modern-day surroundings, the trail takes us back to experience physically the fatigue, heat, isolation, and sometimes danger these pioneers felt as we travel over and examine this unique historic site.

The purpose of this paper is to describe the Hole-in-the-Rock trail as it remains today, a century later, while examining the background and history of its development. Implicit in this endeavor is the plea for greater recognition of and care for this priceless treasure of our pioneer past.

In his book, *The Gathering of Zion*, the Pulitizer Prize winning author, Wallace Stegner, writes of the symbolic importance of the trail:

> For every early Saint, crossing the plains to Zion in the Valleys of the Mountains was not merely a journey but a rite of passage, the final, devoted, enduring act that brought one into the Kingdom. Until the railroad made the journey too easy, and until new

Members of the 1880 Hole-in-the-Rock expedition, c. 1930. Left to right: Parley Butt, Leona Walton Nielson, Margaret Adams, Sarah Jane Wilson, unidentified, unidentified, Caroline Nielson Redd, Sarah Perkins, Charlie Walton, Kumen Jones seated. Special Collections, Marriott Library, University of Utah.

generations born in the valley began to outnumber the immigrant Saints, the shared experience of the trail was a bond that reinforced the bonds of the faith; and to successive generations who did not personally experience it, it has continued to have sanctity as legend and myth. . . .

Symbols of the trail rise as naturally out of the Mormon mind as the phrase about making the desert blossom as the rose — and that springs to Mormon lips with the innocent ease of birdsong. Those symbols — white bows of covered wagons, horned cattle low-necked in the yoke, laboring files of handcarts, booted and bearded pioneers, sunbonneted Mothers of Zion — are recurrent, if not compulsive, in Mormon art, which runs strongly to monumental sculpture and is overwhelmingly historical in emphasis. One might expect to find artistic treatment of Joseph's revelations from God or His angels, the early persecutions and martyrdoms, the massacre at Haun's Mill, the assassination of Joseph and Hyrum Smith in Carthage Jail. But these things, though remembered, have not emerged as abiding symbols. Instead, one finds the trail.[1]

While Stegner accurately assesses the experience of crossing the trail to Utah as a rite of passage which brought one into the Mormon Kingdom, by no means did the pioneering experience end as the last handcart or wagon rolled through the mouth of Emigration Canyon or Parley's Canyon and into the Valley of the Great Salt Lake. These wagons would carry the Saints to over three hundred settlements in the Intermountain West where the community-building experience, unlike that of the trail, would prove an ongoing, never-ending, and sometimes hopeless endeavor.

Perhaps the trail is an important Mormon symbol because it illustrates the pioneer ability to conquer, to succeed, and to endure to the end — essential elements in any scheme to colonize and hold the deserts, valleys, and mountains of this vast land.

In this settlement process nineteenth-century Mormons would draw time and again upon their trail experience. However, as the first band of Mormon pioneers traveled west from Nebraska in 1847 with few problems or obstacles, little did they realize that more than three decades later their legacy would drive a band of fellow Saints to find and open a trail which by all elements of reason should have been judged impossible. For the few whose pioneer saga encompassed both the trek to Utah and the Hole-in-the-Rock trail, the comparison voiced by Mons Larson was no doubt representative: ". . . the handcart journey . . . he made . . . from Winter Quarters to Salt Lake City was not nearly so hard as the journey through the Hole-in-the-Rock."[2]

The settlement of the San Juan area was not an isolated event in Utah's history but followed in logical sequence a colonization effort which encompassed portions of Canada, Mexico, all of Utah, and parts of Idaho, Wyoming, Nevada, Colorado, New Mexico, and California. The process began with the establishment of Salt Lake City in 1847 and continued over the next three decades until Brigham Young's death in 1877 at the rate of about a hundred communities each decade.

The San Juan region was, and is still, one of the most isolated parts of the United States. The country is extremely rough and broken. The canyons of the Colorado River and San Juan River and their tributaries are characterized by sheer-walled cliffs several hundred feet high, while the surrounding mesas, hills, and washes with their bone-jarring slickrock, cedar forests, and sand presented their own obstacles to transportation. In addition, by 1880 the San Juan region was the last area in Utah to be occupied by a large number of Indians, as the San Juan River was something of a natural meeting area for Navajos, Utes, and Paiutes.

Given the ruggedness of the country, the questionable agricultural potential of the region, the availability of more accessible virgin agricultural land in other areas, and the threat of Indian hostilities, it is understandable why the settlement of the San Juan area came in the twilight of the Mormon settlement effort. That the settlement was not delayed longer than 1880 can be traced to the need to cultivate better relations with the Indians, to insure Mormon control of the area and thereby increase the security of Mormon settlements to the west, to open new lands as the older Mormon settlements had reached the limit of usable farmland, and to provide a springboard for future Mormon settlements to the east, south, and north.

Also of great concern to church leaders was the occupation of all usable farm and grazing land, especially if non-Mormons threatened to acquire the land. Additionally, the San Juan region was felt to provide a more satisfactory home for converts from the southern states who found the winters too cold, yet, according to church leaders, needed the pioneer experience to get ". . . a good foundation temporally and spiritually."[3]

Finally, members of the Hole-in-the-Rock expedition were convinced that they were part of a divine plan. As one member of the expedition wrote in later years:

Wagon coming up through Little Hole-in-the-Rock, during reenactment of the Hole-in-the-Rock trek. USHS Collections.

My purpose in this humble effort in writing about it [the Hole-in-the-Rock trek] is to convince my children and my descendants of the fact that this San Juan Mission was planned, and has been carried on thus far, by prophets of the Lord, and that the people engaged in it have been blessed and preserved by the power of the Lord according to their faith and obedience to the counsels of their leaders. No plainer case of the truth of this manifestation of the power of the Lord has ever been shown in ancient or modern times.[4]

Plans for a colonizing mission to the San Juan were announced at the quarterly conference of the Parowan Stake held December 28 and 29, 1878. Although the specific location of the settlement had not been selected, people were issued calls to participate in the endeavor. For many this meant giving up comfortable homes in the older settlements of Parowan, Paragonah, Cedar City, Panguitch, and other communities. While those called were not compelled to go, many firmly believed that the call was divinely inspired and wherever the church authorities directed they would go.

In early January 1879 Mormon Church President John Taylor appointed Silas S. Smith of Paragonah leader of the San Juan Mission. Seven months later Taylor called Platte D. Lyman of Oak City as an assistant to Smith. Because of Smith's absence from the group while securing funds and arranging for supplies, Lyman was the recognized leader of the expedition from mid-December 1879 until after their arrival at Bluff in April 1880.

The 236 individuals included in the San Juan Mission came from sixteen different Utah communities and settlements.[5] Some, such as Woodruff, St. George, Junction, Kanarraville, Kanab, Santaquin, Holden, and Bear Valley were represented by 1 to 5 individuals, most of whom were young single men. Oak City provided 7 for the expedition, all of whom were Lymans. Further south, the settlement of New Harmony produced 16, including Lemuel H. Redd, Jr., and his wife, Eliza Ann Westover. Beaver also provided 16 people including the William Willard Hutchings, Joseph Lillywhite, and Henry James Riley families. Panguitch furnished 20 individuals including the Danielson Baron Barney, James Pace, and George Washington Sevey families.

But it was Iron County that provided the majority of San Juan pioneers. The three communities of Parowan, Paragonah, and Cedar City produced 145 individuals. Parowan was represented by 52, including 21 from the Decker families and the 9 children of Samuel and Ann Rowley which distinguished theirs as the largest family to undertake the journey. Paragonah provided 47 people, including the leader Silas S. Smith, 15 members of four Robb families, and a young man, Amasa Barton, who lost his life at the hands of Indians in June 1887 when they attacked his trading post on the San Juan River at the mouth of Comb Wash. The 46 individuals from Cedar City included some of the oldest and most experienced pioneers of the southern Utah frontier — the Perkins brothers, Benjamin and Hyrum, and Jens Nielson, a member of the 1856 Martin Handcart Company who, at the age of fifty-nine, was the unofficial patriarch of the group.

In the spring of 1879 an exploring party consisting of 26 men, 2 women, and 8 children under the leadership of Silas S. Smith left to explore the trail to the San Juan River and select a permanent settlement location. Traveling southeast into Arizona, they crossed the Colorado River at Lee's Ferry and continued on to Moenkopi where they turned northeast through Navajo country, recrossed the Utah-Arizona border, and made their way to Fort Montezuma on the San Juan River. Here they spent two and a half months exploring the area, building a dam, digging irrigation ditches, and constructing a few houses before returning to the settlements for their families and equipment.

The trail from Moenkopi to the San Juan River had proven very dry, and potential problems with Indians over the scarce water and feed led to the abandonment of this route as a practical way to the San Juan region from the southern Utah settlements. The exploring party returned to their homes by traveling north past the future sites of Blanding and Monticello and to the Old Spanish Trail at the south end of the La Sal Mountains. They followed the trail west to the crossing of the Colorado River at present-day Moab, on to Green River, through Castle Valley, and down Salina Canyon to the Sevier Valley and south to Parowan. In retrospect this northern route along the Spanish Trail would have been the most practical. However, it covered a distance of more than five hundred miles whereas a direct route would be half

Dugway off the slick rocks, Hole-in-the-Rock trail. Special Collections, Marriott Library, University of Utah.

that distance. More exploration was ordered.

During the summer of 1879 Andrew P. Schow and Reuben Collett of Escalante, in response to a request by Silas Smith, explored east from Escalante with a two-wheeled cart carrying a wagon box boat to the Colorado River. After crossing the river they returned to Parowan with a favorable report of the trail. Smith, who was a good friend of the men, was anxious to avoid both the southern and northern routes of the exploring expedition and on the strength of the Schow-Collett report announced in September 1879 that the expedition would proceed to the San Juan via the Escalante route. To those called to settle the San Juan region, the report that a direct route from Escalante to the San Juan River had been found must have been taken as evidence of God's help in the endeavor.

Shortly after the announcement, members of the expedition began their journey to Escalante, then forty miles southeast to the camp and rendezvous point at Forty Mile Spring. From there several exploring parties were dispatched. They returned with negative reports about the feasibility of constructing a wagon road east of the Colorado River. However, the expedition was left with little choice but to push on ahead since the winter snows in the Escalante mountains blocked any return to their former homes, and the prospect of wintering in Escalante was ruled out. According to Lynn Lyman, long-time student of the trail, "Once the decision was made to push ahead, everything the pioneers did was rational and logical."[6] This premise is a very useful guide for locating and documenting the trail today.

The Hole-in-the-Rock trail began about one mile southeast of the town of Escalante where the old route leaves present-day Utah Highway 12 and followed south one mile to Alvey Wash where it continued down the wash to Ten Mile Spring. The spring did not offer much water for those who stopped, and one traveler, Samuel Rowley, claimed the water they found in Alvey Wash ". . . was so hard that peas and beans would not cook in it."[7] Platte D. Lyman, who arrived at the spring on November 20, 1879, found it dry and had to send the stock seven miles to the east for water.

At Ten Mile Spring the road left Alvey Wash and continued southeast across Ten Mile Flat, Cottonwood Wash, Half Way Hollow, and Seep Flat to Twenty Mile Spring. The soft, sandy road provided relatively easy travel, although double teaming was necessary across the washes. From Twenty Mile Spring the road continued southeast across Sunset Flat, where remains of the road are still visible, and on to Dance Hall Rock, approximately twenty-four miles southeast of Twenty Mile Spring. This sandstone formation with its amphitheater-like shelter and smooth floor is a major landmark on the trail and derives its name from its use for dances by pioneers camped a mile away at Forty Mile Spring.

Forty Mile Spring was the major expedition headquarters for more than three weeks as individual groups journeyed there between November 15 and December 5, 1879. The spring offered the best water supply between Escalante and the Colorado River and is presently piped into a tank for watering cattle.

From Forty Mile Spring the trail continued southeast across Sooner Bench along the edge of the Fifty Mile Mountain. Here the trail became more difficult as travelers faced a number of gulches and canyons. Recognizing the accomplishment of building a road the sixty-five miles from Escalante through this area, David E. Miller wrote:

> If the San Juan pioneers had merely succeeded in building a wagon road through that part of the country — to Fifty-mile Spring — and then returned to the settlements, their achievement would have been outstanding. But this was really easy terrain to cross compared to what lay ahead.[8]

The remaining six miles from Fifty Mile Spring to the Hole-in-the-Rock gave the pioneers their first introduction to the slickrock against which they would battle for many miles on the east side of the Colorado River.

Because of the scarcity of water, the camp at Fifty Mile Spring became the major headquarters during construction of the road through the Hole-in-the-Rock. Here approximately half of the expedition remained while those working on the road returned to the camp on Saturday evening to spend Sunday with their families before returning to work on the road Monday morning. Construction of the road at the Hole-in-the-Rock required eight weeks on three major sections: the notch itself; the road from the base of the cliff below the notch to the Colorado River; and the dugway out of the river gorge on the east side of the river which had to be cut from the solid rock wall.

Before work started down through the Hole-in-the-Rock, the cleft was nothing more than a very narrow crack — too narrow to allow for the passage of wagons and with a forty-five foot sheer drop that had to be cut back to provide a steep but manageable slope. Because of the shortage of blasting powder and tools and because of the limited working space at the top of the Hole, the men were divided into three crews and work proceeded simultaneously on all three projects. Those working at the top of the Hole had to be lowered over the forty-five foot cliff with ropes until a suitable grade had been cut. Jens Nielson, Benjamin Perkins, and Hyrum Perkins were in charge of the blasting. The Perkins brothers had become proficient in the use of blasting powder in the coal mines of Wales before emigrating to the United States.

One of the most ingenious and daring road-building feats was the construction of Uncle Ben's Dugway at the base of the notch. At this point it was impossible to continue the straight descent downward and it was necessary to angle the road to the left across the long slickrock slope. Ben Perkins, proposed a suggestion, and with no other choice available the men went to work under his supervision. Charles Redd wrote:

> First Ben directed the smith to widen out the bits of the drills. Then men were set to drilling holes about four feet apart along the down-side edge of the slick-rock where the wagons had to cross. While the grade was nothing like that higher up, it was still

so steep that men swinging the doublejack hammers had to be secured by a rope passed around their waists and steadied by a fellow-worker from above. The vertical holes they drilled were six to ten inches deep and large enough to admit a sizeable oak stake which was driven in and left sticking up two feet. Driftwood logs and poles were then piled against these stakes, and a screen of brush was placed over the logs to prevent the fill-dirt and rocks from seeping through. This crib was then filled to the level with solid matter, and the road bed for the lower wagon wheel was ready to be tried. Meanwhile, along the upper side of the road bed and parallel to the "tacked-on" fill with pick and drill they cut a rut, four to six inches deep in the rock and wide enough for a wagon wheel.[9]

Today the oak poles, rock, and brush have washed away, but the drill holes are plainly visible. By January 25, 1880, the road was completed and the next day about forty wagons were taken down through the Hole-in-the-Rock and twenty-six ferried across the river.

The descent by wagon through the Hole required rough-locking the wheels and attaching long ropes to the wagons so that a dozen or more men could hang on and help slow the speed of the wagon. Women and children walked down through the Hole and were forced to slide down the forty feet at the top because it was so steep they could not walk. Writing to her parents on February 22, 1880, Elizabeth Morris Decker gave this account of the descent to the river.

> If you ever come this way it will scare you to death to look down it. It is about a mile from the top down to the river and it is almost strait down, the cliffs on each side are five hundred ft. high and there is just room enough for a wagon to go down. It nearly scared me to death. The first wagon I saw go down they put the brake on and rough locked the hind wheels and had a big rope fastened to the wagon and about ten men holding back on it and then they went down like they would smash everything. I'll never forget that day. When we was walking down Willie looked back and cried and asked me how we would get back home.[10]

Despite the dangerous descent there was no major tragedy — no animals were killed and no wagons were tipped over or seriously damaged.

In 1880 the Hole-in-the-Rock offered the only possible

crossing of the Colorado River between Lee's Ferry on the south and present-day Moab on the north, a distance of approximately three hundred miles. In 1956 a rock fall in the gorge destroyed much of the road and has made it impossible for wagons, motor vehicles, or even horses to get down the trail. It is possible to hike through the gorge with some climbing and crawling over the fallen boulders. Within the gorge chisel marks remain and at the bottom of the gorge, where Uncle Ben's dugway was constructed, cribbing built and post holes drilled by the original expedition remain.[11]

Today the lower half of the trail is covered by the waters of Lake Powell. The section covered is a long, steep sandy hill on which little construction was done. Fortunately, the most spectacular features of the Hole-in-the-Rock are above the lake level and accessible to boaters.

Once across the Colorado River the San Juan pioneers faced what Platte D. Lyman described as ". . . the worst country I ever saw. . . [it] is almost entirely solid sand rock, high hills and mountains cut all to pieces by deep gulches which are in many places altogether impassable."[12] Yet pass through they must, and the first twenty-five miles east of the Colorado proved a test of their road-building skills almost equal to that required coming through the Hole-in-the-Rock.

Leaving the Colorado River, they cut a dugway from a two-hundred-fifty-foot cliff. This dugway, other shorter dugways onto the bench land above the Colorado, and the road around the north side of Register Rocks — named by David E. Miller in 1953 for the names of several of the original company chiseled into the rock — and part of the trail up Cottonwood Canyon have been covered by Lake Powell.

The road east from Cottonwood Canyon crossed a small stream several times to a grove of Cottonwood trees where camp was established. With the sheer walls of Cottonwood Canyon blocking further passage, the pioneers were forced to turn south and ascend a steep sandy hill, laying a large section of cribbing to provide a level bed as the road rounded the shoulder of what one traveler called a mountain of

Little Hole-in-the-Rock, 1980. Photograph by Allan Kent Powell.

"almost pure sand."[13] On top of the sandhill the road followed southeast a couple of hundred yards to the base of
Cottonwood Hill. Here, putting to good use part of a recently
arrived shipment of a thousand pounds of blasting powder,
the road builders shattered a precipitous dugway from the
solid sandstone's north face.

Judging from the number of accidents this was the most
dangerous spot along the trail. Henry John Holyoak recalled
that when a chain broke the wagon overturned, spilling a
hive of bees which had to be sacked ". . . before we could
start packing the pieces of wagon and the load up the hill."[14]
Later in the spring while returning from a trip to Escalante
for supplies, Platte D. Lyman spilled a load of flour over the
red sandstone hill when on the morning of May 20th his
wagon broke loose from the team ". . . and ran back and off
the dugway and tipped over, breaking the reach, box, bows,
flour sacks and some other things and scattered my load all
over the side of the hill."[15] The accident necessitated a day's
delay while the wagon was repaired and the supplies collected. These were the only accidents reported during
travel on the entire trail in 1880.

Once this dangerous dugway on Cottonwood Hill was
negotiated, the wagons rolled a short distance over a bed of
slickrock, where rock cribbing laid to keep the wagons from
sliding can still be seen, to a V-shaped notch named Little
Hole-in-the-Rock, which leads to the top of a small mesa.
Here the steep pull ends for a time and the trail jars across
the slickrock in an easterly direction for three-quarters of a
mile to Cheese Camp, so named for the forty pounds of
cheese brought from the Panguitch Tithing Office by two
men from that community who arrived to assist in building
the road. The unnamed volunteers worked on the road
through the slickrock and off Grey Mesa for nearly two weeks
before they returned to Panguitch in disgust, claiming "the
road wasn't finished, and never would be."[16]

From Cheese Camp the road continued over the slickrock for two miles to the base of the Chute. Elizabeth Deck-

er described the terrain as ". . . the roughest country you or anybody else ever seen; it's nothing in the world but rocks and holes, hills and hollows. The mountains are just one solid rock as smooth as an apple."[17] Her husband, Cornelius, saw the apple-smooth rocks as resembling "great hay stacks."[18] Today much of the trail is identifiable by the cuts and cribbing that were necessary to allow safe passage across the treacherous sloping rock.

At the Chute, ". . . there was no danger of slipping off the road or tipping over — there was simply nowhere to tip or slip."[19] The Chute is a natural U-shaped notch, barely wide enough for wagons, which rises approximately five hundred feet in elevation in less than a quarter of a mile from the canyon floor to the relatively flat slickrock above.

From the top of the Chute the trail crossed the solid slickrock for a mile and a half and on to the western extension of Grey Mesa for a mile, then down and up a ravine for

Hole-in-the-Rock trail across the slick rocks with a section of cribbing, 1981. Photograph by Allan Kent Powell.

a half mile before reaching the grass and sagebrush table of Grey Mesa. With a magnificent view of the Great Bend of the San Juan River and Navajo Mountain to the right and the peaks of the Henry Mountains to the left, the expedition rolled across the seven-and-a-half mile flat and sandy mesa top without difficulty. Despite the cold and snow there was plenty of feed for horses and cattle. It was on Grey Mesa that Olivia, wife of Mons Larson, gave birth to a son on February 21, 1880. Born within view of the San Juan River, the boy was named John Rio.

The good time made in crossing Grey Mesa was quickly lost in the week required to blast and cut the half-mile of road through the slickrock off the east edge of the mesa which did not have a natural chute like the west end. The route off Grey Mesa was located by George Hobbs, one of the four explorers sent out in December 1879, who followed a mountain sheep — which he labeled a llama — down the slickrock. On February 20, 1880, Platte D. Lyman recorded that after driving seven miles over a smooth bench they camped

> . . . at the top of the smooth rock over which we will build a road. Here the bench terminates abruptly, and a rough broken valley full of sand and low reefs of sandstone lays below us, and to reach it we will have to build a road ½ mile down through the steep hills and little pockets in the rock which extends from the top to the very bottom.[20]

Eight days later the road was completed and the dangerous descent made. Nearly sixty years later Cornelius Decker recalled this stretch of the trail: ". . . we had to drive down a sharp hill to where my lead wagon was on one side of the top of the hill and my trail wagon the other side. It was rainy and slippery, but I got down allright. . . ."[21]

At the top of the slickrock, parts from an abandoned wagon can be found and the trail can be located with little difficulty by the cribbing, dugways, cuts, and wagon tracks that remain.

Once off the slickrock, the pioneers made good time

traveling in a northwesterly direction through what cowboys would later call Death Valley to the east side of Table Top Mesa and on to Lake Pagahrit — a half-mile long, quarter-mile wide, and fifty-foot deep lake which was created when sand drifted into Lake Canyon and formed a large dam which also served as a road for the pioneers. The dam washed away in 1915 under pressure of heavy rains. When the Hole-in-the-Rock expedition arrived on February 29, 1880, Platte D. Lyman wrote: "Cottonwood, willow, canes, flags, bullrushes and several kinds of grass grow luxuriantly, and it would make an excellent stock ranch. On a point of rock jutting into the lake is the remains of an old stone fortification built probably several hundred years ago."[22]

At the lake the travelers took time to repair wagons and gear, wash clothes, and rest after the arduous, month-long endeavor to push the thirty miles from the Colorado River. Today there is ample evidence of Lake Pagahrit in the stained canyon walls and dried deposits of algae on the canyon rim.

Hole-in-the-Rock trail down the east side of the slick rocks showing wagon rut. Lynn Lyman in the background, 1980. Photograph by Allan Kent Powell.

The slick rocks, Hole-in-the-Rock trail. Special Collections, Marriott Library, University of Utah.

The ancient town observed by Lyman is no longer there; however, pottery sherds, flint chippings, and dirt mounds concealing early structures testify that Lake Pagahrit was an important center long before the arrival of the Hole-in-the-Rock pioneers.

After crossing Lake Pagahrit Dam the expedition turned in an easterly direction past a prominent rock cairn placed by the four scouts on their earlier trek. Nearly four miles further east a second rock cairn was placed. Today, approximately a mile further on, the remains of an old wagon manufactured in Dundee, Indiana, and secured to the slickrock by the Bureau of Land Management, can be found. The wagon marked the junction of the Hole-in-the-Rock road with the Hall's Crossing road that was opened in 1881 and proved a much better route west from the San Juan to the southern Utah settlements.

The eastward course carried the 1880 pioneers another seven miles to a ridge that descended into Castle Wash. Here

Platte D. Lyman wrote: "The country looks much better," and as he traveled down Castle Wash the road proved to be "very sandy, but even and tolerably good."[23] Today the original pioneer road has been obliterated by Highway 263 which occupies much of the level terrain along Castle Creek. However, Green Spring and Irish Green Spring, which offered water for the travelers, still flow, and the Indian ruin, investigated by the four scouts in December 1879 while en route to Fort Montezuma, still stands, though not in the pristine condition described by Scout George B. Hobbs who wrote: ". . . there were 7 rooms, the bake oven being in such a perfect state of preservation that by cleaning out the dust it would be ready to bake bread in at this late day."[24]

The ancient residents left not only interesting fortifications and dwellings but also a clearly marked trail the Mormons could follow with little difficulty. The Cliff Dwellers trail, as designated by Hobbs and others, was followed for the three miles off Clay Hill Pass onto Whirlwind Bench nearly a thousand feet below. Here the pioneers worked for a week laying cribbing, making fills, and scratching a passable road out of the sticky blue clay. Much of the pioneer road remains although it takes a careful and knowing eye to discern the old trail from the more obvious road built by the Skelly Oil Company in the 1950s.

On the night of March 13, as the group moved off the Clay Hill Divide, the weather turned bad. A howling blizzard struck the camps and caused Platte D. Lyman to suffer ". . . the coldest night I ever experienced, it was impossible to be comfortable in bed or anywhere else."[25]

Turning in a northeasterly direction the next morning to circle the head of Grand Gulch, the pioneers found the way along the base of the Red House Cliffs to be easy traveling. Here the eighty-three wagons spread out over a distance of thirty miles as those with stronger teams pushed ahead, leaving those with weaker animals to catch up as the expedition reached the cedar forest at the base of Elk Ridge. The sagebrush openings at Harmony Flat, Grand Flat, and Mormon Flat

Hole-in-the-Rock trail across Grand Flat showing tree stumps cut by members of the 1880 expedition. Photograph by Allan Kent Powell, 1980.

offered excellent camping spots while cutters moved in advance of the wagons to hew a passable trail though the often dense cedars. Today this portion of the trail is well marked and can be easily followed around the head of Grand Gulch as the well-known landmark, the Bears Ears, looms above the trail. Stubs of cedar trees cut over a hundred years ago can still be seen. However, in one section near Mormon Flat the trail has been obliterated by a chaining operation to clear land to increase its value for grazing.

After the long detour to the northeast to avoid the impassable canyon of Grand Gulch, the trail turned to the south as it bypassed Salvation Knoll, a promontory about two miles to the east from which the four scouts were able to regain their bearings on Christmas Day when they located the Blue Mountains and Comb Wash. After approximately five miles the trail turned to the southeast for about twenty-five miles, crossing Long Flat then Snow Flat before descending the Twist into Road Canyon and on to the western face of Comb Ridge. The route down the Twist had been marked by the four explorers on their return trip from Montezuma Creek.

Comb Ridge forced the travelers to resume a southerly course as the road followed approximately ten miles "through very bad sand" down Comb Wash to its junction with the San Juan River.[26] By the time the group reached Comb Wash the prolonged and difficult trek had exacted a heavy toll from the participants. Many years later Cornelius Decker recalled his family's plight:

> The night we got down into Comb Wash, just before we got to the San Juan River, our meat and everything else had give out on us. My dear wife and my two little boys had to eat dry bread for their supper. There is where I thought my heart would break; to see them go to bed with nothing but dry bread to eat. My dear wife never did have much of an appetite, with the best of stuff to eat. That hurts me yet when ever I think of it. Yet none of them said a word; even those two little boys ate their dry bread and never said a word about it. I tell you that cut me to the quick. I never slept much that night; I was trying to think what could I do to get them something to eat. The next morning was

no better but that day about noon we landed on the San Juan River about 10 miles from our destination; my brother Alvin killed a calf and gave us quite a big piece of it.[27]

Once on the north bank of the San Juan River the pioneers had hoped to build their road along the north side of the river to Montezuma nearly thirty miles upriver to the east. But as so often on their arduous trek the pioneers found nature uncooperative and geography an especially trouble-some adversary as the cliffs adjacent to the river blocked their passage. Consequently, the journey demanded one more grueling trial of the bone-weary and discouraged travelers. The task to build a road to the top of Comb Wash by way of San Juan Hill has left a colossal, though fragile, monument to the endurance, perseverance, ingenuity, and dedication of the San Juan pioneers. David E. Miller captured the sensation of the first-time visitor to San Juan Hill:

I first examined this spot in March, 1953, in company with Dr. C. G. Crampton. Albert R. Lyman had described the region and told us where to look for the old road; but even then we could hardly believe it when our eyes caught the faint line angling up

San Juan Hill, 1980. Photograph by Allan Kent Powell.

the face of that solid rock wall. What we saw from the benchland near the river bank looked as though it might have been an abandoned horse trail — but surely not a wagon road. However, there was nothing else in sight and no other place for a road, so we climbed up the face of that huge rock swell for a closer look. And sure enough, there was the old road up San Juan Hill![28]

The difficulty of the road up San Juan Hill and the way it exacted the last reserves of strength and determination from the exhausted animals and men was recalled by Lemuel H. Redd, Jr., who was twenty-three years old when he drove his wagon to the top of San Juan Hill. Redd's son Charles wrote of San Juan Hill and his father:

. . . seven span of horses were used, so that when some of the horses were on their knees, fighting to get up to find a foothold, the still-erect horses could plunge upward against the sharp grade. On the worst slopes the men were forced to beat their jaded animals into giving all they had. After several pulls, rests and pulls, many of the horses took to spasms and near-convulsions so exhausted were they. By the time most of the outfits were across, the worst stretches could easily be identified by the dried blood and matted hair from the forelegs of the struggling teams. My father was a strong man, and reluctant to display emotion; but, whenever in later years the full pathos of San Juan Hill was recalled either by himself or by someone else, the memory of such bitter struggles was too much for him and he wept.[29]

After reaching the summit of San Juan Hill, the road followed a northeast direction along the top of Comb Ridge for a couple of miles, then entered Butler Wash which the wagons were able to cross after constructing a set of dugways at what is known as the Jump — about two miles north of present-day U.S. Highway 163. When the four explorers reached Butler Wash in late December 1879 they were fearful that because of the perpendicular cliffs they would have to go many miles up the wash, as they had at Grand Gulch, before they could cross. Three days without food and worried that he would not survive much longer, George B. Hobbs carved his name and the date "Jan 1" in the rock of a small wash which drained into Butler Wash from the west. The inscription was located on May 14, 1960, but destroyed a few years later when the highway was constructed through the wash.

Once across Butler Wash, the travelers were able to resume their eastward course. Platte D. Lyman recorded his last miles on the trail:

> Drove 7 miles over heavy sandy road and camped in bottom of the San Juan 2 miles long where we propose to locate for the present. . . . This land is rich covered with Cottonwood and about 6 feet above the river which runs with a pretty good current, but looks as if it would be hard to handle, the climate appears to be mild.[30]

The San Juan pioneers would find the climate mild except during the blast-furnace days of summer, and the river would indeed prove difficult to handle as it repeatedly washed out the dams and ditches they built.

The historian David Lavender reminds us of the magnitude of the Hole-in-the-Rock undertaking:

> . . . each day there was a causeway to build, a shoot-the-chutes to negotiate, a dugway to chip, a tight-laced forest to hack through with axes. We have heard much about the difficulties of the overland trail from the Missouri to the Pacific, but countless caravans traveled half the continent in less time than it took these Saints to cross the corner of one state. On all the overland trail there was not one obstacle comparable to what they conquered at Grand Gulch, the Slick Rocks, Clay Hills, or Comb Wash, to say nothing of Hole-in-the-Rock.[31]

The trials of these Hole-in-the-Rock travelers did not end once they reached the San Juan River. Indian hostilities were a continual threat to the isolated outpost at Bluff. Unlike other western Mormon settlers who encountered only Indians, the San Juan pioneers were considered interlopers by Colorado and Texas cattlemen who had pushed their large herds westward from Colorado into the easily reached virgin San Juan ranges just ahead of the Mormons. Irrigable land along the San Juan River proved insufficient and extremely difficult to water because the rampaging San Juan River frequently washed out dams and destroyed irrigation ditches. Many of the original group left after a short stay, and those who did remain were usually forced to haul freight or work the mines of Colorado to supplement their meager income.

Yet prosperity did come in time. From the seed of Bluff, communities sprouted at Verdure, Monticello, and Blanding. People persevered in their calling to serve their church as settler/missionaries in this remote part of the Mormon kingdom, even when economic opportunity and the promise of an easier life beckoned from many corners. Adaptations were made — first from farming to cattle, then sheep, and back to farming as the science of dry-farming developed and was applied in the county. Mining and transportation opened new, but initially limited opportunities. The whole process was not simple and certainly not easy. The Hole-in-the-Rock trek was an ample and appropriate foreshadowing of the hardships and trials that awaited those who stayed on to wrest a livelihood from the rugged country.

But even after World War II when uranium, oil, tourism, and recreation greatly expanded and changed the nature of San Juan's economy, the mystique of the Hole-in-the-Rock experience continued to color and shape the character of San Juan County.

NOTES

[1]Wallace Stegner, *The Gathering of Zion* (New York: McGraw-Hill, 1971), pp. 1-2.

[2]David E. Miller, *Hole-in-the-Rock: An Epic in the Colonization of the Great American West* (Salt Lake City: University of Utah Press, 1966), p. iv.

[3]Ibid., p. 6.

[4]Ibid., p. 13.

[5]Ibid. Appendix I contains a list of the Hole-in-the-Rock personnel including the community from which they left.

[6]Lynn Lyman interview, May 20, 1982.

[7]Samuel Rowley's Autobiography in Miller, *Hole-in-the-Rock*, p. 187.

[8]Miller, *Hole-in-the-Rock*, p. 71.

[9]Charles E. Redd, "Short Cut to the San Juan," *1949 Brand Book*, Denver Posse of the Westerners, Denver, Colorado, 1950, pp. 14-15.

[10]Elizabeth Morris Decker to Mr. and Mrs. William Morris, quoted in Miller, *Hole-in-the-Rock*, p. 197.

[11]Miller, *Hole-in-the-Rock*, p. 108. Approximately 150 steps chiseled from the solid rock are found; however, these were not cut by the Hole-in-the-Rock expedition but by citizens of Escalante twenty years later who were establishing an Indian trading post at the base of the Hole. The steps were to facilitate the packing of goods from the trading post to and from the top of the canyon rim.

[12]Platte D. Lyman Journal, December 1, 1879 entry, copy at the Utah State Historical Society Library, Salt Lake City, Utah.

[13]Excerpts from: Sketch of My Life by C.I. Decker, quoted in Miller, *Hole-in-the-Rock*, p. 193.

[14]Miller, *Hole-in-the-Rock*, p. 126.

[15]Lyman Journal, May 20, 1880.

[16]Redd, "Short Cut to the San Juan," p. 21.

[17]Miller, *Hole-in-the-Rock*, pp. 128-29.

[18]Ibid., p. 194.

[19]Ibid., p. 128.

[20]Lyman Journal, February 20, 1880.

[21]Miller, *Hole-in-the-Rock*, p. 194.

[22]Lyman Journal, February 29, 1880.

[23]Ibid., March 3 and 4, 1880.

[24]Miller, *Hole-in-the-Rock*, p. 87.

[25]Lyman Journal, March 15, 1880.

[26]Ibid., April 1, 1880.

[27]Miller, *Hole-in-the-Rock*, p. 195.

[28]Ibid., p. 138.

[29]Redd, "Short Cut to the San Juan," pp. 23-24.

[30]Lyman, Journal, April 5, 1880.

[31]David Lavender, *One Man's West* (New York: Doubleday & Company, 1964), p. 184.

Exploring and Documenting the Hole-in-the-Rock Trail

Lynn Lyman

My experience with the Hole-in-the-Rock Trail started in 1940 when a trip was planned by horseback from Bluff to the Hole-in-the-Rock. We had 82 people and 143 animals — pack animals and riding horses. Charlie Redd was chairman of the committee to make the arrangements. We had several meetings together. Finally in September we met at the Natural Bridges, camped there that night, and began our trek the next morning. Of the 82 people, two had been with the original party of pioneers. They were Aunt Caroline Redd from Blanding and Charlie Walton from Monticello. Aunt Caroline was six years old when she came through the Hole-in-the-Rock. My father was on the original trip too. He was sixteen years old then, but he did not come with us on the pack trip.

We were ten days on the trip. It rained almost every day. We were divided into groups, about eight to ten people in each, who would camp together. At Greenwater it rained and rained. Some of the people camped in the cliff dwelling. This one group — I think it was Charlie Redd's group — pitched camp right in the little draw where the water would come through, and in the middle of the night there was a wild scramble of women and people coming out of that tent seeking a dry place. But the rain made it more interesting and served a good purpose. It filled the water holes — the pot holes in the rocks — settled the dust, cooled the air, and made things really quite pleasant.

We had one Indian with us, old Jim Mike. He was one of the guides. In keeping with the advice of the authorities to make friendly relations with the Indians, it seemed like every group took coffee for Jim Mike.

We camped two nights at the Hole-in-the-Rock and had made arrangements to have a boat there to carry us across the river. We hiked up to the top of the Hole-in-the-Rock and were met by a group from Escalante on horseback.

On our way coming back, after we left the Hole-in-the-Rock, the different groups took out on their own. Some of them wanted to get back sooner, while others were not in such a big hurry. The group that Aunt Caroline was with traveled faster and longer until they made camp in the dark. Aunt Caroline was wandering around in the dark — she was kind of an elderly lady at that time and could not see where she was going — and she fell off into a wash and either broke her shoulder or dislocated it. It was lucky we had a doctor in the group, but there was not much he could do for her except to deaden the pain. The group had one big husky mule. They got Aunt Caroline in the saddle on the mule with

First group to retrace the Hole-in-the-Rock trail coming down Cottonwood Hill, 1940. Photograph by Lynn Lyman.

a man behind to steady her because she was doped and could not ride by herself. My brother George and some other fellow took turns riding behind and holding her on the mule until they got her back to the cars at the foot of Clay Hill and then brought her on home.

Jacob and Lucy Adams were with our camping group. Jacob was not going on the whole trip. He went with us as far as the Lake Canyon. The day we left there, Jacob saddled up his horse and took off to the north up to White Canyon to look after his cattle. That was the last time Lucy ever saw him alive. He went into White Canyon and rode out into a flash flood and was drowned.

That was the end of my exploring for a number of years until the 1950s when David Miller started his research for the Hole-in-the-Rock book. Miller and his group had come to the top of the Hole-in-the-Rock from the Escalante side, hiked down to the Colorado River and crossed it with a little rubber raft, then hiked out this side as far as Cottonwood Hill before hiking back. Later that fall some of the same group made the trip as far as the Chute. On my first jeep trip when we got over to the top of Cottonwood Hill there was an empty Kodachrome film can that contained the names of David Miller and three other men.

About this time Skelly Oil Company decided to drill a well out on Nokai Dome. They built a road up Clay Hill Pass, which was the main sticker up to that time for any vehicles going beyond there. Kay Lyman had just bought a war-surplus Dodge weapons carrier. Kay and his father, Edward, and Henry Lyman, who was an old cowboy from that area that knew the country, and four or five others and I got in the weapons carrier and went up onto Nokai Dome, then headed west. There were no roads. We just started finding our way. We were about four or five miles from the Hole-in-the-Rock road. We headed west, hoping to get over to it. We made it over into Death Valley, where the old pioneer road crossed Death Valley, and camped that night. The next day we hiked to Grey Mesa and the Slick Rock Hill, then came back and camped again in the same spot. The following day we got on the old horse trail, guided by Henry Lyman. We followed it back into the Lake Canyon. Coming up over the Slick Rock following that horse trail was pretty rugged going, but we made it all right.

In 1954 Dave Miller heard that we had been out there so he got in touch with us and came down. We guided him to the foot of Grey Mesa. At the Slick Rock Hill there was no possibility of getting a vehicle up there so he and the men with him hiked to the Chute and up from the river. So now they had covered the entire route. Karl Lyman was with the group. He and I spent a lot of time looking for where we could winch a jeep up onto Grey Mesa. So things rested in that way for a while until another mining company over on the Colorado River decided to build a road into the Rincon. They had to go up the Slick Rock and onto Grey Mesa and then down to the river. As soon as Clarence Rogers and I heard about their work on the road, we were afraid they would follow the old Mormon road and destroy all the work the pioneers had done. We made a special trip out there and talked to the man in charge. He was very cooperative and did not want to destroy any of the old trail. Clarence and I hiked on up the Slick Rock and built a bunch of little monuments along the way. When we came back we told them we had marked a good place for them to go. They just followed our monuments right to the top of Grey Mesa. If there are any complaints about the engineering of that part of the road, it is Clarence's fault.

As soon as they finished their road up there, a group of about seventeen people from Monticello and Blanding got jeeps and went out. I was not with them. They went on Grey Mesa and over to the top of Cottonwood Hill. They came back, told about it, and I got the bug again. The next spring we gathered a group together and went out to the top of Cottonwood Hill, then down the hill. No one had been down the hill in a jeep before. We looked over Cottonwood Hill pretty thoroughly and I finally decided that I could take a

Jeep going up the Chute, Hole-in-the-Rock trail. Photograph by Lynn Lyman.

jeep down. I knew I could take it down, and I thought I could get it back up. We took my jeep down, and soon came to the sand hill where it drops off into the bottom of Cotton-wood Canyon. The road was blown over with sand, which forced us to turn around and come back.

The next time out we were a little better organized, and we took more jeeps. We went prepared with shovels and equipment to shovel the road down the sand hill. We got to the bottom of Cottonwood Canyon, taking five jeeps all the way down Cottonwood Canyon overlooking the river oppo-site the Hole-in-the-Rock.

Once we had fifteen jeeps and thirty-seven people and took five jeeps down the sand hill. We left one at the top of Cottonwood Hill and one at the top of the sand hill where we had a long cable to hook the jeeps together to help pull the others over the bad territory. We had found we could go all the way to the river. We retraced that trip several times, including the steep part of Cottonwood Hill where Platte

Lyman had an accident in 1880. About a month after they got into Bluff, Platte Lyman and my father went back over the road and up the Hole-in-the-Rock to Escalante for a thousand pounds of flour they had left on the way in. When they got back to Cottonwood Hill in order to get footing for the horses they hooked them out on the end of the wagon tongue where they could get up on better ground to work. The wagon broke loose from the team and rolled back down the hill, scattering flour and everything all over the side hill. The next day they spent the whole day gathering the remains together and repairing the wagon. Then they came on to the Lake Canyon.

It was a beautiful lake — Lake Pagahrit — about a half-mile long and quarter-mile wide. There was feed for the horses, and so they decided to lay over a day or two to let the horses recuperate. While they were waiting they hiked down to the Colorado River at the mouth of Lake Canyon, hiked up the river to where Hall's Crossing is now. Uncle Platte said in his diary they thought that would be a much better place to cross the river than the Hole-in-the-Rock. I do not know if they made any recommendations to that effect when they got back, but the next year they did move up and establish a crossing there.

I was asked if any wagons ever went back up through the Hole-in-the-Rock. My father and Uncle Platte went up through there. Platte Lyman, in his journal, says when they got to the bottom of the Hole-in-the-Rock there were three other wagons waiting to go on up the Hole-in-the-Rock. I do not know where David Miller got his information, but he said the route was an established route and used for years for traveling both ways until they moved up to Hall's Crossing. I do not think it was used very extensively. I have to disagree with Miller on that. My father told once how many times they had to rest their horses, going up that hill. They had to rest the teams over two hundred times.

A few years ago David Lavender, a noted author who has written a good many books, came to our home and wanted

Jeep encountering difficulties going up the Chute, Hole-in-the-Rock trail. Photograph by Lynn Lyman.

to know how he could get out to the Hole-in-the-Rock. I could not go with him. He and another young fellow were in a Dodge Suburban four-wheel drive. I described the road to him the best way I could. They took off and got to Lake Canyon where they found Keith Rogers. They got Keith to go with them and went over as far as the Chute and then hiked down to the top of Cottonwood Hill and back. They did not dare take the Dodge Suburban across the Chute.

In June 1962 we planned a real trip. We took thirty jeeps and 110 people to the top of Cottonwood Hill where we camped. Two people came in by helicopter; they were camped over on the top of the Hole-in-the-Rock doing some kind of survey work. I do not know what brought them over, whether they saw some of our fires or what. They came flying over and started to land right in the middle of our camp. You know how much wind a helicopter blows out. It started blowing bedrolls in every direction. They could see what was happening so they went back up, moved over a distance, then set down and came over to visit with us.

I will not try to tell about all the trips I made out there. I cannot even remember them all. In 1962 a Boy Scout troop from Blanding went out. They took a wooden box with a tin cover and put a book in it. Until that time the only record of people who had been there, and there were very few, were those who left their names in the little Kodachrome film can. On the next trip we had 110 people including David Lavender and his wife and David Miller and his wife. David Lavender copied all the names that were in the Kodachrome can. It is a good thing he did because some vandals came along and tore off the box that was bolted down to the rock, took the lid off, and left the book out in the weather. My wife and I gathered up what was left of it and brought it in, thinking there might be a little information in it. You can see some of the names. Kent and Fern Frosts' names are in there quite often where they took parties out. I have been out with the BLM a number of times helping to spot the trail and mark it. I have been out with Kent Powell and some of the Utah State Historical Society staff a number of times. It was quite interesting having these writers with us.

In June 1966 we made our last trip, with a question mark, to Hole-in-the-Rock. I think we have made that last trip about ten times since then. I do not know how many more we will make. Not very many, I think. I made it again this spring with Kent Powell and some of his friends from the Historical Society. We have explored every chance we got. But there are some mistakes. I have been out with BLM personnel a number of times trying to establish where the pioneer road went. It is a hard thing to do. You can take a jeep through the country and after one good wind storm you can not tell where the jeep has been. That is the way it was with this road. But if you know a point here and a point over there, you naturally select the best way to get between those two points. That is what we have been doing.

Those people — the original settlers — knew what they were doing. They were picking out the best roads. You might doubt that, considering they chose to come across this way instead of going another way, but I think there was a purpose in that. I talked to Jay Redd in Monticello, and he agreed with me that this was a mission. These men were called here for a specific purpose. I think they were divinely guided in what they were doing, and I think the Lord directed them across this way for a purpose. Jay says if they had gone on around the other way and landed in Moab with those streams coming down out of the mountain and a lot more land available than there is in Bluff, they would have stopped right there and would not have come any farther. Kumen Jones says that if they had got through to here in six weeks, like they intended when they started, instead of taking six months, they would not have stopped in Bluff. They would have probably gone on to somewhere else. But when they got to Bluff their wagons were worn out, their teams were worn out, and the people were tired of fighting the terrain. They could see enough land there to get a foothold, so they stopped in Bluff. They did not even get up to Montezuma Creek which was their intended destination.

There was not enough land in Bluff for everyone in the party. Bluff is one town that was bigger the day it was settled than it ever was after that. The Holyoaks went up the San Juan River almost to Shiprock, New Mexico, where they established a little town called Holyoak. Other people went over to the San Luis Valley and other points farther east.

At the top of Clay Hill, where the road starts down, there is a big boulder with an inscription on it, "Make Peace with God." I do not know who wrote it or anything about it but it is there and you can see it today. At the top of San Juan Hill, engraved on the cliff there, is an inscription, "We thank thee Oh God." I do not know if the pioneers did that or somebody else trying to help history.

There is room for argument about the section of road from Long Flat down through Snow Flat. The way it is marked on the map follows south along the present road toward Mexican Hat then makes a right angle turn to the east toward Snow Flat. The pioneer road, however, is toward the north and east. It follows in a southeasterly direction from Long Flat to where it intersects the present road to Snow Flat.

There is also some confusion where the present road goes around the head of Death Valley. The old pioneer road went straight across Death Valley to the dam across Lake Canyon. We know the pioneers crossed on that dam. While we were there in the spring with the group from the State Historical Society we were talking about that. Somebody said, "Why did they choose this place to cross instead of some other place?" Melvin Smith, director of the Society, said, "Well it's a damn sight better place than any other place to cross." Which is true. In some places you can follow the old road straight to Castle Wash. You cannot see any road, but if you were at a given place and had to get to another you would pick the best way. That is what you have to do when you are looking for the old road.

We have had many people out on our trips. It is a rough trip. You bounce over those roads for two or three days and you are pretty well beat when you get back to civilization. Many people say, "Well I'm glad I went but I don't want to go again." In about three weeks they call me to ask, "When are you planning another trip to Hole-in-the-Rock? Let me know when you go again." That's the way it is. It gets to you.

Editor's note: The following unsolicited comment about the involvement of Lynn and Hazel Lyman in guiding groups over the Hole-in-the-Rock Trail was made by Gene Blickenstaff following Mr. Lyman's comments in Blanding on September 8, 1982. "It was my privilege to be out there with Lynn and Hazel on several of these trips and I think Lynn is due some more recognition. He is the authority on this side of the river on the Hole-in-the-Rock. He is due credit for searching out the exact trail. Some of it is still in question. I know that Lynn and his wife spent lots of hours helping people that were out there. There were the jeeps; on some of these big trips there were jeeps that never should have left

Lynn Lyman walking along Hole-in-the-Rock trail up San Juan Hill, 1980. Photograph by Allan Kent Powell.

Blanding. It is a tough trip — that is where they separate the men from the boys. If the equipment breaks down out there, it is a long ways from the parts house; but Lynn took extra parts. He was thoughtful. He was the commander-in-chief on every trip I ever went on, and he was not seeking glory for himself but he just wanted to make sure that everybody was comfortable, that everybody was fed, and that they were not left out some place broke down and could not get back to camp. It was a privilege to me and to everybody else that went on one of those jeep trips. We owe a debt of gratitude to Lynn and Hazel. They are great people."

PART FOUR

Communities

Aunt Jane Allen in front of her home in Bluff, 1907. USHS Collections.

Blanding: The Making of a Community

Gary L. Shumway

In the early spring of 1905 young Albert R. Lyman stood near where the Parley Redd Merc is and watched a herd of mustangs emerge from the trees that then covered the land. Breaking into a spirited lope as they started down the hill where the high school now is, they followed the draw toward the southeast, crossed it near the Utah Navajo Development Council offices, and disappeared into the taller sagebrush covering a large Anasazi ruin where my parents later built their home. That moment — when this land still belonged to such free spirits — is not really separated so long from this moment in time, yet this day and that are separated by a long series of experiences, each destined in an inexorable way to turn a sagebrush flat possessed by wild horses into a thriving community with a red stoplight in its navel.

The founding and settlement of the town of Blanding is at least chapter two of the community history of this site. In another day, there was another people who loved this land and had faith in its ability to sustain them and received inspiration from the beauty of these same mountains and canyons. It is intriguing to realize that those people had a name for this community, although it probably was not Blanding, and the name probably was not changed to obtain a library. They also had a name for Blue Mountain, Elk Mountain, the Knoll, Westwater, Lem's Draw, and Recapture.

While there is much not known about the Anasazi, there is a great deal known, and every person who ever lived in Blanding has been richer because of them — richer not only because of the fascination for their pottery, arrowheads, cliff dwellings, and crumbling mesa-top ruins but because we know that another people loved this land also and remained for a thousand years. The Anasazi were gone by 1400, many appearing to have left precipitately, as if they feared that they might change their minds if they lingered.

For five hundred years no one seems to have claimed White Mesa as a permanent home. The Utes living to the east almost certainly crossed it often, stopping to drink from the all-seasons spring in Westwater Canyon as they hunted or lived for a time in the area. After Ouray's treaty, when they lost most of their land in western Colorado, some of the Utes refused to go to their new reservation in Duchesne County, Utah, choosing instead to disappear into southeastern Utah whenever any pressure was put upon them. One of the well-traveled Ute trails from Colorado to the security of Navajo Mountain comes onto White Mesa near the confluence of Lem's Draw and Recapture Canyon, where Ashton Harris's

Blanding Bank, 1983. Photograph by G. B. Peterson, © 1983.

field is east of town, and crosses the width of the mesa, leaving on the west where Posey and his followers left in March 1923.

The trail seems to have been followed in reverse by some of the country cousins of the Colorado Utes, the Paiutes from western and central Utah. Although the precise date of their arrival here is not known, nor even the entire motivation for their exodus from further west, it would appear that their migration was related to the series of Mormon-Paiute skirmishes that lasted for much of the third quarter of the nineteenth century and was more bloody and disruptive to Paiute culture than most Utahns have realized. If their decision to remove to southeastern Utah was based in part upon the feeling that Mormons loved Lamanites but hated Indians, some of their later intransigence is explained.

Navajos, a very few of whom may have lived in San Juan County prior to 1861, became more numerous in the southwestern corner of the county between 1861 and 1864 when it seemed as if the whole world had declared open season on them. A group probably numbering several hundred chose not to surrender to Kit Carson and go to Fort Sumner on the Texas-New Mexico border, vanishing instead into the wild canyon country surrounding Navajo Mountain. There they stayed, unchanged, until their reconstructed tribesmen, having promised never to steal from or fight the Beliagaana again, returned from Fort Sumner in 1868. Unlike those returning from Huelte, the Navajo Mountain Navajos had not known the ignominy of utter defeat and four years of captivity. Believing they had escaped by clinging to the old ways, they ignored most of their returning tribesmen's descriptions of new foods, ideas, languages, and crafts. The Navajo Mountain Longhairs became a conservative, traditional force that has influenced the history of the Navajo in southeastern Utah to the present, including the Blanding community as Navajos have played an increasing role in it.

Besides the undefeated Longhairs, there were other Navajos who made a decision to stay in San Juan County.

Much of the background of the Navajo beginnings is nebulous, but it appears that there were a few Navajos living as far north as Green River prior to 1861 and east through the La Sal Mountains to Norwood, Colorado. For a time at least, they seem to have lived on fairly good terms with the Utes, even occasionally trading corn for Ute children, who were incorporated into the Navajo families.

Although some of these families survived the attacks of the 1860s and like their Navajo Mountain counterparts never went to Huelte, by the late 1870s they found their old homes being taken over by white cattlemen and settlers who told them to go south to the reservation. On their way south, several families settled in the Recapture Canyon-Montezuma Canyon-McCracken Mesa area north of the San Juan River where they remained relatively undisturbed for about sixty years. During that time they built up sheep herds and worked amicably for some of the local stockmen. They, too, represented a conservative Navajo element that one day would have a significant impact on the quest for community in Blanding.[1]

One final non-Mormon group should be introduced as part of the mix existent at the time of Mormon settlement of White Mesa. Stockmen who had learned the basic truth that cows are machines that convert government grass into silver dollars were attracted to southeastern Utah in the 1870s by the tall grass and adequate water. For a time the clamor for beef in the western Colorado mining camps, the belly-high grass covering both summer and winter range, and the freedom from any form of taxation beyond an occasional tribute of a cow butchered by an Indian created a thriving cattle industry, especially from the northern part of the county south to the LC Ranch on the edge of White Mesa. But weakening markets and range conditions, personnel changes, the increased activity of cattle rustlers, and the establishment of San Juan County with an indefatigable tax assessor led to the eventual withdrawal of the larger cattle companies.[2] Their remaining assets fell into the hands of rather rough individuals, most of whom the Mormons at least viewed as less than desirable community members. Although almost none of these Gentiles ever considered becoming a part of the Blanding community, their influence was, in fact, rather pronounced; and the lingering tradition of inhospitality toward strangers in Blanding may partially be attributed to the proximity of undesirable strangers during the formative years of the community.

It was into this uncertain milieu with its tenuous associations that Mormons from the mother colony of Bluff came to forge a community.

In the summer of 1880, a youthful Walter C. Lyman first saw White Mesa. There are several variations to the story of why he happened to go there. The account given by his son Lynn says that while waiting for his older brother Platte D. to return from Durango, Colorado, Walter and his brother-in-law Kumen Jones rode north from Bluff Bench toward the white-rimmed mesa visible in the distance.[3] As they rode over the rim onto White Mesa, they stopped to assess the land before them. The immediate impression that came to Walter was of the breathtaking beauty of the cool mesa, almost imperceptibly tilted from the north and covered with tall sagebrush and cedar and pinyon trees, while in the distance the majestic Blue Mountains, timber covered and with patches of snow still remaining, watched protectively and promisingly. It was a beautiful site, and as Walter looked at the spot partway up the mesa where the blue sagebrush melted into the cedars, he had an overpowering feeling that there lay his destiny. Riding further up on the mesa, Walter stopped to scoop up a handful of the rich red earth and to think of its implications. To persons who had been reconciled to the fact that the sandhills of Bluff Bench and the San Juan River banks afforded the best soil available, the abundant grass, the height of the sagebrush, and the size of the cedar trees of White Mesa seemed to promise a better alternative. If a ditch could be dug to bring enough water from one of the streams in the spring to be stored in irrigation reservoirs,

the natural rainfall could be augmented sufficiently to produce excellent crops.

Walter Lyman returned to Bluff afire with enthusiasm for
such a venture, although he probably understood from the
outset that it would have to wait, as the people of Bluff were
not yet at liberty to leave the mother colony.

During the years to follow, Walter Lyman never forgot
his feeling for White Mesa. Instead, after visiting Blue Mountain and spending a long solitary time looking down on the
mesa, he believed a vision was opened to him of a burgeoning town there, with well-laid-out streets, educational facilities, and a temple. When in 1897 three LDS general authorities came to Bluff, urging the settlers to remain but telling them that expansion into the streams coming from Blue
Mountain would be considered a fulfillment of their calling,
Walter Lyman had already spent the previous few weeks on
the north part of White Mesa, surveying a line for a ditch
from Johnson Creek. By the end of that year the surveying
was far along, a short tunnel was being driven, and a rough
dugway had been made from Bluff onto White Mesa.
Throughout the next summer a number of Bluff settlers
worked on the ditch and the Little Tunnel until fall, when so
many were called on missions that work stopped.[4]

Not until 1902 was the plan for preparing the mesa for
settlement reactivated, at which time Joseph A. Lyman moved
to the LC Ranch and he and others resumed work on the
ditch. That year, or early the next, Walter Lyman helped
Peter Allan survey the townsite, and by the spring of 1903
water ran through the ditch and the Little Tunnel from
Johnson Creek onto White Mesa. In 1904 members of the
Lyman family were living at the LC Ranch and at the Park
four miles above the townsite; but it was not until April 2,
1905, that Albert R. Lyman, his wife, Lel, and oldest child,
Cassie, came to start their home. Recalling that evening when
they arrived, Albert later wrote:

> At long last we had come to abide on the appointed site of Sidon,
> the city-to-be. It had taken the first San Juan Pioneers nearly six

months to get to Bluff after they made their start in that direction. It had taken us more than seven years to get to the edge of the cedars after it had been appointed as our promised land. Into the hush of the twilight, as we kindled our cheery fire, came the ominous voice of an owl in a nearby tree and the slim howl of a coyote from away among the cedars. They put into that solitude a meaning unlike that of any camp I had ever made in the past. We would not be going on from that camp in the morning; we had stopped there to remain, to meet the unknown and unguessable future and to hazard the failures and calamities which the popular prophets of evil had predicted.[5]

By the end of the summer of 1905 there were six families in town. That fall, the Fletcher B. Hammond family, the only family not related to the Lymans, moved to Monticello, and Walter Lyman took his family to Bluff for the school year. The other four families stayed the winter and ate Christmas dinner together.

The next summer the Will Nix, E. F. Thompson, Willis Rogers, Jense P. Nielson, Ezekiel Johnson, and Hyrum Stevens families came to stay, and in 1908 the Will Young family came immediately from New Mexico but with years of

L. H. Redd cabin in Bluff. Special Collections, Marriott Library, University of Utah.

L. H. Redd sandstone house in Bluff. Special Collections, Marriott Library, University of Utah.

experience in the Mormon colonies of Mexico and acquaintance with a number of good people there who soon would need a new home.[6] By 1910 when the Shumways came — along with the families of Benjamin D. Black, Azariah Brown, and Bailey Lake — the town possessed more than twenty-five families.

By then an important new pattern had been set. At the outset most of the settlers had been relatives or close friends of the Lymans or Bluff stockmen who saw the advantage of the more central location between their summer and winter range. Increasingly, however, the settlers were coming from farther away: the William Young, Benjamin D. Black, and Peter Shumway families from New Mexico and others such as the Carrolls, Porters, Kartchners, and Hursts, from as far as Old Mexico. When some of the original settlers learned of the reason for this far-flung interest, they were somewhat concerned. Many of the stockmen, who tended to view land tenure in correlation with water supply felt that a small pastoral community was preferable, but Walter Lyman had been to the mountain and had seen an impossible dream of a large, vital community; and as he attended general conferences, as he visited the far-flung reaches of the San Juan Stake as its president or met Mormons for any reason, he searched for the kind of people he felt would provide a basis for a great community. Once determining that they were fit material, Walter Lyman used his intellectual charm, his spiritual strength, and his certain persuasive skills to entice them into the Garden of Eden. As we have intereviewed those early settlers in the Southeastern Utah Oral History Project, one of the recurring stories they tell is how Walter Lyman appproached them and so fired their enthusiasm with his description of White Mesa that they made a decision to throw in with the country sight unseen.

Those who became a part of this deliberate selection process fell rather easily into the sense of mission so strongly permeating the San Juan frontier. There would always be differences of opinion, sometimes rather loudly expressed or stoutly defended, but these differences were largely over how best to achieve an objective, not over the objective itself. Indeed, a careful study of the evidence has led this writer to the conclusion that the amount of basic difference within the community was much less than most have assumed. Even the often-repeated story of the major division between the Hole-in-the-Rockers and the Old Mexico Mormons, or Pachecoites, somewhat falls to pieces under the weight of other evidence. The local tradition is that there was a major cleavage between the wealthy, elitist, aristocratic Hole-in-the Rockers, who had divided up among themselves the economic opportunities of the area, and their poor struggling fellow Mormons forced to leave all of their possessions in Mexico as they fled a maniacal Pancho Villa. As a local historian, this writer has worked very hard to document this cleavage, having long accepted it as fact. By asking the right people the right

Riley Hurst in his Blanding Westside Market, 1973. Photograph by Ken Hochfeld, USHS Collections.

questions and through sheer perseverance, some examples of hurt feelings were found but nowhere near the magnitude expected. Furthermore, the examples found do not clearly indicate that this was a Hole-in-the-Rock versus Mexico Mormon controversy. Who were these Hole-in-the-Rockers that were so inhospitable? The Lymans, who worked so very hard to welcome newcomers, even to the extent that Walter, who might have owned much of the mesa, died ultimately with no land at all? Were the Nielsons, then, the culprits? It was never this writer's understanding from his Blanding beginnings that the Nielsons, though relatively wealthy, were anything but model citizens in encouraging the development of a community spirit, nor has he found anything from his oral history documentation to indicate otherwise. The Bayleses? One theme that emerges from almost every interview with Old Mexico Mormons is that the Bayles family worked very hard to provide jobs at a respectable wage and to assist in any other way possible to alleviate the problems besetting those coming from Mexico. The Redds? Unfortunately for the tradition, most of the Redds who settled in Blanding, while having family who were Hole-in-the-Rockers, actually came from Old Mexico.

That there were slights and disagreements and even occasionally affronts is not disputed. But these will happen whenever humans live next to each other. It now appears that those settlers from Old Mexico, coming as they did from an embittering experience in their last town and not always possessing the most finely honed social skills, were as culpable as were the Hole-in-the-Rockers for any unpleasantness that may have occurred. In fact, as much strife could be documented between various Mexico Mormon families or between, or even within, various Hole-in-the-Rock families, as between the two larger groups.

Almost as an aside, but something that could definitely stand clarification and further research, there is at least one other problem with the tradition of the mistreatment of those unfortunates fleeing the wrath of Pancho Villa: virtually all of the Old Mexico settlers of Blanding left Mexico before Pancho Villa himself had any wrath and some of them before any kind of unusual threat to life or property in Mexico had occurred. It woud be incorrect to suggest that the Mexico Mormons did not live under conditions where there was always at least a latent threat of violence — the experiences of the Harvey family in Colonia Diaz or the Stevens family near Pacheco are grim reminders of this threat — but for many, such as the Carrolls and the Kartchners, the Lakes, the Hursts, and the Redds, the inconveniences and ordinary dangers of living in Mexico, not Pancho Villa, compelled them to leave.

Rather than dwelling on any real or imagined stresses within the community, one should emphasize that in fact the melting pot did melt a host of rather strange individuals into a very viable community. The Nixes would come from Moab, and Brother Nix would serve as ward clerk for thirty years, besides providing a great deal of entertainment for the entire town in the early days, as he pedaled his bicycle in pursuit of some hardened criminal, such as a teenager driving his father's car without a license.[7] This was a town where the only jail was a stray pen where cows that had committed some crime against society such as getting into Brother Jones's corn patch would be incarcerated until their owners redeemed them. Brother Nix, or some other person designated as the town's peace officer, lived a more placid life than did his counterpart in many frontier towns.

From Jewitt Valley, New Mexico, in 1910 came the Shumways, with twelve grown or nearly grown children and one hundred cows for which Peter Shumway, perhaps too optimistically, hoped to find grazing room. Having a very high standard of honesty for himself, and being rather inflexible in expecting the same in others, Grandpa Shumway was easily offended when he thought that others diverged from that standard. He spent much of his later life being offended, and the Shumways searched for many years for a way to make their own contribution. Once they found it, in extracting wealth from the uranium-rich sandstone strata of the area, they became an integral, even vital part of the community.

Two large families of Hursts came out of Colonia Juarez, Mexico, making the long journey in covered wagons to the place someone had convinced George Arthur Hurst was the veritable Garden of Eden. Once in Blanding, and acclimated to the rather unpretentious Garden, the Hursts dug into the community with a vitality and depth of talent that was most impressive. Especially in fulfilling their cultural and civic responsibilities, the Hursts made Blanding a better community than it would have been had they not come.[8]

The Blacks, two great families of them, would come from New Mexico and Old Mexico and stay to make bricks and flour and electricity and roads and become healers of bones and of spirits and of social ills. Few people, even those from Blanding, have adequately perceived the contributions of Benjamin D., David P., Morley, and other Blacks.

Along with the Blacks were the Redds, most of them from Old Mexico, but already with family and a heritage in

Pack train preparing to depart from Blanding for the Natural Bridges. USHS Collections.

The Grayson Co-op Store in Blanding. USHS Collections.

Blanding. Their commitment to hard work and their talent for making money have provided an economic credibility for southeastern Utah that might not have existed otherwise.

If there were Blacks and Redds, there would have to be Browns, and there were — a large family of strong, intelligent, humble, spiritual people who loved the soil with the passion of true farmers.

Whether they were Blacks or Redds or Browns, they were white, and along with the Guymons, Harveys, Hawkinses, Helquists, Hunts, Johnsons, Joneses, Palmers, Rowleys, and others they were Mormons. Between 1923, when the Utes and Paiutes under Posey made one final, poorly orchestrated protest, and 1953, when new roads and two simultaneous mineral booms joined to break down the insularity of the area, Blanding enjoyed a peaceful, contented era of gradual development. Few new families moved into the community, but few had to, when Albert R. Lyman had fifteen children, the twelve Shumway children busied themselves with raising large families of ten or more, and the Blacks, Redds, and most others did likewise. A number of schoolteachers, attracted by Superintendent Joseph B. Harris, became so enamored by the combined charms of the country and some members of the opposite sex that they stayed to make an effective and essential contribution.[9] A few others came, seeking high-grade trees or big-foot wolves or, for one brief but very significant moment, a place in the sun as the CCC brought in large numbers of inquisitive and appreciative young easterners.[10]

Growing up in Blanding in that era was a privilege for which few participants failed to be grateful. There were picket gates to swing on and hollyhocks to trap bees in and ditches of water in the spring to jump or wade or float homemade boats in. There were bonfires to sing around or listen to stories of Old Mexico or the Hole-in-the-Rock, trips to Bluff for cliff flowers or watermelons or swimming and to the Grove on the mountain for Twenty-fourth of July celebrations. There were bluebird nests with sky blue eggs and sky blue skies with puffy white clouds, and always there were the

Dedication of the "New Church" at Bluff, February 23, 1895. USHS Collections.

Blue Mountains, hovering protectively to the north, providing water for thirsty crops and promising a full measure of water for many more people if the community was willing to work hard for it. And ultimately, before that era ended, the people of the community made that effort. Perhaps there is no greater symbol of the success of Blanding in that era than its transformance of some foul smelling "frog soup" ponds into the excellent water system enjoyed today, involving second-feet water rights to Indian Creek, a mile-long tunnel through Blue Mountain, and a pipeline from Johnson Creek. Those of us who know of the forty-year-long dream of Walter Lyman and David Black, and the several-year sacrifice of Vet Bradford and Marvin Lyman in putting through the tunnel, never take a drink of excellent Blanding water without remembering the strained frogs of past years and blessing those with foresight enough to push through the tunnel and pipeline before the neccessity of environmental impact reports and other government restrictions would have made it impossible.[11]

If Blanding was many good things to waves of young people who grew to maturity here during those years, perhaps most of all it was Albert R. Lyman. In "Little Church," which as a sacrament meeting counterpart to Junior Sunday School was itself unique to Blanding, in fast and testimony meetings, in stake conferences, at Scout campouts, in his cobbler shop, in the books we read, in the patriarchal blessings we received, and especially in all of the seminary classes taught during that entire thirty-year period, Brother Lyman spoke from deep in his heart of his love for the church, this community, and its mission to be a center for learning and for service to the Indians.

It was that destiny of service to the Indians that eventually brought an end to the pastoral little Mormon community. The change began quietly enough. Almost from the beginning, Scotty Jones and a few others trod across Westwater — Navajos who for some reason were permitted to live there by the good-natured Utes. By the late 1940s there was an unobtrusive but fair-sized group there: Grandma Johnson, Old Lady

Tree, Old Man Oshley, Fanny Reid, Bert Atene, Paul Goodman, and their families, along with others. On Christmas Day
most were out early with their long seamless sacks to be
filled with "Christmas Givit" and at other times during the
year they satisfied their simple financial needs by hoeing
weeds, cutting wood, herding sheep, or performing other
tasks that townspeople hired them to do. Never feared, or
even disliked, they nevertheless were rarely truly befriended
and were never expected to live by the same norms as the
people across the canyon. If someone had thought to ask
Grandma Johnson, she would have said that she had left her
home near Nakaito to come to Blanding after having decided
she wanted her family to be raised here with the Mormons.
Old Man Oshley came from the same general area with the
same major objective. This tall, stately Navajo and this di-
minutive, mischievous, ubiquitous woman suffered the slights
and the condescension along with the other Navajos of the
area, many of whom also may have come with the hope that
they or their posterity could one day be a part of the community.[12]

Most of the townspeople remained oblivious to the fact
that at least some of the local Navajos wanted to be a part
of the community, and the Westwater Navajos seemed willing
to accept their lot, but others were not. Almost imperceptibly, a series of factors combined to ultimately change the
contours of the community. In about 1935, with the establishment of the Taylor Grazing Act provisions, the local
stockmen were faced with the problem of formally dividing
up the range land in a way that would be acceptable to individual ranchers and to the Grazing Service. This distribution
process bubbled with emotion and other complications, and
it took many months, climaxed by a marathon talk session
lasting more than twenty-four hours, before an agreement
was reached.[13] From the beginning, however, it was agreed
that no Navajos should be with their herds in the area north
of the San Juan River, and a fence was built for the purpose
of keeping the Navajo sheep off the white stockmen's winter

grazing range. Most of the Navajos were convinced through one means or another to keep out, but one Navajo named Jim Vijil persisted in returning to his home near the mouth of Recapture. After several efforts to dislodge Vijil from the winter range, a Blanding stockman took his problem to a peace officer. The following story was told by Vijil and may be full or errors, but it at least demonstrates his perception of the event. Driving up to Vijil's hogan, the officer took out his shotgun, walked up near the dwelling, and called for Vijil to come out. When he stepped outside, the officer told him that he had thirty seconds to be heading back to the reservation or be shot. Rather than beginning to run, Vijil stepped up closer to the two men and said, "Do you see that rock over there? My father is buried there and this was his home. The only way you will get me to leave is to kill me." The officer cocked his shotgun, aimed it at Vijil and repeated his demand. Vijil stood there, looking down the barrel of the shotgun. There was a long pause, then the officer lowered his shotgun and said, "You damned old Navajo," and he and the stockman walked off. Not too long afterward, the reservation was extended to cover Vijil's claim, and other Navajos began a slow encroachment that even before the annexation to the reservation of the sizeable, oil-rich Aneth-McCracken Mesa area, seemed to establish a pattern of inexorable Navajo expansion.

In the midst of this expansion came an even more immediate and cataclysmic threat to the community's status quo. In the late 1950s Hugh Benally, one of the grandsons of the Navajo White Horse who had settled in Montezuma Canyon, used some oil royalty money to buy a school section of land in Montezuma near where he had been raised. Blessed with a large number of intelligent children, Benally began to wish they could attend the Blanding schools, where they could receive a good education and return to their own home each night. His first request for the admission of his children was denied, as were the second and third, but he persisted, pointing out that he paid property taxes on his land

and, therefore, his children had a right to attend tax-supported schools. Ultimately, the system buckled under his persistence and logic, and his son Clyde Benally graduated from San Juan High School in 1964, the first non-foster-child Indian to do so.[14]

The opening of the Blanding schools to the Benally children released the flood gate, and soon hundreds of small children, as well as older ones, were groping along snow-covered trails in the dark to cross a slippery foot bridge over the San Juan River and run a mile and a half down to Saint Christopher's Mission, where, just as it was getting light in the winter, they boarded a bus for the trip to Blanding. After a long, and sometimes overwhelming, day at school, they would reverse the process, arriving at home long after dark to do their studies by a kerosene lantern in a one-room hogan shared with ten or so other members of their family, then retiring to get up at 4:00 a.m. to begin the new school day.[15]

Few of the Blanding people, who saw their own children's education being diluted by the massive infusion of Navajo students, ever understood how much it meant to those children to have the opportunity to be in Blanding. And, when the Navajo parents decided that at least for the winter they would move to Blanding to ease the difficulties of their children in getting to school, many in the community interpreted this simply as a desire to be closer to the welfare offices, whose headquarters had been moved to Blanding, or to toothache medicine in Monticello. Some even saw a more ominous portent in the burgeoning birthrate of the reservation, the steady, determined advance of the reservation since it first entered Utah after 1900, and the growing economic power of the Utah Navajo Development Council. Feeling that the coming of large numbers of Navajos, more than CCC camps, uranium or oil booms, or missile bases had changed the pastoral cohesion of the community, some began to fear that Blanding would become a Navajo ghetto. But even in the gloomiest times, many who had learned to love the Navajos

for their industriousness and their gift for understatement, remembered Albert R. Lyman's repeated insistence that the mission of the community was in great part to be of service to
the Indians, and they saw in the Navajos' presence the literal
fulfillment of Walter Lyman's vision from the mountain.

As the community has agonized over alternatives, events
have transpired to lessen some of the shock of radical change.
The decision, supported by most of the people, both Navajo
and white, to build excellent schools in areas more accessible
to the reservation has diminished the need for Navajo families
to leave their land and possessions to move to Blanding and
has at least bought time for more orderly absorption.

Perhaps even more significant, just as this important decision regarding the future of the community was being made
and put into effect, a new influx occurred, even more suddenly, that again drastically changed the community. Escaping
from the poor economic situation of the East Coast and elsewhere and the poor social conditions of cities throughout the
nation have come people, finding in the same clear air, pro-
tective mountains, and whispering canyon breezes the attractions that brought the first settlers. Some of these are people
who were born here, but were forced through economic
necessity to leave, and have now found it possible to return.
Others are Mormons who received the same clarion call concerning the Garden of Eden that Walter C. Lyman once gave.
Many are other good people of the earth willing to share
their wisdom and knowledge and skills in building up the
land. Whatever the reason and whatever they have to give,
they are here, perhaps nearly as many having come with the
past two years as came during the first seventy-three.

April 2, 1980, was the seventy-fifth anniversary of the
settlement of the town. A great deal has happened since Albert R. Lyman stood watching that band of mustangs start
from the spot where the high school now stands. Albert R.
Lyman and Walter C. Lyman are dead, as are Will Nix and
Ben Black and Parley Redd and Peter Shumway. And so, in
many senses, has the community passed away that they knew

and loved. But perhaps as they watch the development of Blanding from an even greater vantage point than Blue Mountain, they will be proud of what they see.

NOTES

This chapter was originally presented as an address at the annual meeting of the Utah State Historical Society held in Blanding in September 1979. It was later published in the fall 1980 issue of *Utah Historical Quarterly*.

[1]See interview of Hugh Benally by Gary Shumway, July 11, 1972, no. 1234, Southeastern Utah Project, cosponsored by the Oral History Program, California State University, Fullerton, and the Utah State Historical Society. Copies of this and other interviews are available at the sponsoring institutions and the Blanding library unless otherwise indicated.

[2]Franklin Day, "The Cattle Industry of San Juan County, Utah, 1875-1900" (M.S. thesis, Brigham Young University, 1958), passim.

[3]Interview of Lynn Lyman by Mark Collins, May 29, 1978, no. 788b.

[4]Albert R. Lyman, *A History of Blanding, 1905-1955* (n.p., 1955), p. 9.

[5]Albert R. Lyman, *The Edge of the Cedars: The Story of Walter C. Lyman and the San Juan Mission* (New York: Carlton Press, 1966), p. 79.

[6]Loyd L. Young, *William L. Young, 1875-1929* (Monticello, Ut.: Author, 1980).

[7]For a delightful account of Brother Nix's law enforcement efforts, see interview of Vincent Jones by James D. Redd, September 3, 1971, no. 1090.

[8]See interviews of Retta, Riley, Parley, George, and Phillip Hurst; Luella Hurst Rogers; Margie Hurst Lyman; and Dora Hurst Bayles.

[9]See Jessie L. Embry, "Schoolmarms of San Juan County," MS, Utah State Historical Society; La Ray Alexander, "Backboards and Blackboards" (Fullerton: California State University Oral History Program, 1977); interviews of Beth Guymon, Irene M. Redd, and Louise E. Redd.

[10]See interviews of Frank Montella, Thomas Wozniak, Michael Camberlango, Edward Keele, James Hunt, Phillip Hurst, and Floyd Nielson.

[11]See "Pages from the Lives of Marvin and Margie Lyman" (Fullerton: California State University Oral History Program, 1974); interviews with Sylvester Bradford, Douglas Harvey, and Grace Shumway.

[12]See interviews of Oshley and Johnson by Gary Shumway and Clyde Benally in the Doris Duke Indian Oral History Collection, American West Center, University of Utah.

[13]See interview of Reed Bayles by James D. Redd, September 21, 1971, no. 1091.

[14]Interview of Hugh Benally by Gary Shumway.

[15]Interview of the Sampson family by Gary Shumway, August 1968, Doris Duke Indian Oral History Collection.

Personal Reminiscences of San Juan County

Clarence Rogers

Shortly after the settlement of Bluff in 1880 some of the San Juan pioneers began looking for another place to live. One day Walter C. Lyman got on his horse and headed north. After about fifteen miles, he came to a high mesa called White Mesa. Looking north a vision passed before his eyes and he saw a beautiful town. The place was beautiful and the crops were green. People asked him later how big the town was and I recall him saying, "I wouldn't dare say how big it was. You would think I was absolutely crazy." In the vision he also saw a temple there on a hill.

My father, David John Rogers, was living in Bluff at that time. He and Walter became good friends. My father was just as interested in White Mesa as Walter was. Eventually, the two of them went to survey a ditch from Johnson Creek on to the mesa. The only instrument they had was a carpenter's level, which is now in my possession. They used a long board about 18 feet long with a leg about 2½ feet long on each end. Walter carried the back end with the carpenter's level and my father carried the front end, placing it where Walter told him to. They were going through trees, brush, and arroyos when my father came to a pile of rock. He could see it was manmade and quite new. He asked Walter what it was. Walter replied, "I was up here looking for a route where I thought we could build a ditch. I piled that rock up where I thought a ditch might go." They surveyed right through that rock pile and that is where the ditch was built.

They started work on the ditch with the help of the Jody

Lyman boys and others. It came down from the creek and around the side of the mesa for about two miles. At one point there were a hundred yards of solid rock. They built a tunnel through that area. They worked from both ends of the wall, with Rogers in one tunnel and Lyman in the other. One would pound on the wall with his hammer and the other would listen, and vice versa. Then they both took their hammers and hand drills and drilled toward the sounds they heard. They put some powder in the holes, set off the blasts and broke through. There was great rejoicing.

There was a Texas cattle outfit called the LC Ranch located on Recapture Creek. It belonged to Mrs. Lacey. Her cowboys, riding up the canyon to look after the cows, could see the men working on the ditch. They would laugh and joke about those crazy old Mormons who thought they could make water run uphill. To look at it now, it does look like it is running uphill. Later, when the water ran through the ditch and on to the mesa, the cowboys said, "The crazy old fools did it, didn't they!"

The Lymans moved to the town and called it Grayson.

Early Bluff log cabin, 1983. Photograph by G. B. Peterson, © 1983.

154

Drilling artesian well number 1, Bluff, 1908. USHS Collections.

Not until several years later was its named changed to Bland-ing. Other men came up to work their farms, and in the spring of 1907 my father moved his family there. People that came talked about how big the town would be. Some said it would be wonderful if there were 500 people. Others said there would never be enough water for 500.

The first year the water was in the ditch, it ran about to the middle of town and then dried up. That was all they got that year. Later, they enlarged the ditch and got a little more water each year. Over the years, when more families moved in and more water was needed, they were able to find it and bring it in. Now with a population of 3,500, there is yet a shortage of water and people continue to look for ways to develop more.

Two groups who had a great influence on the people of the area were the Navajo Indians south of the San Juan River and the Ute Indians who roamed the country. Even before Bluff was settled, the government tried to contain these people. After white settlement there were a few instances of violence between Indians and whites, but nothing very sig-

Jim Mike, 1973. Photograph by Ken Hochfeld, USHS Collections.

nificant. The last one — the so-called Posey War — happened during the first part of this century.

Old Posey had a son named Jess Posey. He was a fine man. He had two wives and lived in a one-room hogan. One of the wives had children, the other did not. When they went for their meat supply Jess would take both wives. He would shoot the deer and they would dress it, clean it, and put it on the bushes to dry. They would get enough meat for a year. This family was honest and honorable and they were good workers. I became good friends with them and liked them very much. Their boys worked for me and were good workers with cattle and sheep. I could trust them. Jess Posey finally died and was buried about six miles southwest of Blanding.

Jim Mike was a Paiute Indian, born and raised in Piute Canyon near Navajo Mountain. He discovered Rainbow Bridge and guided the first white party to see it. I became friends with Jim Mike after he moved to the Blanding area with his horses and sheep. His livestock was better than most belonging to the Utes. I found him to be trustworthy and honorable.

How Jim found the bridge and guided the white party to it is a matter of record. He told me about it in these words, "Me go canyon," and he motioned with his hands showing it to be crooked. "Canyon turn here, me come around, me see 'um," and he pointed to the air. "What it is I don't know. Me heap scared. Me go back. My father he wait back there and we go camp."

A Navajo man was given credit for having found Rainbow Bridge and guiding the first white party to it. When I heard this, I supported Jim Mike, because I knew his story was true. I have a picture of the first white party to see Rainbow Bridge. Jim Mike was in the picture, the Navajo boy was not. When I tried to tell the story to the *Deseret News*, they would not listen. However, the *Denver Post* heard about the "weird" story, looked me up, and believed what I told them. They investigated and assured themselves the story was true.

Through their efforts, the National Park Service eventually recognized Jim Mike, had a party for him, and gave him a $50 bill and a beautiful Pendleton wool blanket. After his death in September 1977 and interment in the Blanding Cemetery, the family gave me the blanket. It is still in my possession.

Another group who contributed to the development of San Juan was what were referred to as the Mexico people. They had been sent by the LDS church to colonize Mexico but returned to the U.S. between 1912 and 1916. Many came to Blanding. I believed they were sent for a special purpose. The town was just started and needed help. There were ditches and roads to build, schools and churches to construct. These people were handy at most work and were willing to give a day's work for a day's pay. Little has been written about them, but they contributed much to the building of Blanding. There were the Blacks, Youngs, Redds, Hursts, Porters, Hardys, Palmers, Carrols, Johnsons, and others.

These people came with only their teams and wagons and what was on their backs. There were men here, like L. H. Redd, Hansen D. Bayles, and Kumen Jones, who had herds of cattle and sheep. They hired the Mexico people, enabling them to provide for their needs. Some of these people were good road builders, others were brick makers, others were good carpenters. Some knew how to run sawmills. Eventually there were several sawmills in and around Blanding.

When the Mormons from Mexico and New Mexico moved to Blanding there was great need for manpower and horsepower. The city needed a schoolhouse, a church house, and private dwellings. Ben Black built an adobe mill and went to work. The adobe mill was four cedar posts set in the ground in a square about 6 or 8 feet apart with 2 x 12 boards fastened on all sides to a height of about 6 feet, making a large box. In the center was placed a large post extending up about 3 feet above the box, and secured with wooden bearings to the corners. Four paddles were attached to the bottom. Then a long pole about 18-20 feet long was secured with heavy bolts and iron straps to the top of the post. In

Olin Oliver, Bluff, 1973. Photograph by Ken Hochfeld, USHS Collections.

making adobes, a horse was hitched to the long pole with harness and single tree. The horse then walked around and around turning the paddles that mixed the mud. One group of men with teams and wagons hauled dirt. Another group hauled sand, and another water. These ingredients, in the right mixture, were put in the mill. An opening about 12 x 14 inches was cut into the box at ground level. As the horse went around in a circle the mud was mixed and squeezed out of the hole.

A hole was dug in the ground about 3 feet deep and 2 feet wide and 3 feet long for a man to stand in to take the mud with his hands and put it in a mold box that held three or four bricks. This mold was about 4 inches wide and 3 feet long. Then some men or boys would carry it to a place pre- pared for it, dump it out, and return for another load. After the adobe dried it could be used to line buildings or other purposes.

They also piled the bricks up in a stack or kiln about 20 feet long and 10 to 20 feet wide — or whatever size they needed for the number of bricks they were making.

About every 3 feet a hole through the brick pile was made as the adobes were stacked about 2 to 3 feet high and 20 inches wide. Wood was then hauled and a fire made in the long holes. Long trees were trimmed and pushed back in the kiln and burned for a week or more until the adobes turned to brick.

Mr. Black and his helpers made enough brick to build a large schoolhouse, church house, and several large dwellings in Blanding.

The first thing the Mormons built, after a church, was a school. So they needed schoolteachers. Joseph B. Harris came from Salt Lake. He taught in Bluff one year and moved to Blanding. Wherever he was he wanted the best for the town — the best streets, sidewalks, water, the best of everything. Blanding had a difficult time getting these things because there were not enough people to do the work. Joseph Harris would let school out on Friday so the kids could work on roads. They would shovel dirt or roll off rocks and be ready to work again on Saturday. That is how the roads got built — farmers with their teams, and men and boys to help. Harris spent his whole life doing this type of thing. He became school superintendent, bishop, mayor, and stake president. While trying to make a living teaching school and developing his little farm, he kept busy with other things. But he spent his life for the public. Little has been said about him. He died in 1963. I believe there should be a monument, preferably a college, dedicated to this man.

Walter C. Lyman, referred to earlier, was also a great man. He could have been rich, but he did not try to be. He had an engineering mind. He could take a carpenter's level and survey a ditch. He, like Joseph Harris, spent his life in the advancement and development of this town. A city park north of town has been dedicated to him, but that is not enough. I believe there should be a plaque put up showing his accomplishments.

Dorothy Nielson, Bluff Post Office, 1973. Photograph by Ken Hochfeld, USHS Collections.

A man named Burnheimer also made a contribution. He spent 30 days in the country each summer for 8 to 10 years hunting for Moki dwellings and sending his findings to the American Museum of Natural History and the Carnegie Institute. He made four or five trips to Rainbow Bridge. He loved it and was trying to find a better way to get there. On his last trip he brought tools and blasting powder and shot a trail down the cliff so you could come from Navajo Mountain Trading Post directly to the bridge without going around the mountain, so people who did not have horses could walk. I was with Mr. Burnheimer on his last trip and found him to be a wonderful man.

Mr. Evans was a surveyor. He spent several summers surveying the country so people would know where it was, what was here, and how to get to it. John Wetherill was a great explorer of the Four Corners area. He was the first to explore Grand Gulch, Mesa Verde, and many other canyons around the country. Earl H. Morris worked for the government. He spent many years in the canyon country investigating the ruins and gathering facts and figures to study. I was fortunate to be in his company and listen to him talk. Zeke Johnson lived in Blanding and was a natural guide for the Four Corners country. He loved the natural bridges and taking people to see them. He accompanied Mr. Burnheimer on his trips to the bridges and to Rainbow Bridge. I was also able to learn from him.

One of the first cowboys in the area was Al Scorup. He came from Salina to White Canyon with about 100 head of cattle. It was terribly hot and dry, and most of the first bunch of cattle died. He returned to Salina and brought another bunch. From his first experience he had learned how to run cattle in this country, so the second experience was successful. He eventually developed a herd of 3,000 to 4,000 head. He married one of the Bluff girls and made his home there.

An interesting story involves Scorup and "wild cattle." When cattle drifted from the main herd and ranged among the many trees in the country, they would become very wild.

The only way to catch them was to outrun them, rope them, tie them up for about two days, and then go back and lead them out. The cowboys all tried to outdo each other to be the best "wild cow man." They usually rode after the wild cattle in the winter when there was little else to do. They would camp for about a month, riding out each morning to look for wild cattle. One day Tom Jones was riding with Scorup and other cowboys near the natural bridges. They scattered, each to follow a different critter. Tom found a little red bull and chased him, finally caught him, threw him, jumped off his horse, and grabbed him before he could get up. He put a halter on him and tied him to a tree and then went after the rest of the cowboys, hoping to catch another cow.

About the third day after the incident, Tom told Scorup he thought he would go get that red bull and bring him to the canyon. So Tom went out, but he could not find the bull. He hunted all day but there were no tracks to follow; the ground was frozen and the trees were thick. So he went back to camp that night and told the other cowboys. One said, "I

Bluff, 1908. L. H. Redd house and haystacks in the foreground. Bluff church and school in the left background. USHS Collections.

can find him. I know where he was. I'll go with you." They rode out together next morning, hunted all day, but still could not find the little bull. The following day all the cowboys in camp went to search for him, but he was not to be found. Several years later, Scorup was riding through the trees in this area and found a little pair of horns tied to a tree.

In 1940 a large group of relatives of the "Hole-in-the-Rock" people decided to follow the Mormon trail to Hole-in-the-Rock on horseback. They were to assemble at Edwin Bridge in the bridges area. Jacob Adams, an old cowboy from Bluff, wanted to go with this group. He arranged for his cowboys to tend the cattle and meet him at a certain place when he returned. Jacob and the cowboys found a cave and horse pasture in one canyon and had the cattle grazing in other canyons. This was in September, and one night there came a rainstorm that caused a big flood in White Canyon where Jacob and the cowboys were camped. In the morning, they saddled their horses to go to the south side of the canyon where the cattle were located. The cowboy who was riding lead came to the stream which was in flood. The noise of the rolling rocks and rough water scared the horse and he would not go into the water. Jacob said, "Oh, let me show you. I can make my horse go." He forced his horse into the water, but then they both went down. Jacob was a large man. He had on a new pair of chaps, extra big and heavy, a big overcoat, because the days were cool, and heavy boots and spurs. He was pretty well hog-tied. When the horse was swept off its feet, Jacob went head first into the stream. The cowboys followed him along the edge of the water, trying to throw him a rope, until they came to a cliff where they could not go any farther. They watched helplessly as Jacob went over a 12-to-15-foot high waterfall a little farther down the stream.

One of the cowboys went to Kigalia Ranger Station, phoned Blanding, and told us what had happened. Several of us took our pickups out to see what we could do. Early that morning the men dispersed in different directions. We searched all day. Jim Scorup, who was keeping track of us, found me late in the afternoon to let me know the body had been found. I told him I would get Harv Williams, the other cowboy who had been searching with me, and we would meet the rest of the party back in camp. We assumed they would have the body in one of the pickups.

When we got to the camp, however, we found they had not moved the body out of the canyon. It was almost sundown and was important to do this before dark, if possible. We talked about lowering a rope into the canyon and pulling him out, but rejected that, as the canyon was 200 to 300 feet deep. I finally said I would get Jacob's mule, put a pack on it and see if I could get him on the mule. Milt Rogers, a boy, and I went to get the mule and started down the canyon. Harv Williams and another boy, De Reese Nielson, got on a horse and caught up with us. Lynn Lyman had gone to look for a flashlight, and when he had found one, he got on a horse and started down. As we started down, we met the three men who had found the body. We did not say much, but found out the body was about 3½ miles down the canyon. We thought one of the three men would come back and show us where it was, but none of them offered.

It was very dark — one of the blackest nights I had ever seen — and the canyon was rough, with sharp, twisting turns and cobblestones on the path. Lynn led, shining the flashlight on the bank of the creek as we went along. After we had gone about three miles, I suggested we leave the horses and proceed on foot so we would be sure and not miss the body. I figured when we found him we could come back and get the horses. Harv said he would stay with the horses, and the rest of us went on. About 200 to 300 yards on down the creek, Lynn flashed his light on the body, which was on the edge of the creek. I had been thinking I did not like that canyon. It was spooky and dark and there was a dead body in it. I surely did not want to stay with the body while the others went back for the horses. So I spoke up quickly and said, "I'll go get the horses." Lynn had apparently been thinking the same thing because he said, "I'll go with you." So we left those two kids in the dark, spooky canyon with the dead man while we went back and got the horses.

When we got back to the body, I took the blankets from the pack and adjusted them in the panniers. We rolled the body up in a tarp and put it across the mule. We put another tarp across the body and tied it with a salt hitch. I thought it would stay and it did. The body never moved an inch. Lynn walked behind and I led the mule, and we came out without any trouble. We got back to Blanding just as the sun was rising the next morning.

One might think there would be little to do for recreation in an isolated area as this. But the town had a good recreation department. The church sponsored most of the recreation. We had a dance every Friday night and everyone would attend, old and young alike. In the winter we would put on several dramas and musicals, using the piano, trombone, violin, etc.

The first post office we had in town had a high porch, the width of the building and about 6 to 8 feet deep. On the sunny days of February and March, after we had been cooped up all winter, many of the cowboys would congregate on that porch, and visit and whittle. When there was not anything else to whittle on, we would whittle on the flooring. We whittled up two porches before they got rid of us, but we surely had fun.

Northwest of Monticello, in the slickrock hills, there was one place in the rock with a deep hole about 20 feet deep and 12 feet wide. The walls were almost perpendicular. An old cowboy lived in the area. He was without a wife and was left alone with three or four little kids. He generally took his responsibility well and cared for those children. The story goes that when he went to Monticello to drink beer with the boys, he would put the kids in the hole. It was aptly named the jailhouse. One day he put the kids in the hole and rode into town. He had so much beer that day he forgot to go back for about three days. The kids were surely glad to see

L. H. Redd Company store, Monticello. Special Collections, Marriott Library, University of Utah.

him. He pulled them out and they went back to their camp in the hills and lived happily ever after.

About 25 years ago a buffalo herd was started near the Henry Mountains in Utah. The rangers kept track of the herd, which increased and grew. Finally, they decided they could have a hunt without jeopardizing the herd. They decided to allow ten permits. The people made applications and a drawing was held to see who got the ten permits. I was lucky and drew one. I asked my brother to go with me on the hunt, and we shot a beautiful bull. When we got back to town, I decided to have a barbeque so the townspeople could have a taste. We took one-third of the meat and barbequed it in a pit overnight. The next day we had a buffalo dinner. I thought the meat would be tough and strong, but it was neither. It was tender and good. We had a real party that day.

PART FIVE

Farming & Ranching

Roping and tying a calf, 1973. Photograph by Ken Hochfeld, USHS Collections.

San Juan: A Hundred Years of Cattle, Sheep, and Dry Farms

Charles S. Peterson

More than a hundred years ago a construction crew of young Utahns made their way across San Juan County from the southeast. Among them was William T. Tew, my wife's grandfather, who kept a journal of their trip. They entered the county somewhere west of present Dove Creek, worked their way down a rugged drop known as Three Step Hill into Dry Valley, paused at Cane Spring, passed through Moab, ferried the Colorado River, and proceeded on to their homes at Springville and Nephi. Like thousands of other Utahns that year, they had been grading railroad. Unable to find farms as their pioneer fathers had done and with the doors of the educational frontier as yet unopened, they were the "drawers of water and choppers of wood" who opened the plateau country of the Four Corners area, grading and laying much of the track for both the Denver and Rio Grande Western and the Santa Fe railways.

This particular crew had been in the railroad camps all winter. Their diet had consisted mainly of cornmeal, and as they worked their way north they tried to relieve the tedium of their limited menu. Some stopped at roadside saloons and others fished for the so-called white salmon of the San Juan River and hunted deer, all with poor success. But their luck seemed to change on Thursday, April 7, 1881, as they ground their way up the slope of the La Sals to Coyote Springs, near which several case-hardened families had made the first ranches in the north end of San Juan County. In the cedars a few miles beyond Coyote Spring, as my grandfather told the story, "some of the Nephi boys killed one of the longest-taled Dear I ever saw." While his entry seems to imply disapproval, my grandfather nevertheless took one quarter of this "longtailed buckskin" for the mess with which he traveled and stood by while others dug "a hole and buried" the hide and head. Full of good beef and enjoying rare good weather they pushed on in high spirits the next day "to the cane Springs," passing through "whole mountains of sollid red and stone rock" over the "roughest roads" they had yet encountered. Shortly after they stopped for lunch two grim-eyed men rode up and joined them for dinner. Having eaten some of the evidence, the strangers mounted their horses and one of them announced:

> . . . some of our outfit had killed one of his Steers and wanted to know who he was. Two men said they did not know any thing about it. He replied that we all knew who they were and if we did not settle for it there he would make it cost us a damed site more. He had us by the heels, so we asked him how much it would cost us. He said that it would cost us $100.00 to get out

One thousand foot long rip-rap dam on the San Juan River at Bluff, 1910. USHS Collections.

172

of it so we let him have a Horse and $30.00 cash . . . $3.65 each.
With a little play on words Tew dryly concluded that it was
"pretty dear Beef."[1]

The San Juan country was then, as now, recognizably different. In part its difference was natural — red rock, sand,
canyons, and the incredible distances included in its 4.9 million acres, which amounted to nearly 10 percent of Utah's
total area. In part the difference was also the product of San
Juan's remoteness and its heavy emphasis upon ranching. It
was cattle country first, then sheep country, and then both.
Still later it was also the promised land to hundreds of dry-
farm families. While its ranching tradition is truly the key to
the way in which San Juan stands apart from other Utah
localities, this difference is much more complex than the
mere fact that in old San Juan the ratio of cows to men exceeded any other Utah locality.[2] The purpose here, then, is
to tell the story of cowboys, cattle barons, sheepherders, and
dry farmers in such a way as to point up certain conflicts and
adjustments that have given the country character and color.
This process might be summarized by saying that Texas
ranching converged with Mormon living practices to create
a different experience in San Juan's vast expanse. As cultural
clashes go, this confrontation was not violent nor bitter, but
it has been in process now for more than a century and does
much to make this country interesting.

Only five years old as a place for white human habitation
when the Springville and Nephi railroad builders passed this
way, San Juan County was already a ranching county, its character foretold by the timing of settlement and the places from
which settlers came. Hidden behind the nation's most impos-
ing geographical barriers, the San Juan country had come to
the general attention of Americans only after 1870.

Surveyors like John Wesley Powell began to fashion its
image as color country. It was a region so unlike other frontiers that its development would require significant adaptations in the modes of settlement and ranching to wrest it
from the Indians who had been crowded into it as develop-

ments elsewhere forced them from earlier homelands. Indeed, until the early 1870s Indian hostilities had stretched a barrier to white penetration along the Wasatch Plateau a hundred miles or more to the northwest. To the east Indians continued to impede white expansion through the Uncompahgre and San Juan mountains. That whites were killed at Moab and surveyors harried off the La Sal Mountains in 1875 and that at least four encounters worthy of the name "Indian battle" took place in the next decade gave emphasis to the reality of Indian resistance.

Between 1877 and 1885 mounting pressure finally began to breach the barriers, and ranch settlement picked up. This first influx consisted of small ranchers who drifted before the movement of the larger frontier. They came from two directions — some from Utah and some from the Four Corners country and the rest from beyond in ranching country dominated by Texas cattle and practices. From the northwest along the line where the Denver and Rio Grande Western Railroad was then building came an individualistic smattering out of Utah, some of them Gentiles, some Jack Mormons, and a handful of Mormon stalwarts. Moab, Spanish Valley, Coyote, and old La Sal were destinations for these people. Choosing an altogether different road and thus marking themselves as a different sort came the Hole-in-the-Rockers, in whom the fires of Mormon destiny burned strong. Three major avenues of access also gave recognizable character to different localities. For Castle Valley and Moab the Colorado River and its valley were a high road — making connection with Grand Junction and the mining country beyond. Perhaps a hundred miles to the south was a second major access, the San Juan River, while the great sage plain of the Dove Creek-Monticello country became another natural line of ingress through which had moved the Old Spanish Trail and long-riding Texas cowboys and sheepherders.

But in the early 1880s the first small ranchers ran cattle on the north, the west, and south slopes of the La Sals and on the north and east slopes of the Blues. The Hole-in-the-

Rockers dug in at Bluff. They built diversion dams and water wheels, shoveled sand from washed-in ditches, worked in Colorado for subsistence, quarreled among themselves, and watched the river carry off their tiny farms. But in the first years they ran only a handful of livestock on the ridges immediately around Bluff rather than getting into the business in any effective way.

Between 1882 and 1887 big outfits and bitter competition came to San Juan's cattle ranges. Preston Nutter rode into the country north of the Colorado River. The Pittsburgh Company bought out the small ranchers at La Sal and Coyote. The Carlisles, English noblemen with ranching connections in New Mexico and Kansas and marital connections with Texas, did the same on the north Blues, making headquarters at the Double Cabins or Carlisle and at Piute Springs near the state border. Near Verdure the LC or Lacey Company from the Texas Panhandle also established itself, grazing Montezuma and Recapture creeks and the southeast slopes of the mountain while another Texas outfit, the ELK, dropped below the Mormon outpost at Bluff, running longhorns from the Rincon through Comb Wash onto Elk Ridge.

Hard pressed and divided by poverty, the Bluff Mormons shifted their emphasis after 1885 from the farm village practices that had characterized Mormon settlement throughout southern Utah to cooperative livestock management. A cattleman from northeast Utah named Francis A. Hammond was called as stake president. Together with the Lymans, Nielsons, Joneses, Bayleses, Redds, and other famililes of the original settlement, he organized the Bluff Pool. Pursuing tactics that earned them the name of "Bluff Tigers" among non-Mormons, they dickered immediately with Piutes and Navajos for grazing rights on Elk Ridge. Later they invaded "no man's land," a region west of Monument Valley designated by Teddy Roosevelt as a reserve for Indians, and fought back when Indians objected to encroaching stock along Montezuma Creek and on White Mesa. Ranching towns were established at Monticello and Verdure in 1887, and settlement attempts at the

Rincon on the San Juan River and Mormon Pasture on the Elk
Mountains failed. As county assessor, L. H. Redd was tireless
in collecting taxes on transient herds, thus reducing the
county's appeal to wintering Colorado cattle and generally
enhancing the cause of the Mormons who always controlled
the country politically.

Town dwellers by preference and by church calling, the
Bluff stockmen did not regard themselves as cowboys. Like
Mormons elsewhere they managed stock cooperatively to
support community life rather than as an end in itself. Herders were hired or line riders assigned cooperatively, but few
of them lived with their cattle year round or gave themselves
to the outfit with the complete loyalty of old-line Texas cowboys, many of whom had no other life whatever. As a type,
cowboys were feared and avoided socially and their life-style
and values denounced. Indeed, so sharp a social line did the
Bluff and Monticello stockmen draw between themselves and
the cowboys and cattle barons that a "Mormon cowboy" was
for several years something of an oddity. Albert Scorup, for
example, who had punched the wildest of cows in the Rob-
bers Roost country and White Canyon, living in caves for
months on end and coming into town only occasionally, was
greeted at Bluff in 1891 by what historian David Lavender
called "a committee of the whole." Thirteen or fourteen
"cowboy shy" girls had come to see this loner who continued
to style himself "the Mormon cowboy."[3]

Before many years Scorup had become the hard-riding
manager for the Bluff Pool, and a few dozen other young
men, including Frank Adams, Monroe and Wayne Redd, and
several boys of the Butts family, would certainly have been
called "Mormon cowboys." In time even the very stalwarts of
the Hole-in-the-Rock group gave themselves to livestock as
well as to the church and to their families. Like their
stockworking counterparts from the general frontier, they
adapted ranching ways that originated in Texas to local conditions and their own values. The product was a set of practices, unique in many ways to San Juan County, that still

176

needs to be examined in detail and compared with cowboy-ing practices elsewhere.

Although the Bluff Mormons were often desperate for work, there is no evidence that they punched cows or worked otherwise for the Carlisles or the Lacey outfit. The former had Texas connections through the wife of Harold Carlisle and her son, Latigo Gordon, and are said to have hired long riders from Texas in hopes that the cowboys' well-known loyalty to the outfit would reduce losses to rustling and mavericking. The Lacey outfit had driven cattle directly from the Texas Panhandle to Recapture Wash in 1879 or 1880. Whether they all came from Texas or not is not known, but a long list of relatives including the husbands of Mrs. Lacey's two sisters were involved in the company's management and in successor outfits at Indian Creek, Cross Canyon, and Moab. Prone to violence, the Lacey people hired drifters, died with their boots on, and at least one of them carried a gun regularly long after he became a Moab banker. But the real point is that Mormons from the south end of the county worked for neither outfit. The lone reference suggesting that any Bluff Mormons worked for outsiders is A. J. Scorup's account that he and Frank Adams made a drive for Elk Mountain Texans to Ridgeway, Colorado, in 1890.[4] By contrast, a large list of Mormons worked for Cunningham and Carpenter, who bought the Pittsburgh Company in 1895. A few of them, including Hile Savage, appear to have also worked for the Pittsburgh, suggesting a fundamental difference in the lines of social interaction in the south and north ends of the county at extremely early times.

Not surprisingly, Mormon standoffishness and the aggressive tactics of the Bluff Pool produced a reaction. At the cowboy level the response was direct and personal. Young and full of life, cowboys undertook to invade the Mormon towns socially. As Fred Keller's Blue Mountain song recounts, they drank at the Blue Goose Saloon, traded with Mons's store, and "danced at night with the Mormon girls."[5] Occasionally there was gunplay, much of it in drunken but dangerous fun, but now and again with tragic results. Two 1890 shooting sprees involved children. In the first, drunken cowboys shot up the school. Running out of ammunition they broke into Mons Peterson's store and returned to the beleaguered schoolhouse. They stopped only when a thrashing crew rushed to the scene with loaded rifles. On another occasion a group of cowboys had lifted a case of brandy from a stalled freight wagon and coming into town the next morning fired at the feet of two small girls. One cowboy reflected the real feeling behind the episode when he shouted "nits make lice" as he shot at the frightened children. More tragic was the July 2 celebration in 1891 when Tom Roach, a Texan reputed to have killed six men, initiated a shooting spree at a dance where Mrs. Jane Walton and a cowboy who had tried to intervene were killed.

More important to the character the community took was the fact that a dozen or so outside cowboys married Mormon girls. Frequently these men stayed in the country. A few, like Harve Williams, became Mormons. Some located in Moab or in neighboring Colorado towns where most of them became the relaxed channels through which Texas and Mormon customs evolved.

Over the long haul the cow outfits were overmatched by village settlements and the Mormon Pool. Not favored by homestead legislation, they lost key spots held only by customary use to homesteaders and forfeited water rights when "dummies" or company entrymen defected and sold their filings to Mormons. But on the range the companies managed livestock competitively. Mormon animals were scattered and their cowboys were threatened. Al Scorup, for example, told of returning to his

> old stamping grounds in White Canyon, [where] five armed Texans surrounded me and said, "See here, youngster, we've scattered your cattle and we mean to use all this feed for our own stuff. You'd better go way back where you came from." I looked around and saw there were several more Texans playing cards . . . . I said, "All right, brothers! If that's the way you feel about it, you can have all these dried up canyons and long-horned

cattle. I know where there are greener pastures and better cattle! So long!"[6]

Occasionally, stock belonging to the Pool were killed, usually for camp meat, but according to one report, at least once, stock was killed in wanton and destructive anger. Henry Honaker of Cortez, Colorado, who worked for the Carlisle Company as a "young chap," recalled that

> the foreman took me to a swale and pointed to a pile of bones bleaching in the sun. "See what happens to Mormon cattle when they come on our range," he said with an oath, "there was 300 head in that bunch."[7]

Although early settlers thought Honaker's story was exaggerated, some Monticello residents evidently felt that grudges did lead to grazing Carlisle stock on streams used for culinary water with intent to contaminate drinking water with tragic, though unintended, results much later. Writing in 1911, Forest Supervisor Henry Bergh explained:

> Monticello . . . has withstood many hardships; for a time the health of the community was threatened by the pollution of the water by sheep. The sheep belonging to Carlisle & Gordon, before the creation of the La Sal National Forest, and every year since the creation of the Forest, until this season, have grazed and bedded along the banks of the two Montezuma creeks, which waters had to be used by the residents of Monticello for culinary purposes. It is claimed by the Monticello people that this company had a grudge at them and that they adopted this means of vindicating themselves. At the outset, at least, the residents of this village were unable to protect themselves and they were just compelled to put up with it. During the season of 1910 a great typhoid epidemic broke out in the town and quite a number of fatalities were reported [eleven deaths according to one report]. The results of this being that the town incorporated, elected appropriate officers, and the sanitation of the town and water question was looked into. Plans have, I understand, been perfected for the piping of water from ... the National Forest for ... the town.[8]

Whether or not the typhoid epidemic of 1910 was the direct result of bad blood between the livestock companies and the Mormons, other developments do seem suggestive. Monticello had lobbied for an 1892 law prohibiting livestock from watersheds within seven miles of towns and worked unsuccessfully in 1900 to get teeth put into that law. With the epidemic fresh in mind, the town built its water system in 1912 with the blessing of Mormon Stake President Lemuel H. Redd, who signed the note financing the project. It is also likely that the epidemic had more than a little to do with the fact that the residents of Bluff associated themselves the following year, to purchase "the entire holdings of the Carlisle & Gordon ranch."[9] A stated intention was to establish a town to which Bluff's citizens, washed out by floods, could move, as well as new homeseekers attracted by the dry-farming boom that was just then gathering steam.

But whatever the later outcome of enmity between contending factions, the late 1880s and early 1890s were the heyday of the big outfits. It was a ranching bonanza that made fortunes for absentee owners, adventuresome English noblemen, and members of Moab's blue-blooded "500 Club" as well as giving some credence to the oft-repeated boast of the previously impoverished Bluff Tigers that Bluff was the wealthiest town per capita west of Kansas City. It was a moist era. Good growth of grass and browse, plus naturally stored surpluses, provided feed for cattle estimated as high as 100,000 head.[10] Markets were good. Progress was made in breeding herds up. Great roundups employing as many as 75 to 100 cowboys were held annually, and as many as 25,000 animals are said to have been collected in Dry Valley and other winter ranges.

But all this began to change almost before it was established. Hard times struck nationally after 1893. A new era of drought was initiated about the same time which ended only in 1903. Competition and the imbalance of winter and summer ranges led to overgrazing. And for some, what had been adventure became boredom, and longing for the conveniences of civilization replaced enthusiasm for frontier life. Thus, by 1895 bonanza had turned to near panic and the big outfits began to fall apart or get out.

Most tried sheep. Some sold to younger members of families and corporations. Some turned local operations over to trusted ranch hands, and a few had sons or sons-in-law who wanted to stay on. New operations of considerable size formed and broke again as times changed. Mormons — both Jack Mormons and the Hole-in-the-Rock variety — seemed generally to be better stayers. In 1895 Cunningham and Carpenter purchased the Pittsburgh Ranch and combined it with widespread ranges at Paradox Valley and on the Book Cliffs and in eastern Colorado. By 1900 the Carlisle Company was prostrate, and its remaining interests turned to sheep under the management of Latigo Gordon, a colorful hard-riding Texas cowboy who had not only accepted sheep but married a local girl and settled down. The Elk Mountain Texans were long gone and the remnants of the Lacey outfit scattered from Cross Canyons in Colorado to Indian Creek and Moab where their interests extended to fruit farming, merchandising, and banking, as well as sheep.

Sheep entered the county from the southeast with first Indians and then New Mexico sheepmen bringing them. By 1886 the Bluff Pool had found it necessary to buy one sheep operation to control where its sheep grazed. But elsewhere in southeast Utah sheep came only slowly until the cattle bonanza began to collapse. With a U.S. marshal riding shotgun, the Taylor brothers of Moab breached the sheep deadline from the north in 1895. There was complaint but very little violence, and within three or four years virtually all the big outfits had turned to mixed operations of sheep and cattle. In 1900 some of them, including Cunningham and Carpenter as well as L. H. Redd and other Mormons, clearly contemplated shifting entirely to sheep. Sheep, like cattle, quickly passed their zenith, and well before 1910 the San Juan grazing industry had stabilized to accommodate both sheep and cattle.

An important social development was that with the sheep came Mexican herders. Most of these came from northwestern New Mexican villages like Coyote, Abiquiu, and Cuba and maintained close contacts there. Like the Texas cowboys before them, they were skilled stockmen whose lives revolved around their work. Largely without ideas of social conflict and lacking a labor-class mentality, they were loyal to their employers. If they were not utterly without aspiration to change, they at least lacked the strong opportunism that made it difficult for many an Anglo stockworker to keep his mind on the outfit's interests rather than upon his own progress up the ladder of ownership.

Initially, only men came from New Mexico. They often returned home for a month or two during the course of the year, but while in Utah they rarely left the herds. In time a few families also came, and at one time a Mexican homestead district was planned and a few homes established at a lonely spot on the south slope of the Elks. Later, little enclaves of Mexicans lived in dilapidated housing in most of the San Juan towns and bigger ranches.

As it worked out, this system provided an ideal work force until at least 1960. Men of great native ability and sound experience, but with limited opportunity otherwise, devoted their lives to their San Juan County employers. There are observers who think that the devoted intelligence of good stockworkers more than financial wizardry or even the

Shaded sheep, 1979. Photograph by G. B. Peterson, © 1983.

chance developments of weather and markets has been the making or breaking of the livestock industry. One who holds such an opinion is Chet Smith, longtime cattle foreman at Redd Ranches. He has said again and again that good men at the stockworking level have been the key to Redd Ranches' success as much as Charlie Redd's management. When pressed for examples of such stockmen, it is interesting that Smith came up with a list that included only Mexicans with one exception — Joe Redd, a relative of Charlie who, like the Mexicans, gave himself to the ranch with rare singlemindedness for many years.[11] Right or wrong in his assumptions about whether management or workers played the more important role, Smith was correct about one thing: good stockmen made the difference. Like the Texas-trained cowboys before them, the San Juan Mexicans made real contributions to the county's character that need careful and appreciative examination.

But in the decade after the turn of the century, dry farming was the new El Dorado, and the old-time outfits continued to change hands and break up. With hundreds of homesteads and a few giant steam tractors already clearing the sage plains to the east, the Carlisle successors sold out in 1911 to a Bluff consortium to whom the idea of farming districts and villages seemed more compatible. For similar reasons Cunningham and Carpenter watched with jaundiced eyes as homesteaders moved into Paradox Valley, old La Sal, and into the flats and bottoms around their main ranch at La Sal after 1909. Finally in 1914 they too sold out to the same group of Mormons who bought the Carlisle ranch plus a few emigres from the Mormon colonies in Mexico who were looking for homes. It is clear that the Mormon purchasers intended to continue ranching operations, but it is also clear that the old Mormon inclination to expand the bounds of the kingdom through farming settlement was very much alive among them, and homesteading in the locality accelerated immediately as settlers moved in from other Utah regions. In 1915 La Sal townsite was surveyed about two miles west of the ranch. A school was built and a Mormon ward of upwards of 400 members established.

Termed "an island of hardcore poverty" by one writer, the La Sal dry-farm district was indeed hard pressed.[12] Like earlier pioneers, the La Sal homesteaders led a hand-to-mouth existence. They subsisted on what they raised, lived in mud-roofed cabins, and as they hacked out sagebrush and built adobe houses on the townsite they trapped, freighted, and worked for the company (Redd Ranches) or at copper mines and on oil rigs to make an occasional dollar. Once in a while there was a windfall, as when Roy Musselman, an "out East" homesteader, trapped a notorious wolf called "Old Big Foot," which had left a trail of bloody destruction over a range of 700 miles, and collected the $1,000 reward that had been raised by the stockmen.[13]

But windfalls notwithstanding, the season of good rains passed. The drought tightened and "ditch companies sprang up everywhere." Some were "co-operative affairs, some pure swindlers." At one highly advertised tract in East Paradox which filled solidly with squatters, a wag posted a sign, "Homesteaders, Beware: It's water you want — NOT HOT AIR."[14] At La Sal they struggled to develop dry-farm ditches, ran bills at the company store, went deeper in debt, and finally sold out to the La Sal Livestock Company or just walked away from land that had no value, as did the owners of millions of acres throughout the West. A few stayed in the country. A handful got educated and came back to work for Redd Ranches. One or two hung on to diminishing ranches, finding solace for a lonely existence in hatred for the company or by contrast finding friendship and status in their connection with it. Resentments flared in the thirties and forties. Arsonists mistook the company's shift from the previous generation's interest in community building to ranch making to be a naked quest for power and put the torch to threshing machines, barns, shearing sheds, and other buildings.[15]

In addition, one or two misfits remained. Living like hermits or raising families in conditions as primitive as the first settlers had found seventy-five years before, they gave little thought to bettering themselves. One such was Skeeter Stocks, who had raised nine children in a lonely three-roomed cabin through the roof of which the sky could be seen. Something of his attitude toward development as well as dry humor was apparent in his comment to a visitor that he had been waiting for ten years for a large dead pinyon pine near his cabin to fall so he could drag it in for wood.[16]

In the neighboring rimrock country of western Colorado historian David Lavender described the "limp fields" of a half-dozen dry farmers held "helpless in the iron grip of poverty." Their children were "ill-educated," raised up in an "incredible mental vacuum," and their bodies "bent and hardened under adult labor." Some reached "maturity without entering a church or sitting down before a white tablecloth. They never flushed a toilet or saw a railroad or stepped on a cement sidewalk." In the face of such conditions some withdrew within themselves, reflecting their rejection of humanity by ill-treatment of friend and foe alike. That some showed the results of withdrawal in physical appearance as well was evident in the demeanor of one stooped, sharp-faced bachelor whose humorless and "tiny rosebud mouth" cowboys said was so "tightly pursed . . . that you couldn't drive a needle into it with a sledge hammer."[17]

Yet as Lavender tells it, homesteaders were not deficient in pride and determination. To survive a particularly terrible winter one "tore up his mattress and fed the straw" to his milk cow, wrapped his feet in gunny sacks, and butchered his burro, telling his hungry children that it was a deer. When summer came he walked to the county fair where handbills offered $25 for staying in the ring three rounds with a traveling slugger. "He was knocked down seven times, lost three teeth and part of the hearing of one ear. But when he walked home he had twenty-five dollars to give his wife" for a trip to see her ailing father.[18]

One has the feeling that most La Sal homesteaders were also not deficient in industry and commitment to education.

Indeed, their commitment to the better things of life was in final analysis the reason the town failed. Their views were larger, and they moved on to fulfill them.

Although it began earlier, Blanding was also the product of the dry-farm boom. Apparently established first as a hay ranch by Bluff stockman about the turn of the century, it grew as a community after 1905. The new town was first called Grayson and then changed to Blanding after the family of a philanthropist who purportedly gave the town a library in exchange for the name change.

To a degree, Blanding's early fortunes were influenced by the experimental farm established in 1903 a little north and west of Verdure by John A. Widtsoe from the State Agricultural College. Widtsoe, who along with William Smythe and President Theodore Roosevelt, was one of America's great advocates of the idea that the nation's real vitality came from country living, developed the science of dry farming. Throughout Utah he experimented with its possibilities, demonstrated its methods, preached its virtues, and founded arid farm companies and communities. Proteges of Widtsoe in San Juan County were his students Dan Perkins and Will Brooks, who "loved this man and looked upon him as our guiding star."[19] With his encouragement they ran the experiment farm and with money borrowed from Hans Bayles made a down payment on 3,000 acres of state land, taking out enlarged homesteads of 360 acres each for themselves. During 1909 they cleared land, built fences, and broadened their partnership to include Dan's brother Soapy, who had a few hundred head of cattle.

The press of debt, however, became a major problem. The first winter Brooks taught school at Liberty, New Mexico, in part because they needed money desperately and in part because church leaders called him to. Later, both partners worked in local cooperatives, at trading posts, flour mills, and elsewhere. Newly wed, Perkins's wife was a casualty of the typhoid epidemic in the fall of 1910. Brooks himself laid at death's door for ten days; through a thin board wall he heard her die and nearly gave up the ghost himself. The shock barely slowed them. Indeed, 1911 was a year of great promise. Brooks went into partnership on a store, hired a clerk, and camped out "working on his land project." As he later recalled:

> I can hardly explain how good everything looked to me in San Juan this summer of 1911. I took stock in a new flour mill that was being set up to handle some of our wheat; I helped to manage the State Experiment Farm; my homestead included some wonderful land and water, and our big collective farm seemed to have boundless possibilities. Perhaps they were only a young man's dreams, but I thought I could see a good comfortable life ahead for me, and a chance to become wealthy.[20]

But Brooks had taken a wife who proved unequal to the new frontier, and by mid-1912 he pulled out. With the boom well underway he salvaged $8,000 from his interests.

Earl Halls's experience in the "out East" dry-farming district was more typical. Circumstances, rather than the vision of a great social planner like Widtsoe, brought him to the country. He was born in Mancos, Colorado, but had returned to his ancestral home at Huntsville, Utah, where he had ranched, learned blacksmithing at the Agricultural College, and ramrodded an Idaho hay ranch for an uncle. In 1915 another relative went into partnership with Frank Adams at Monticello in a garage and began encouraging Earl to join him. Friction between Halls and his uncle led him to make a trip back to San Juan late in the summer of that year. Once there he worked at Barton's sawmill at Verdure during the fall and sawed cord wood for Monticello people with a "one lunged," water-cooled gas engine during the winter. As he put it:

> Sure was slim pickings that winter. We had to take flour, spuds, or whatever we could get, for pay. There was no money in the country. Someone, generally a cow-man, would write out a check, possibly for $5, and the check would pass around, for change, until it was worn out. Then someone would take it back to him and he would make out a fresh one. That was the way they had to make change. There was no change, very little money.[21]

It was a hard winter. Monticello's famous wind worked

overtime, and snow drifted to six-foot depths in the streets. Halls recalled attending a silent movie in a "barnlike place made of lumber, and covered with tin. The snow would drift in, and the wind howled." Walking home they crossed Main Street in which lay a five-foot drift. His wife "crawled across on her dress, and I wallowed through . . . . After we were through, a little fellow about five feet tall (full-grown man) started across, but sank in all over, and he started to shout, 'Somebody come and help me.'"[22] But even this story pales by comparison to Will Brooks's account of a monumental storm the spring of 1909 that

> never slacked until it had covered all the fences. We made paths and tunnels to the barns, and sat out a full six weeks of repeated storms. We just settled down in the homes, but had parties almost every night. During that time I met all the people of Monticello, the best class of people that I ever associated with in all my life.[23]

As bleak as things looked, Halls struggled out to Lockerby in February 1916 where he homesteaded 320 acres, bought a team and wagon in New Mexico, and pitched a tent on his property. The first summer he cleared twenty acres and hauled lumber from a mill to Monticello to pay for some wood from which he built a one-room shack and a floor on which he pitched his tent. Within three years he had cleared a total of 65 acres, proved up on the place, and, just as prices began to fall and the drought to close in, mortgaged his land to the Federal Land Bank for $1,800. With this he bought a small tractor and leased an adjoining farm of 110 acres. One year a neighbor's child set fire to his stackyards by accident, and he only survived by gifts from neighbors. Another year the Monticello banker from whom he was leasing talked him out of hiring a thrashing machine to thrash grain that could have been sold at the machine for $2.50 a hundred so they could use the bank's own outfit. By the time the bank's machine got to his place it was December 7, a foot of snow was on the ground, and it had been raining. He recalled:

> I lost 600 bushels of wheat that was too wet to thresh, and there was no market for wheat. The land owners brought a herd of

hogs out from Monticello to feed around the straw stacks so they didn't lose. Next spring the bank had my wheat hauled out to the railroad and gave me credit for 50 cents a hundred for it on my note. I had to borrow money to farm with.[24]

Halls also had his trouble with cattlemen. One named McCabe was determined to run the squatters out. But let Halls tell the story.

> They would cut our fences and turn a big bunch of cattle in to our crops. One or two hundred cattle can clean out a home-steader in one night. But we hung together. One neighbor shot two bulls worth two or three hundred dollars each. One day the cattlemen drove a herd in on his land, and he drove the bunch out, down the canyon. I should say, here, that we farmed on the top of a plateau. We were on top; and canyons below us. These cattlemen would bring a bunch of cattle up a draw with ledges on either side, cut the fence, let them in, and ride on. On this particular day, as we dogged the cattle out, we met McCabe down below and asked him which way he wanted his cattle to go, up the canyon or down. In answer he got off his horse and pulled his rifle out of the scabbard and I rode back out of sight and set the dog on the cattle. They went down the canyon and into his other bunch. Another time a neighbor sent word that cat-tle were in my corn. I had ten acres. I got on my horse and rode over. The field was across the canyon from our house and rest of the land. There were some 30 or 40 cattle in. I drove them out, but one little long-horned cow refused to go. I could hear her running between me and the canyon rim, I jumped off the horse and waited until she came in sight. I shot and got her in the backbone and down she went. Another shot in the ear finished her, and I pulled her one end at a time, until I was able to push her over the ledge, down 40 feet. I guess she is still there. Another farmer about five miles west of us put a 30-30 bul-let in a post by the elbow of a cowman who had just cut the top wire of his fence. He had his sons holding a bunch of cattle in the trees ready to put them in a farmer's field. The cowmen soon found out the homesteaders weren't to be fooled with, and became friendly. A year or so later a neighbor and I ate dinner with McCabe at his cow camp, and were treated royally. I also cleared some land for him in exchange for a horse.[25]

Apparent in Halls's memoir are antipathy for bankers who let him carry the rap and some showing of violence be-tween stockmen and squatters. But occasional conflict also broke out between homesteaders themselves. Sometimes they fought over where schools should be located. On one occasion some of them even stole a school, pulling the one-room structure from one site to another. Other times conflict over water, land, or right-of-way was at the core of discord. Two men named Bradford had harassed one named Stevens for months over a road he had to use to get to some of his property. Finally, Stevens took to carrying a gun, and on one occasion told Halls that the next time he and the Bradfords met "one of them would eat breakfast in hell the next morning." Another time when Halls stayed in Stevens's cabin one night while the owner was temporarily away, he awoke "with the flicker of a match in my face, and a 38 revolver pointed at my head, and Stevens said 'It's you, is it?' Well, I stayed there . . . [but] will say here that the hole in the end of a 38 revolver looks pretty big, even by the light of a match."[26] Later, Stevens bushwhacked the Bradfords as they returned from Monticello in a two-horse buggy.

> Stevens started to shoot, first striking Charlie, and the team ran. He shot through the back of the seat, hitting Charlie again. George got out, but was hit, and hid back of a log. The team ran home with Charlie still in the buggy. Stevens walked up to the log and finished George. Stevens headed for the canyons and a posse tried to locate him, but didn't want to, I think. After two weeks he came to the county attorney's home one night, about three in the morning, and gave himself up. He was put in jail and in a week or so was let out on bail. He is still out on bail. Apparently no one ever tried to find him. Everyone in the county that knew the Bradfords knew that they had it coming.[27]

By 1922 the "country had gone to pot." Gas was 60 cents per gallon and jackrabbits swarmed the dry farms. There were "for sale" signs "on every farm" but no buyers. Neither Halls nor his neighbors could pay the interest on their loans much less pay anything on the principal. Many people just left and let the banks sue them. Halls signed his deeds over to the Federal Land Bank, tried to sell what he could, and planned to store his tractor, for which there was no sale at any price.

But San Juan's dry-farm bonanza was not yet through with him. On the way out of Monticello he was stopped by the county attorney who asked if he "wanted to manage a large ranch." The next morning he looked it over with a

> man by the name of LeFete who had just bought 1,100 acres of farm land, and seven or eight sections of range land. We went to the ranch, seven miles north of Monticello. LeFete told me he wanted to build barns, hog pens, graineries, reservoirs and so forth, and wanted me to be foreman. I would be paid $125 a month with a house to live in, and garden and meat furnished. Well manna had started to fall from heaven, and I took the job. The rest of that fall I had as many as 35 to 40 men to herd. Mostly I rode a horse between jobs. We bought 16 head of horses, 75 head of pureblood cows and other range cattle, and 35 head of pure-blood pigs. The drouth came — blew grain out of the ground, roots and all, with large piles of dirt at the ends of the fields like snowdrifts. Jack rabbits were so thick they could clean a hundred acre field overnight. There was no water to irrigate with. We hauled 200 pigs to Dolores, Colorado. They weighed 90 to 110 pounds each. We got $2.30 each for them. They were used to make hog cholera serum. We hauled them 78 miles in wagons. It was either that or let them starve to death. Grain was too high to feed pigs at that time.[28]

In September 1924 "the ranch boss came from Kansas City," closed down the operation, and leased the ranch to Jude Bailey. After nine years Halls headed back to Huntsville. He had not done as well as Brooks but doubtless had fared as well as many. Established families with livestock interests and support from commercial enterprises, mining, and other activities survived. Extended drought and depression closed many others down. The county's population had soared from slightly more than 1,000 in the years before the boom to 3,379 in 1920; the number of farms rose from 157 in 1910 to 405 in 1920. By 1925 farm numbers had fallen again to 263.[29]

With the break-up of the big outfits and the initiation of the dry-farm era after 1910, change and development continued to characterize San Juan County's livestock industry. Although the number of people who ran stock increased

Comparative Grazing Data for the La Sal and Manti Forests

Year	Number Permitted				Number of Permits				Permit Averages			
	Cattle		Sheep		Cattle		Sheep		Cattle		Sheep	
	*LS	M	LS	M	LS	M	LS	M	LS	M	LS	M
1909	15,770	19,764	61,509	191,984	157	1,031	25	583	100	19	2,460	329
1915	25,856	25,321	35,418	146,537	169	1,235	19	510	153	20	1,863	287
1920	23,560	21,987	37,987	128,209	150	1,600	37	644	157	14	1,026	199
1924	16,935	20,599	24,682	130,338	130	1,382	17	670	130	15	1,452	195
1929	13,430	15,945	40,970	139,412	64	933	36	826	209	17	1,138	170

*La Sal (LS) and Manti (M)

sharply, it was still characterized by relatively large herds owned by a relatively small number of people. Elsewhere, Utah was absolutely unique in the large number of farm-based operators that ran a few dozen head of sheep or cattle. A rough idea for the comparative position of San Juan to other counties may be gained by comparing La Sal National Forest grazing permits to Manti National Forest grazing permits.[30]

With the early outfits gone and an increasing number of stockmen using the range (up to 160 cattlemen and 25 or 30 sheepmen), the big roundup of earlier days gave way to what locals have referred to as "greasy sack" operations. Cattle were scattered over vast areas — 3,000 square miles according to one writer. Cowboys rode widely in all kinds of weather and knew every draw and ridge in the great triangle formed by the Colorado, San Juan, and Dolores rivers. In the "long season of death which in happier climes is known as spring," herds trailed off State Line Hill or crossed the Colorado River in boiling runoffs to maintain schedules set by hard-nosed bosses who never signed contracts but whose word was their bond. Cowboys slept in the mud, ate their own greasy compounds, and drank what one called "venomous coffee." They lived alone in caves or shared line shacks so small "a cocked elbow" made them dangerous, read pulps on the wild West, and felt chesty to see "their drab trade glorified."[31]

At first look they were a nondescript, varied lot. Among them were tenderfeet from the East like John Riis, whom John Cunningham palmed off on the Forest Service in time to head off a mutiny among his other riders. Some were boys full of romance but at home on their granddad's outfit, like Bill Allred, or who looked at cowboying as God-sent relief from the tedium of life on the dry farm, as did Milton Jameson. Others, like Allred's cousin Ardin Johnson, rode horses or worked cows only under duress, turning by preference to machinery or visiting among the ranching and dry-farm neighbors. Still others were relics of the past. Cy Orr, who carried no more meat "than a yucca blade" holed up winters near

Paradox in a filthy shack known locally as the "Boar's Den" but summers still trailed cows beween Scorup's Indian Creek country and Al Lavender's Lone Cone Summer Camp. His face was terribly eaten by cancer, and his thin frame shivered at the slightest hint of cool. To combat the chills he drank himself senseless on home brew he made from potatoes. Yet he had pride in his work and a certain dignity, perhaps held over from remembered days when he came to western Colorado from England by way of Texas.[32] Another partial cripple was Lee Larson, who, as Bill Allred tells,

> needed no babying because of his missing leg . . . . Using one crutch, he jumped around, saddled his horse and hopped up from the right side into his saddle. A strap from the cantle to the left saddle forks cinched around his waist gave him balance and he stuck like a burr on his horses. Some of them were frisky and bucked a little. Lee had guts, pride, and plenty of cow savvy and didn't want anyone doing his work for him.[33]

Donnie Marsden, whose "long, limp face and long, limp mustache" were always partially hidden under a "high steepled" Mexican hat, had been scalped by a lariat, but notwithstanding the idiosyncrasies of his appearance, was a good cowboy.[34] Latigo Gordon and several others had lost fingers and one Moab boy an arm working the dallies of rawhide ropes. Some, like John Scott, were superb cowboys but subject to moods beyond their control. "Grotesquely homely," he plastered his "thin black hair . . . to his bony skull" and had "a red, bulbous, pockmarked nose and green eyes set so close together it was said you could not put a cigarette paper edgewise between them . . . He camped at sheep outfits and cursed his fellow cattlemen to the Mexican herders; he joined the Mormon Church when riding in Utah," and on going "to Colorado could not think of enough evil to say of his religion."[35] Dave Lavender, who spent some of his best and some of his worst hours with Scott, recalled:

> He could track wild animals like an Indian and could tell more lore in a more fascinating way than any man I ever knew. But he was always looking out for John Scott. When I was a youngster he lazily used to take but one bed along on the rides, saying we

could sleep together and save the bothers of extra packing. Many a night I did not sleep, however. He snored like a lumber mill. He shoved me with his knees and rammed me with his elbows until he rolled me out on the cold, stony ground. In desperation I would steal a blanket, wrap up in it, and crouch by the fire, hating him until my arms trembled and my mouth turned dry and hot. In the morning he was enormously surprised and blamed his antics on nightmares. I never believed him. I think he wanted the bed to himself and manufactured his dreams to get it.

A first-rate cowboy, Scott nevertheless reached his greatest heights as a storyteller. With an "ear for dialect" and a "mimicry of mannerisms" that was both "shrewd" and "mercilessly exact," he held his listeners. "His hard, knobby body leaned forward. His green eyes snapped, and his crabbed red face grew full of magic. The ugliness disappeared," and he swept listeners "irresistably into a fairyland of word and sonorous tone, of soft gesture and biting allusion."[36]

Of a similar cut was Amasy Larsen of Moab, who for years rode the San Juan and Grand county ranges. According to Faun McConkie Tanner, he was born in 1866, drank heavily, and when sober talked plainly, but when drinking had a pronounced lisp. "He was lanky, hardly wide enough to hide a bottle, long in the back, and his shirttail was always flying in the breeze." Because of a badly set broken leg he walked on the side of his feet. Arrested once in Grand Junction he was taken before a judge for drunkenness. When he pled not guilty, the judge asked why it was he had been "wobbling down the street." At this Amasy pulled off a boot, "shook it in the judges face, and lisped, 'Judge, if you can walk thtraight in that boot, I'll plead guilty.'" The charges were dropped. As a boy he spent only two days in school and could neither read nor write. A Grand Junction newsboy who tried to hawk a paper to him was turned down because "I'd be wasting my nickel, I can't read." Quick in his reply, the boy retorted, "You could smell it — its all bull anyway." Quick to appreciate the point, Amasy bought the boy's entire stock.

Faun McConkie Tanner tells two other stories that convey not only the man's personality but the humor that char-

Round up and branding time in San Juan County, 1973. Photographs by Ken Hochfeld, USHS Collections.

196

acterized the cowboy fraternity:

> One day he dropped into his favorite barber shop. The barber slapped a hot towel on his face. Amasa reared up in the chair and bellowed, "Jethuth Chritht, Krug! When thith dod-damned towel getth cool enough tho you can thtand to take hold of it, would you pleathe take the dod-damned thing off my faith!" So far as he was concerned, there were only two ways to travel — both of them on horseback. Once a year he deviated from this theory when he drove his steers to Thompson and rode the cattle train with them to the eastern market. He was perhaps more awed than the rest of the townspeople when the first bi-wing airplane flew over the valley. He moved into the street with the rest of the residents and squinted at the mechanized bird until it disappeared in the horizon. "Amasa, how'd you like to be up there with that pilot?" someone asked. The old cowboy seemed to reflect a moment, then replied soberly, "Id'd a dang thight rather be up there with him than without him!"[37]

Names too were colorful. Fred Keller points this up in his Blue Mountain ballad. "Yarn Gallus with gun and rope" refers to Henry Goodman, a Texas rider who was variously said to hold his pants up with a single string of yarn or to dutifully wear yarn suspenders knit by his mother and sent him from Missouri. "Doc Few Clothes" was Tom Trout, one-time Carlisle rider whose tall body left an ample length of bare back and a bit of cleavage showing between his shirt tail and his low-riding Levi pants.[38]

More seriously, there were dozens of riders still in the country who were of good humor and quick wit but better remembered because they worked cattle well or got on with other men. Some showed an almost unbelievable commitment to the work of handling cattle. Among these was A. J. Scorup who by constant riding built a spread that is said to have operated on more than a million and a third acres of canyon-wracked public domain. Another was his foreman Harve Williams who, with obvious reference to the Biblical Jacob's fourteen years of cattle management to win a bride, used to say that he had worked for forty years before Scorup had given him one of his daughters. Yet another was grey-eyed bachelor Chet Smith, cattle foreman for Redd Ranches, for whom, as I have good reason to remember, dairy cows and the choreboys who milked them were a special anathema.[39]

Cattle were hated, coddled, abused, handled with deft skill, but one suspects almost never loved. The huge five- or six-year-old steers were gone except for a few "snakes" that still haunted remote cedar points. In their place, cowboys of the era after 1910 worked yearling steers with most of the longhorn bred out of them and with Hereford rapidly replacing the Durham and Shorthorn of the early Utah strains.

In 1918 Albert and James Scorup, two brothers with fantastic dedication to desert cowboying and more than a modest spirit for adventure, joined William and Andrew Somerville of Moab to buy the Indian Creek Cattle Company from David Goudelock and other Moab stockmen in a deal that sent reverberations through every part of the country and involved at least eight transactions in which cash and property totalling over $850,000 changed hands. A hard winter in 1919-20 in which the Scorup-Somerville outfit lost 1,500 head of cattle drove the Adams brothers, who had taken over other Scorup ranches, to the wall. Reabsorbing these operations and staving off disaster as prices fell and drought took the country in the 1920s, the Scorups headed what was known as the Indian Creek Cattle Pool for a number of years before incorporating as Scorup-Somerville in 1926. By 1937, when they acquired private ground on the La Sal Mountains from Goudelock and others, Scorup-Somerville ran on more than 36,000 privately owned acres and upwards of 1.3 million acres of public domain and national forest. The outfit's forest permit (sometimes reported to be as many as 7,000 or 8,000 head) is said to have been the largest single permit in the United States.[40]

Meantime, the La Sal Livestock Company extended its operations. The company barely survived the hard times of the early 1920s, and its manager, Charlie Redd, diversified his interests to build buffers for his stock business, bought out an increasing number of the earlier stockholders, and picked up small bits of property as broken homesteaders left the country around La Sal. By the mid-1930s the home ranch, which in the Cunningham-Carpenter era had included about 900 acres of farm land, had been enlarged to nearly 2,000 acres of farming and improved pasture ground. More important, the ranch found opportunity to buy out Colorado ranchers with whom it had long dealt and by the later 1930s had, according to one source, 47,000 acres of deeded land and large forest permits, as well as vast acreages of Grazing Service or Bureau of Land Management permits.[41]

Other San Juan operators had also moved increasingly into western Colorado. The interaction between the two areas had always been strong. But for years the movement appeared to be primarily from east to west. First came Colorado cattlemen, later sheep, then cattle buyers and dry farmers. But San Juan-based Utahns had always depended upon Colorado. First they worked there in the mines and grading railroad tracks. Then they looked to banks at Durango and Grand Junction, which often provided handier credit than Salt Lake institutions. Winter range was in better supply in Utah, summer in Colorado. To keep Colorado stockmen from invading their winter range, Utahns had only one alternative — fill winter ranges and expand into Colorado for summer grazing. As a consequence, Utah stock had always been summered in Colorado either under the care of their Utah owners or by new Colorado owners to whom they had been sold. In addition, markets for Utah cows as well as sheep and wool lay to the east, beyond Colorado, at Kansas City, Omaha, or Chicago. Stock driven to Colorado was on the way to market; consequently, animals and the ranging customs of Utah were drawn eastward by the workings of market systems.

Two important points remain. First, the long-range calculus of social and natural forces had worked to bring the country under control of stockmen of Mormon background. The metropolis from which they drew was closer at hand, and they tended to be of bigger families, allowing one to replace another if he pulled out of the country. For several decades the sense that San Juan was Mormon country, part of the kingdom to be settled and held, also made them better stayers. They lived in San Juan with less of a sense that they needed to return to Denver, St. Louis, or Los Angeles. If they did go to the city, it tended to be Salt Lake City or to Provo, as it was in the case of both A. J. Scorup and Charlie Redd.

But in the final analysis, the Mormon sense of religious destiny that had guided the first generation of San Juan County's community builders did not extend to the second generation. Indeed, it would seem that both Charlie Redd and A. J. Scorup built ranches in the traditional sense. They were in effect more ranchers than Mormon settlers. For them the effective agenda was a money-making outfit, not a country held by the Mormons and congenial to their ways. With the passing of time the old "near nationalism" that guided Mormons in the early days had become a dead letter. True, Mormons believed the millennium was still coming, but their agenda called less for the expansion of its physical or geographic base and more for personal righteousness and conversion of new members to the church.[42]

How the current crop of small ranchers and farmers fit into this context is not known. Recent decades are too close to us — the data is not in. But it is safe to say that San Juan long remained a frontier remote and sparsely settled. It lay between the Texas-influenced livestock frontier of the broader West and the Mormon Great Basin. Profoundly influenced by each of these cultures, San Juan was nevertheless isolated enough over a relatively long period of time to develop a character of its own — one that, for this writer at least, is among the most interesting to be found in the American West.

NOTES

[1]Journal of William T. Tew, entries for spring 1881, copy in author's possession.

[2]Don D. Walker, "The Cattle Industry of Utah, 1850-1900: An Historical Profile," and "The Carlisles: Cattle Barons of the Upper Basin," *Utah Historical Quarterly* 32 (Summer 1964): 190, 268-84.

[3]David Lavender, *One Man's West* (New York: Doubleday and Company, 1943), p. 192; and Stena Scorup, *J. A. Scorup: A Utah Cattleman* (n.p., n.d.), pp. 26-27, 30.

[4]Scorup, *J. A. Scorup*, p. 25.

[5]Fred W. Keller, "Blue Mountain," copy in author's possession.

[6]Scorup, *J. A. Scorup*, pp. 26-27.

[7]Cornelia Adams Perkins, Marian Gardner Nielson, and Lenora Butt Jones, *Saga of San Juan* (San Juan County: Daughters of Utah Pioneers, 1968), p. 106.

[8]Henry A. Bergh, *Cliffdwellers Echo* 1 (January 1912), Records of the La Sal National Forest, pp. 58-60, National Archives; and James Monroe Redd Oral History, July 21, 1973, p. 3, Charles Redd Oral History Project, Brigham Young University.

[9]Henry A. Bergh, *Cliffdwellers Echo* 1 (January 1912): 58.

[10]Francis A. Hammond was responsible for this estimate, which according to tax records and census information was much too high. See his Journal, December 17, 1885. Others have repeated the figure; see James Monroe Redd Oral History, August 20, 1973, p. 2, for example.

[11]Chester B. Smith Oral History, October 19-21, 1973, pp. 21-22, Charles Redd Oral History Project.

[12]B. W. Allred, "Cattle Roundup, Mountain Style," *Corral Dust: The Brandbook of the Potomoc Corral of Westerners* (1966) (p. 17 in MS in author's possession).

[13]*Times-Independent* (Moab), April 1, 1920, and Charles S. Peterson, *Look to the Mountains: Southeastern Utah and the La Sal National Forest* (Provo: Brigham Young University Press, 1975), p. 204.

[14]Lavender, *One Man's West*, pp. 142-43.

[15]Fires at Redd Ranches in the 1930s and 1940s are described in numerous oral histories from the Charles Redd Oral History Project.

[16]Austin E. Fife, Moab, Utah, August 6, 1955, Fife Mormon Collection, Series I 923, p. 4.

[17]Lavender, *One Man's West*, p. 151.

[18]Ibid., p. 209.

[19]Juanita Brooks, *Uncle Will Tells His Own Story* (Salt Lake City: Taggart & Company, 1970), p. 134.

[20]Ibid., p. 137.

[21]Earl Halls, "Incidents in the Life of Earl Halls" (May 16, 1968), p. 9, copy in author's possession.

[22]Ibid.

[23]Brooks, *Uncle Will Tells His Own Story*, p. 116.

[24]Halls, "Incidents in the Life of Earl Halls," p. 13.

[25]Ibid., p. 10.

[26]Ibid., p. 10-11.

[27]Ibid.

[28]Ibid., p. 14.

[29]*San Juan County: Basic Data of Economic Activities and Resources*, compiled by the Utah State Planning Board (Salt Lake City, 1940).

[30]Peterson, *Look to the Mountains*, p. 174.

[31]Allred, "Cattle Roundup, Mountain Style," and Lavender, *One Man's West*, pp. 101 and 117.

[32]Lavender, *One Man's West*, pp. 119-21.

[33]Allred, "Cattle Roundup, Mountain Style."

[34]Lavender, *One Man's West*, p. 126.

[35]Ibid., pp. 150-54.

[36]Ibid., pp. 153-56.

[37]Faun McConkie Tanner, *The Far Country: A Regional History of Moab and La Sal, Utah* (Salt Lake City: Olympus Publishing Company, 1976), pp. 319-21.

[38]Ibid., pp. 316-17, B. W. Allred Oral History, June 2, 1973, pp. 42, 60, Charles Redd Oral History Project, also provides good descriptions of Goodman and Trout.

[39]Charles Peterson leased Redd Ranches' dairy herd from 1953 to 1956 but to his chagrin was always referred to locally by the traditional ranching term "the choreboy."

[40]Scorup, *J. A. Scorup: A Utah Cattleman*, especially pp. 38-46; Harve Williams Oral History, June 13, July 6, August 7 and 10, 1973, Charles Redd Oral History Project, also contains much information.

[41]For general information on Redd Ranches see Kathy Redd, "History of La Sal, Utah," in Perkins et. al., *Saga of San Juan* pp. 170-93; also see various oral histories from the Charles Redd Oral History Project.

[42]Klaus J. Hansen, *Quest for Empire: The Political Kingdom of God and the Council of Fifty on Mormon History* (East Lansing: Michigan State University, 1970) deals with Mormon assumptions about the millennium. Charles Peterson, *Utah: A Bicentennial History* (New York: Norton and Company, 1977), pp. 78-105, treats nation-like inclinations of early Utah Mormons.

Comments on "San Juan: A Hundred Years of Cattle, Sheep, and Dry Farms"

Hardy Redd

Chas Peterson has done a delightful job collecting information, putting it together, and interpreting the result. I agree with almost all he says. I am particularly delighted by such expressions of his as "a few like Harv Williams became Mormons, and more located in Moab or in neighboring Colorado towns *where most of them became the relaxed channels through which Texas and Mormon customs evolved.*"

As a preface to my comments, I would like to relate what Chas has said about San Juan County in another essay, "Cowboys and Cattle Trails," published in 1979 in a companion volume to this book, *Emery County: Reflections on its Past and Future*. In comparing Emery, Grand, and San Juan counties, Chas writes:

> The village and cooperative pattern of settlement gave a distinct Mormon flavor to the San Juan area. The character of the Moab, La Sal, and Castleton district was more consistent with the general frontier. It was not that Grand County was without Mormons. Indeed, people who affiliated in some way with the church constituted a majority of its population. But taken with the other settlers they did not add up to a Mormon community the way the San Juan Mission did. With few exceptions Grand County Mormons had come unbidden, prompted by their own ideas of opportunity rather than by the mission call by which Mormon colonizing was so often carried out.

From earliest times Grand County gave itself unabashedly to economic development. . . . By contrast to San Juan, Grand County was not selfconsciously involved with its own identity. . . . Grand County was less clearly under attack from outside livestock interests, Indians, and the outlaw culture of the times, and thus found no real need to surround itself with a defensive identity.

The Moab area had few heroes. Those it did have were successful businessmen or . . . closely associated with the cowboy tradition. . . .

San Juan, on the other hand, was concerned with inner self and developed strong traditions of its uniqueness. To an amazing degree it was preoccupied with what may be called the Hole-in-the-Rock mystique. . . . They had done their duty. Once on the San Juan many questioned the wisdom of staying. Survivors, however, assumed an even more assertive position, that their work was unique and that they were a chosen community. . . . San Juan produced its own heroes . . . like old Indian scout Thales Haskell. . . . Uncle Ben Perkins, an illiterate shotfire from the mines of Wales, who blasted the road down the Hole-in-the-Rock. In Moab the figure of Bishop Jens Nielson, feet and legs twisted and crippled by frostbite, could never have emerged as the single dominant folk hero. But Nielson, Haskell, and Perkins all lent themselves admirably to the Hole-in-the-Rock mystique. Like the character of the community for which they became symbols, they were people apart. (pp. 82-84)

Turning back to the paper on San Juan County, from this point most of my comments are where I take exception to the emphasis placed on some things, interpretations, and implications, or where I amplify.

Quoting Peterson's: "The Hole-in-the-Rockers dug in at Bluff. They built diversion dams and water wheels, shoveled sand from washed-in ditches, worked in Colorado for subsistence, quarreled among themselves, and watched the river carry off their tiny farms." I say that they did not quarrel much. Mormon frontier communities were pretty close-knit, and Bluff especially so due to difficulties with the ditches and water and the threat of Anglo and Indian thieves. Ninety-nine percent of the time they worked in cooperation with each other building diversion dams, keeping the ditch free from sand and washouts. People who let their leader allocate scarce water irrespective of water turns were pretty united.

"Hard pressed and divided by poverty, the Bluff Mormons . . . ." I would more likely say "united" by poverty, because poverty usually unites families and communities more than it divides.

During a six-week period of protracted storms in Monticello in the 1920s, Will Brooks "met all the people of Monticello, the best class of people that I ever associated with in all my life." The enforced confinement to home and community put people into more contact with each other and they were living under adverse circumstances. This had the tendency to bring out the very best in them.

"As county assessor, L. H. Redd was tireless in collecting taxes on transient herds, thus reducing the county's appeal to wintering Colorado cattle and generally enhancing the cause of the Mormons, who always controlled the county politically." The main purpose of tax collection was to raise funds for county government. Taxes fell equally on Mormon and Colorado cattle, giving no advantage to the Mormons.

Pioneer Days Rodeo, Monticello, 1973. Photograph by Ken Hochfeld, USHS Collections.

I am not sure "the large San Juan County ranches were a bonanza that made fortunes for absentee owners." It would be an interesting research project for a budding historian to find out if they really did make money. My comment is that the ranches did make money some years but in other years did not; on balance, they were similar to other agricultural enterprises — making money some years and losing in others, depending on prices and moisture conditions. The fact that many of the ranches in San Juan and western Colorado were sold in the late 1890s or early 1900s indicates they were not all that profitable.

I agree that Mormons gradually expanded and took over the county for a number of reasons. Primarily, because they were better "stayers." A few years ago, I visited Boise City in the panhandle of Oklahoma. When I asked who farmed the land, one family was prominent. When I asked how they got so much land, the reply came: "During the depression and dust bowl of the 1930s, *they stayed.*" In San Juan, the Mormons "stayed." J. A. Scorup came from Salina and worked under tough conditions that almost no one else would tolerate. He was enterprising and was willing to take chances and risks. He "stayed."

There is a tendency among some writers and historians to assume that because some succeed in business and others fail, or some farmers and ranchers acquire more property and others sell, the survivor must use some nefarious or underhanded methods. While I do not doubt some of this happened, most of the time the survivors were just the better operators — more frugal, more careful of expenses, harder working, more foresighted, had more ability to plan and execute toward goals, did a better job with livestock, crops, fertilizing, irrigating, etc. Over time, most of us get what we deserve in economic as well as spiritual realms.

Chet Smith is correct when he says that the men who worked at La Sal were as much a part of Redd Ranches' success as was Charlie Redd. Charlie had the ability to manage and get the best out of men. Anyone who knows Chet Smith knows that it would take a combination of diplomacy and toughness to work him. That Charlie was able to do this with Chet and Spanish-American sheep and cowmen such as F. R. Lopez, Merejeldo Valdez, Roque Garcia, and many other men is an indication of his ability to manage men. This should take nothing away from the men themselves; they were dedicated, hard-working, loyal, competent people who did the careful, painstaking work that makes or breaks a ranch.

As a young boy I was greatly embarrassed by how harshly my father would speak to the men. I wondered why they liked him and why they did not quit after being spoken to so sharply. I think that because my dad was so vitally interested in the work and in improving their work habits and abilities, the men took it and worked even harder. Once my father visited Lewie Willson who was trailing cows and calves on Monogram Mesa. It was June; the weather was hot; it was painstaking and difficult work — hurry up and wait, taking care all the while not to miss a calf lying down under a bush, a dreary kind of work. My father came to the noon camp and berated Lewie severely for the way things were going and his performance in general. "But when your dad left," Lewie said, "he put his hand on my shoulder and told me, sincerely, that he had faith in my ability and knew I could get the cattle to Summer Camp in good shape. He made me feel capable and a valued person. I felt ten feet tall and was determined to do the best job I could."

Charles Peterson suggests arsonists set many of the fires on the La Sal Livestock Ranch during the 1930s and 1940s. Although the shearing shed fire near La Sal Junction was apparently set by arsonists, most of the other fires, I suspect, were caused by lightning or carelessness. An attempt was made to poison sheep in Lockhart Basin, but these incidents were exceptions rather than the rule. Most people, even cattle and sheepmen fighting over range and water rights, cooperated more often than they fought.

I was bothered by David Lavender's quote that some of the homesteaders' children reached "maturity without entering a church or sitting down before a white tablecloth. They never flushed a toilet or saw a railroad or stepped on a cement sidewalk." My immediate response is to wonder if these things measured a person. My father remembered that many of the Indian people and so-called "uneducated Anglos" were some of the finest in character, integrity, inventiveness, and persistence. They may have been somewhat unsophisticated and lacking in polish, but many of them were fine, generous, high-type individuals in spite of their lack of white table-cloths, flushing toilets, or cement sidewalks.

Charles is correct in saying the La Sal homesteaders had a commitment to the better things in life. They just could not make a go of it in the arid desert without irrigation water. I am not so sure their "views were any larger" than those who stayed; rather, small farm dry-land homesteading in the La Sal area was not economically feasible. The shift from small to large farms, shown in the following table, was common in the United States settlement and accelerated in the arid West as homesteaders found that they could not live or support a family on 160 acres of dry land.

Average Size Farm in Acres[1]

Year	U.S.	Utah
1850	203	51
1900		212
1940		354
1970	374	—
1975		1000
1982	429	1000

The national trend, and particularly in Utah, has been toward fewer but larger farms. Those who were less efficient, less frugal, less well situated, usually left first.

The number of Utah farms is illustrative:

Number of Utah Farms[2]

Year	Number
1859	926
1920	25,000

1936	31,000
1960	19,000
1970	14,000
1982	13,000

In 1900 it took one person to feed three; in 1982 one farmer fed seventy-five people. This has freed a vast number of people from back-breaking hand labor and allowed people to provide the goods and services that give Americans the highest standard of living in the world.

I disagree that the "Mormon sense of manifest destiny that had guided the first generation of community builders did not extend to the second generation. Indeed, it would seem that both Charlie Redd and J. A. Scorup built ranches in the traditional sense. They were in effect more ranchers than Mormon settlers. For them the effective agenda was a money-making outfit, not a country held by the Mormons and congenial to their ways." I would suggest that one of those who started this transition was Lemuel Hardison Redd, Jr., who came with the Hole-in-the-Rock expedition to San Juan as a young man and constantly expanded his operations. He set the stage for Charlie Redd and the La Sal Livestock outfit. I suggest that L. H. Redd's impetus and purpose to acquire land and ranges were an extension of, rather than a departure from, the San Juan mission. He realized that the sons and daughters of the original Hole-in-the-Rock pioneers needed room and employment, hopefully close to home. If the limited land resources in San Juan were held by non-Mormons, the increasing Mormon population would have to go elsewhere. Part of the reason the Gentile outfits were purchased was to avoid conflict between Mormons and non-Mormons, to avoid cultural shock, and to create communities with a good environment for the raising of children that could be somewhat controlled by a dominant Mormon population. L. H. Redd may have felt (or rationalized) that the San Juan mission had to be on a solid financial base, without which the purpose of the mission — converting Indians — could not be accomplished.

It is interesting to note that, with the establishment of a solid financial base in Blanding, many are expending their time and effort in church leadership positions and missionary work on the Navajo Reservation. There is much more Indian missionary work going on now than when the San Juan Mormons were struggling to survive in Bluff and Blanding. The secure economic foundation now allows the descendants of the Hole-in-the-Rockers and Mexican refugees the leisure and wherewithal to make these efforts.

Another reason the Mormon people stayed in San Juan, while those left who came here merely for profit, may be found in a comment made by a Nazi Germany concentration camp inmate:

> How did people stand it? I fear I must disappoint you. With regard to the purely physical aspect, not the young, the strong-looking boys survived best, but most shorter sinewy men.
>
> But far more important than the purely physical angle is the mental one. In all concentration camps we found that the death rate was lowest among political and religious prisoners who had suffered for their convictions, and highest among the tramps and petty criminals who were by far the strongest physically. It is also interesting to note that not the young people of college age were the best to survive, but the middle-aged group — those between 35 and 50. The explanation of this fact that simply the greater spiritual and ideological resistance offered by men whose character had matured. . . . As a rule, a weak body with a strong mind survived. . . .[3]

The staying power of many San Juaners is illustrated in a Charlie Redd history of the La Sal Livestock Company:

> We got along very well until the fall of 1919 when World War I ended. A deep depression spread over the country, prices dropped, and cattle were very low for about 5 years and the major part of our livestock was investment in cattle.
>
> We sold cows for 2 or 3 years to the Holly Sugar Company, shipping them from Thompson, at from 11 to 13 dollars a head. The La Sal ranch had been bought on time, only part of the debts had been paid off, and the Monticello Store had gone into receivership just a short time earlier. We really had a time holding onto the property. It looked, for a number of years, like we would lose it.

Bunkhouse at the La Sal Ranch. Photograph Copyright 1979 Steve Lacy Wild Bunch Photo.

Prior to his death in 1923, my father (L. H. Redd, Jr.) told me, "I don't know what the end will bring, but I wish I could be sure of two things: that my debts would be paid and that my families will get along." I was deeply moved. The estate was very heavily in debt. He had borrowed money for the water and power systems for both Blanding and Monticello. His total debts, those he owed directly and indirectly, as I recall, totaled nearly $600,000. It was initially considered by our creditors that we were busted.

We were advised to take out bankruptcy or go into receivership. I would not allow my mind to even consider it. For some reason, bankruptcy, failure to pay bills, was a very serious offense, almost like murder. I wouldn't allow anybody to tell me we were busted. I persuaded my brothers and creditors that I thought we could make it.

We were lucky to be dealing with people who had confidence in us and who were fair minded. Cunningham and Carpenter were helpful in extending the notes. Continental Bank and Trust, with Mr. Walter Cosgriff as President, was very generous.

Even then it was a struggle. When I was asked why I kept going when it looked hopeless, I answered, "I don't know how it will turn out, but I have a simple philosophy: I am working hard — harder than I ever have in my life. I'm doing everything

I can to protect the property, maintain numbers, and look after it. I'm cutting expenses to the bone. Now if this thing does turn around, I will be able to hang onto the property and have something. If conditions continue bad and we finally go broke, I can look myself in the face and say 'Well, I did my damnedest; I did all I could.' "[4]

As mentioned above, the reason some ranchers survived was their frugality. It is reported that Harv Williams of the Scorup-Somerville outfit drew only 25 cents of his wages one year and that was spent on cigarette paper which he wet and stuck to his lips so they would not chap and crack in the wind and sun.

Charlie Redd's advice to his children gives a hint of his and his father's background and why their livestock operation survived:

> Sometimes I feel I've stressed saving and thrift too strongly. I still feel that it is a better part of wisdom to be thrifty, industrious and to waste nothing.
>
> I want you to know that the property is to be enjoyed, the income wisely spent for your joy and comfort. I'd like to see all of you do more traveling, spend more time reading, looking at beautiful things, and visiting with wholesome folks. Sometimes property makes people selfish and scrubby. Sometimes it makes spendthrifts, wastrels, and drunkards of them. I have confidence that you children will use it wisely, but I want you to give careful consideration to wise spending. I'd like to see you take trips; I'd like to see you broaden your knowledge and experience, strengthen your culture. Money and wealth is valuable only as it adds to the happiness and growth of those who own it. I'm sure you'll all be modest and humble in your feelings about these possessions. I see no evidence of any of you being boastful and arrogant or feeling self-sufficient because of anything you have or will have.
>
> I don't need to moralize. I know you know the blessings as well as the evils that can come from material wealth. I would be very sad if I discovered my life's effort to build up an estate for each one of you was the means of your downfall. Having property means added responsibility. You must be a little more stable, a little more honorable, a little more charitable, a little more helpful, and a little more kind. Property is to be used and not abused. I hope you will always be humble about your possessions; to boast or brag or strut because of any possessions you may have

is an evidence of immaturity and shallowness. You are acquainted with some of the get-rich-quick people who are so eager to advertise their wealth that they are not highly regarded, and they are very unwise.

There is an old adage about "rags to riches and back to rags in three generations." Some families are so speedy that they can make the circle in two generations.

My reward will be sufficient and all the sacrifice, worry, work, and strain involved in my 45 or 50 years at La Sal will be rewarded if you boys and girls develop into fine, solid, wholesome, and kindly men and women.[5]

NOTES

[1]Cultural Statistics of the Utah Department of Agriculture Report, 1981.
[2]Ibid.
[3]Anonymous letter published in the *Daily Californian*, April 7, 1948.
[4]Minutes of Redd Ranches Stockholders meeting, August 4, 1960, at La Sal, Utah, copy in author's possession.
[5]Ibid.

A Perspective of the Agriculture and Livestock Industry in San Juan County, 1959-1982

Preston G. Nielson

The story is told of a farmer who recently won a lottery with a prize of a million dollars. When interviewed by the media as to how he was going to spend it he replied, "I guess I'll just keep on farming until it is all gone." This illustrates the present state of agriculture in this county and country. Few farms or ranches are making a profit. Most are being run on borrowed money from the equity they have in the land. While the expenses of running a farm or ranch operation continue to rise, the prices received for goods produced are less or the same as years ago.

The principal crops raised in southern San Juan County are wheat and beans. They are raised on dry farms with many more acres being used for wheat than beans. There are also several thousand acres of irrigated ground used for raising alfalfa hay.

Up to this point there has been much effort and expense put into clearing new land for farming. Most of it has now been cleared and is in production. The government is not selling any more land to farmers. There are no more homesteads to be acquired; therefore, most of the land that could be used for farming in this area is in production.

Few young people used to go into farming. However, now there is a new generation beginning to run the local farming operations. Most of these are family farm situations. The old generation is being replaced by their offspring.

There are more hobby farmers now than twenty-three years ago. They farm small acreages and hold down a full-time job. A full-time job permits them to farm after work and on weekends and holidays. There are few farming operations in the southern part of the county that derive all their income from farming. Most have some additional source of income.

Perhaps the increase in size and efficiency of farm machinery has kept the farmer in business. He can farm larger acreage in less time and do it better. Too much cannot be said about this fact.

Irrigation farming has become more efficient over the last few years. Many farmers are using sprinklers. Wells are much more abundant. Land has been leveled and pipelines laid. Many of these irrigation projects would not have been possible without technical assistance from the Soil Conservation Service and financial assistance from the Agriculture Stabilization and Conservation Service. Many of the farm improvements would not have been made without these two organizations. They provide a great service and assistance to the county farming and ranching industry.

Farmers continue to have the same problems and challenges with insects, wheat smut and other plant diseases, and noxious weeds. Clisbee Lyman, a prominent local farmer, says the biggest problem facing our farms here today are the noxious weeds. They have increased tremendously over the last twenty-three years.

The Recapture Dam Project, now in its initial construction stages, will provide for more acres to be irrigated and will supply a consistent source of water throughout the growing season. Heretofore, the farmers had to depend on the runoff from Blue Mountain as their only source of water. After the runoff was finished so was all irrigating.

Blanding ditch with Walter C. Lyman, developer of the ditch, in the center of the photograph. Copyright 1979 Steve Lacy Wild Bunch Photos.

The County Master Plan calls for many thousand acres of government land to be added to the farming acreage. If this ever occurs it will greatly affect the farming industry in this area.

Local farmers hope and believe that there is a better financial position for them in the years ahead. They feel that fertilizer will have to be used more extensively to keep up the yields of their product. Plant scientists are continuing to improve varieties of wheat and alfalfa which will be of great help. It appears that commercial farms will increase in size in the future and that there will be more hobby farmers.

Now for a quick look at ranching. In the mid-1870s this county was a rendezvous for outlaws. It was estimated that 35,000 head of cattle roamed from the Blue Mountain to Dolores, Colorado, seventy miles away. Southeastern Utah was too remote for natural expansion and colonization; therefore, people had to be called to come and settle here. This they began to do in 1880.

The 1959 census of agriculture for San Juan County listed the total number of cattle (cows and calves) at 16,272. The 1981 agriculture statistics show total numbers at 27,100 cows and calves. Perhaps as dramatic as the change in the number is the change in the kind and size of these cattle. In the late 1950s almost all herds were comprised of straight Herefords. Now there are few, if any, straight Hereford cattle herds. Crossbreeding is a common practice, yielding bigger calves that bring more money. The most common cross with the Hereford is the Angus. The exotic cattle from Europe such as the Semmental, Charolais, Limousin, and others have been used extensively with mixed results. Nevertheless, these cattle have left offspring that are bigger in every way, have increased milking ability, and generally bring a greater net return. I believe we have much better cattle today. This has come about through using better bulls and also through much better management of available resources.

The sheep industry used to be a viable part of the ranching business in this area. Today there is not a single herd of sheep left that is owned by an Anglo. The Navajo people continue to run lots of sheep on the reservation, which are made up of many bands owned by individual families.

Most of the cattle in this area are run on Bureau of Land Management and Forest Service land. Private lands supplement these permits with smaller herds of cattle run entirely on private land. We have not begun to tap the rich potential of these government lands for grazing. There are literally hundreds of thousands of acres that could be reseeded and improved for cattle grazing. Many restrictions, multiple-use policies, and environmentalists, along with a lack of funds, keep this from taking place. The BLM put a moritorium on any reseeding projects in the 1960s, which will continue to be in effect until the environmental impact studies are done. The Forest Service continues with some projects for range rehabilitation as funds permit. Many of the projects completed in the late 1950s and early 1960s are in bad need of maintenance. However, because of a lack of funds and many environmental restrictions, even basic maintenance of existing projects is nearly impossible. This has been very discouraging to the rancher. There are few things that could be done that would benefit him more than reseeding lands and then being able to maintain them.

Reseeding and range rehabilitation projects pay many dividends. Over the last twenty-three years they have helped to increase fertility, significantly increased weaning weights, increased cow size, permitted more cattle to be run, and made the calf crops much more uniform.

It is significant to note that the four-wheel drive vehicle has opened up many areas previously closed to proper use by the cattlemen. These areas can now be reached in the wintertime, making it possible to take in feed and supplements to the livestock. The improvements in roads have also helped a great deal in getting to and from the ranges. Water trucks and tanks have opened grazing areas that had little or no use in times past because of the unavailability of water. This has been so critical in reseeded areas. The development of springs, reservoirs, windmills, and wells has helped the rancher use the land more effectively, thus guarding from overgrazing. The availability of veterinarians has really increased the health of our cattle. Through better management and nutrition, heifers calve at the age of two and then serve in the herd for ten to twelve years. The feeding of grain and protein supplements on the winter ranges has greatly increased the vigor and fertility of the cattle. We have much more winter range than summer range in this part of the county. Many cattlemen truck their cattle to Colorado to spend the summer and fall months. In years past they drove them over and back and did not take nearly as many.

Because of the inability to develop government land for grazing, many ranchers have turned to reseeding state school sections. All revenue generated from the lease of these school sections is given to the state uniform school fund. This amounts to millions of dollars each year coming mainly from mineral and gas and oil leases along with grazing fees and other uses. Ranchers must do this development themselves, but it greatly benefits their operations.

Much technical assistance is given the cattle industry here by the Soil Conservation Service and the Extension Service of Utah State University. Financial assistance on some development projects is given by the Agriculture Stabilization and Conservation Service.

The cattle industry can have a very good future in this county if more development and maintenance of livestock projects can take place on government land. With increased cooperation with government agencies and an improvement in the economy the livestock industry will continue to make a great contribution to this area.

Any discussion of San Juan County livestock must include mention of the Utah Strip. This is an area of the Navajo Reservation stretching from Lake Powell to the Four Corners area, covering about a million acres. It is estimated that there are forty thousand cattle, sheep, horses and goat units running in this area. There are no grazing boards or co-ops. The

Barn and pasture at Verdure, 1979. Photograph by G. B. Peterson.

Granary at Verdure, 1979. Photograph by G. B. Peterson, © 1983.

livestock is run by family or extended family units. It is evident that the quality of the animals is increasing due to better management and seedstock.

Many improvements have been made in the last twenty years. Most grazing areas have been fenced off from the major highways. Wells and windmills have been established in many areas, thus dispersing the livestock over a wider area. Irrigated hay farms have been developed in the Aneth and Montezuma Creek area. Four farms are in this area with one being privately owned and three operated by co-ops. They provide much needed supplemental feed for the wintertime plus a cash crop.

The operators in this area seem to be raising more cattle and less sheep. Also there is more emphasis on raising goats for their mohair than sheep for their wool.

Through the Utah Navajo Development Council there are several range rehabilitation projects planned. In the Navajo Mountain area they plan to do chaining, burning, and reseeding projects in the pinyon-juniper stands. On Macraken Mesa sagebrush removal and reseeding projects are planned for the future. There is much potential for development of this kind on the Utah Strip. Many family organizations may start fencing off their grazing allotment, thus making way for even more improvements.

PART SIX

Roads & Resources

Utah-Arizona state line, May 1941. USHS Collections.

San Juan County Roads: Arteries to Natural Resources and Survival

Jay M. Haymond

Since the initial settlement of San Juan County in 1880, roads have been the means to survival in a land that gives up its substance grudgingly. As with other government functions carried on in a vast area by a small number of people, road construction and maintenance has been a struggle. Most San Juan roads have been built because of the need for access to the county's natural resources. These resources have not only been the reason for much road construction but have also been the source of funds to pay for maintenance. Federal funds have also been important in the development and maintenance of roads in the county. Today few, if any, roads would be built without federal funding.

After the construction of the Hole-in-the-Rock road from Escalante to Bluff in 1880, San Juan pioneers built roads to the mountains. These one-way or "dead end" roads were built first to reach the much-needed timber, then later as part of the development of water resources in the mountains.[1]

Of equal concern was the early establishment of roads connecting San Juan communities with other parts of Utah and nearby Colorado. In 1881 the Hole-in-the-Rock was abandoned in favor of a new route to Escalante by way of Hall's Crossing on the Colorado River. However, the Hall's Crossing road was a primitive trail, not much better than the original Hole-in-the-Rock route. Roads were also built northwest from Bluff to Cane Springs, Spanish Valley, and the community of

Moab on the Colorado River. Pushing east, a road was built to Dove Creek, Colorado. These early roads were built under the direction of George W. Sevey, the county's first road supervisor.[2]

County efforts were reinforced by those of private business. Some roads were built for business reasons, then donated to the county. An example of such self-interested generosity is found in the 1909 report of County Road

Wagon tracks in the sandstone at the head of Cow Canyon northeast of Bluff, 1966. Crampton Collection, Marriott Library, University of Utah.

228

Supervisor M. A. Barton to the newly organized State Road Commission:

> In order that we could have a better road west of the Navajo Hill into the oil field proper, instead of going up Comb Wash and over Lime Ridge, several men came to me and said if I could have a route marked out they would spend a few thousand dollars on the road and then after it was finished the County Commissioners might accept it as a county road or state road. In order to get the public sentiment, I called a meeting on December 9, by order of the County Commissioner, and the result was very favorable. Three men were appointed by the meeting to designate a better route than the old one and a much more direct one, and I was informed within a week that at least $5000.00 had been raised to improve the way to the oil field and it is expected to be finished by January 1, 1912.[3]

Until 1909 all roads were the responsibility of the county. Vehicular traffic was light and usually only local in nature. There were few automobiles. The truck, a phenomenon of World War I, would not be seen until the 1920s. Because roads were primarily for local use, the county carried the entire burden for public improvements on them. Modification of this philosophy began in 1916 when "post roads" were subsidized with federal funds to assist counties like San Juan where long distances made the cost of roads, and therefore the transportation of mail, very expensive.

With the establishment of the Utah State Road Commission, state officials recognized the growing need for better roads and a state road system. A boon to the isolated rural counties, the developing state concern meant that more money would be spent and attention paid to construction and maintenance of roads located in areas of few people who otherwise could not afford to pay for them.

Beyond San Juan County's small population, the nature of the country — rough terrain, loose sand, and long distances from road-building material — created more difficulties and greater expense for road construction. In his 1912 report to the Road Commission, M. A. Barton argued for money to improve the road between Monticello and the Grand County line. Beyond the fact that this section was part of the Utah

State Road System, Mr. Barton reasoned that the route to Moab "is the only feasible outlet for San Juan County over suitable material for road construction." Barton's plea, and those of his successors, would not be recognized for many years.[4]

The idea for a centralized road construction responsibility developed from a nationwide "good roads movement" and a national awareness that if the growing American population were to take advantage of the rapidly unfolding technological innovations for travel and conducting business, a more dependable transportation network was needed. Utah was in the mainstream of these concerns for a number of reasons, including a proposed transcontinental road which would pass through the state. Known as the Lincoln National Highway, the road was promoted by the Lincoln National Highway Association, whose members included makers of automobiles and automobile parts.[5] Construction of the Lincoln Highway was delayed by disputes, lawsuits, and World War I.

Animals were essential in road construction, reservoir building, and digging irrigation ditches and canals. Photograph Copyright 1979 Steve Lacy Wild Bunch Photos.

Fortunately the idea of good roads was supported by Congress in the Federal Highway Act of 1916. The act authorized funds to match those of state and local governments for "post" road construction and maintenance. Companion state laws allowed counties to bond to raise needed matching money. The Lincoln National Highway was completed in 1923 but lost its patriotic name in favor of a number as part of the uniformity of a national system. Thus, in Utah the Lincoln National Highway became U.S. 30 and later Interstate 80.[6]

The authority to assign numbers and designate routes was given to states in the 1921 Federal Highway Act. This act also increased federal participation in new-road construction from 50 percent to nearly 75 percent in Utah. This percentage corresponded to the proportion of Utah land under federal management. This feature in the law recognized the vast distances in the West over which roads had to be built and the lack of local tax revenues with which to pay for roads. The new formula applied to Federal Aid Project (FAP) roads or those segments of the state system that were "trunk" roads.[7] In San Juan County the route 451-7 from Moab to Bluff and later on to the Arizona line was the designated trunk road. In 1924 grading work on the segment between Moab and La Sal Junction was completed. The Road Commission reported the route improved after it was graded in 1928. Though graded, the road was not graveled. Pavement did not come until 1938 when the first three-mile segment of the road to Monticello was surfaced.[8]

In 1921 San Juan County reported 116.1 miles of state roads, none of which were paved or graveled. However, San Juan County was not alone. That same year twenty-one of Utah's twenty-nine counties reported no pavement of any kind. Fourteen counties stood with San Juan, having no pavement or gravel on their roads. The 1921 report listed 728 miles of San Juan County roads. That biennium $14,549.09 was collected in gasoline taxes. Over $38,000 was spent for road and bridge construction; $45,995.18 to retire part of the

Owachomo Natural Bridge, Natural Bridges National Monument, 1983. Photograph by G. B. Peterson.

Sipapu Natural Bridge, Natural Bridges National Monument, 1979. Photograph by G. B. Peterson, © 1983.

bonded indebtedness; and $45,549.39 to match federal funds, for a total state expenditure of nearly $130,000 for roads.[9]

The decade of the 1920s was especially difficult for Utah and other western states. After World War I the sharp demand for food products and mineral ores dropped quickly. In San Juan County the wartime demand for beans and vanadium followed this general trend and local tax revenues fell accordingly.

Fortunately, when state and local revenues fell short for essential road work, federal government agencies were able to pick up part of the burden. In 1924 the La Sal National Forest, which was established in 1910, built two roads on the forest in San Juan County. One road went from Blanding west to Natural Bridges, and the second east from La Sal Junction to Paradox, Colorado.[10] These were not new roads but rather improvements of existing wagon tracks upgraded to accommodate anticipated increased traffic from timber cutting, mining, and automobile sightseers. The primitive nature of these trails was observed by Herbert E. Gregory who made geological reconnaissance trips to San Juan County between 1909 and 1929. Speaking of the route to Natural Bridges he noted: "A few trails are kept open by cattlemen and in many places the topography marks out feasible routes for pack trains."[11]

During the 1930s road building was integrated into a broader program of improving existing community assets and promoting recovery from the economic depression by putting people to work. Congress poured money into labor intensive projects such as road construction. In the first Emergency Highway Appropriations Act, of the eighty million dollars appropriated, Utah received four million. An important use of these funds in San Juan County was the surfacing of part of its trunk roads.

The Civilian Conservation Corps was a prominent recovery program in San Juan County. One of the CCC's primary activities there was road construction. Though records documenting the importance of road maintenance and construction activity by the CCC and others in San Juan County are not extensive, a comment by Mr. H. K. Thurber in the Moab *Times-Independent* on January 9, 1936, sheds some light on the contribution of good roads to the county's economy. Speaking of the new interest in carnotite mining in San Juan, Mr. Thurber observed "the carnotite industry is moving the ore for a tithe of what it did in the past due to better roads."

World War II halted road construction all over the country except for roads essential to the war effort. In San Juan County some mine access roads were built but most work was not undertaken on the state road system.

After World War II traffic on San Juan's state roads increased as travelers, no longer restricted by wartime gas rationing, took to the roads and as mining activity continued to expand. The increased traffic, especially by the enormous ore-hauling trucks, raised questions of safety on the San Juan roads and brought road engineers to study ways to widen or straighten sections that posed safety hazards.

One such hazard was the dugway at Cane Springs which was realigned in 1948. The realignment included straightening the road along the mesa to the top of the dugway, then widening and improving the grade to the Cane Springs rest stop and patrolman's cottage. The contractor used local labor as much as possible on the project. Some of the workers found a "uranium tree" just off the right-of-way and sold the find to an Atomic Energy Commission buyer for ten thousand dollars — a fabulous sum in those days. This event was a harbinger of things soon to come as uranium fever would sweep across the Colorado Plateau in the early 1950s.[12]

Traffic demand is the obvious motive to build roads. In 1949 San Juan County recorded the next to the lowest road use in the state, as determined by the number of cars passing a given point in a twenty-four hour period. Only Garfield County was lower.[13] However, the boom in prospecting for uranium during the early 1950s jolted the quiet pace of Grand and San Juan counties into a feverish race. Access roads could not be built fast enough. In 1951 the Atomic Energy Commission, working through the Utah State Road

Commission, "rented" state equipment, operators, and supervisors to build a road from Blanding to Natural Bridges and grade the road from Natural Bridges to the Hite Ferry crossing. These agencies pushed road construction into the wilds of San Juan County without even a preliminary survey.[14]

Such extraordinary measures by the Atomic Energy Commission and State Road Commission are strong evidence of the national and state interest finally paid to isolated and remote San Juan County. Sections of today's U.S. 95 between Comb Wash and Natural Bridges were laid out by Jim Hurst, an inspector for the State Road Commission at Green River, Utah, who flew his airplane down each week and used it to scout the road line, keeping just ahead of the road-building crew working on the road he was inspecting between Blanding and Comb Reef.

Construction of a road through Comb Reef was a rigorous challenge. Prior to building that road, the only way west toward the Colorado River from Bluff or Blanding was over the forest road. which passed to the north of Comb Reef, or

Early road up east side of Comb Wash. USHS Collections.

across the Navajo trail west of Bluff near where the San Juan River cuts through Comb Reef. Surveyors chose a place near the halfway point between the two existing passages, possibly because of local stories about the "Posey Trail" and its potential as a route through the north-south running obstacle.[15]

Comb Reef had a break at the top of its jagged formation where the contractor started a road south by southwest through the first fifty feet of red rock before encountering a smooth and nearly vertical two hundred foot slickrock barrier. While work proceeded on the upper section, a second crew was sent into Comb Wash to push the road from the bottom toward the top. Living in a ranch house in Comb Wash, the second crew cut a road up the talus slope matching the grade of the line coming down from the break at the top of the reef. Both crews then attacked the treacherous slickrock. Drilling and shooting the vertical smooth rock throughout the winter of 1952-53, the crews finally met near the middle. Grading work on the road into Comb Wash was completed that summer, and construction crews pushed west beyond the wash as fast as the broken terrain would permit.

The road provided miners with better access into what had been one of the most remote sections of the county. After prospectors found what they were looking for and mines were developed, haulers had a much easier time getting the ore to processing plants. Later, in the early 1970s, another cut was made through Comb Reef to improve the alignment for Highway 95 which, through Comb Wash, passed south of the original road.

San Juan's road system and uranium industry was supported by federal funds under the Defense Highway Access Act to provide better access to producing uranium mines. In San Juan County these funds went to the following projects:

Bears Ears to Wooden Shoe Buttes Road	16.6 miles
Natural Bridges Junction to Red Canyon Road	33.0 miles
Red Canyon to White Canyon Road	6.8 miles
Utex Mine Road	6.8 miles
Montezuma Canyon Access Road	24.0 miles[16]

The first three projects were for a total of 56.4 miles of graded roads and the last two projects for a total of 30.8 miles of graded and graveled roads.

During this period improvements in the main trunk road were completed by the State Road Commission. The dugway at Peter's Hill was changed in 1954; Devil's Canyon realigned in 1953-54; and the road and bridge in Recapture Wash rebuilt. The following report from the State Road Commission indicates the tremendous effort in building and improving roads throughout the county:

	State Roads		County Roads	
	1948	1954	1945	1954
Oiled surface	36.1 miles	86.9 miles	5.5 miles	156.2 miles
Oil treated	1.1	0.0	0.0	0.0
Graveled	85.7	79.3	175.0	338.1
Graded	41.9	59.3	—	—
Unimproved	—	—	198.4	406.4
Primitive	74.5	40.3	345.3	56.0
Totals:	239.3	265.8	724.2	946.4[17]

The next important surge in road building took place about 1964 with the discovery of oil in the Aneth Basin. To provide better access into the new oilfield, the old road from the bottom of the hill off White Mesa to Hatch's trading post was rebuilt. When oil was found near Mexican Hat, the road to the Navajo reservation was improved. In 1964 the road west from Bluff was rebuilt to improve the section through Butler Wash and improve the alignment through Comb Reef into Comb Wash. Butler Wash was especially dangerous because of an old one-way Bailey bridge which spanned the wash. That bridge was replaced by two ten-foot diameter corrugated metal pipes. The road was constructed south of the original right-of-way. A new bridge was built in Comb Wash as part of the contract, which is currently still in use.[18]

In conclusion, roads in San Juan County were built because of the need for natural resource development. Federal money was an important supplement to private and local

Early San Juan County road across Grand Mesa near the Bears Ears. Photograph Copyright 1979 Steve Lacy Wild Bunch Photos.

government road-building initiatives. In the future, the construction of additional roads will be subject to further demands on the county's natural resources, to include scenic and recreational attractions.

NOTES

[1]Charles S. Peterson, *Look to the Mountains: Southeastern Utah and the La Sal National Forest* (Provo, Utah: Brigham Young University Press, 1975), p. 210.

[2]Cornelia Adams Perkins, Marian Gardner Nielson, and Lenora Butt Jones, *Saga of San Juan*, second edition (San Juan County: Daughter's of Utah Pioneers, 1968), p. 264.

[3]Public Documents, Highway Department Report, 1911-12.

[4]Ibid.

[5]*The Lincoln Highway*, Lincoln National Highway Association, 1935.

[6]Public Documents, Highway Department Report, 1923-24.

[7]Ibid.

[8]Public Documents, Highway Department Report, 1939-40.

[9]Public Documents, Highway Department Report, 1921-22.

[10]Public Documents, Highway Department Report, 1925-26.

[11]*Utah: A Guide to the State* (Salt Lake City, 1941), p. 427.

[12]Interview with Harold Whiting and Melvin Haymond, Utah State Historical Society.

[13]Public Documents, Highway Department Report, 1939-40.

[14]Interview with Harold Whiting and Melvin Haymond.

[15]Ibid.

[16]Public Documents, Highway Department Report, 1955-56.

[17]Ibid.

[18]Interview with Harold Whiting and Melvin Haymond.

San Juan County Roads and Resources

Calvin Black

Originally when people came here, they came to settle under the instructions of Brigham Young. They had to have roads and access and resources to survive. As people developed resources, for example gold mining along the Colorado River, they had to have access. The uranium, the oil, and other things have also demanded a need for access and they have created our ability to pay. Let me give you an example. In the early 1950s and up to the middle 1950s the total assessed valuation of San Juan County was 3.8 million dollars. We were one of the poorest counties in the state of Utah, the largest and the poorest school district in the state. The revenue from that assessed valuation — the maximum levy that counties could collect — brought in less than $50,000. By 1960, with the development of uranium ore, oil, and gas, the assessed valuation had gone from 3.8 million to 132 million. We were, at that point in time, the second wealthiest county on a tax base in the state of Utah. We did not stay there too long because the assessed valuation of the wealth from uranium, oil, and gas is dependent on the production of that resource and in some cases on the profitable production. So we went back down, then we went back up, and now we are going back down. Again, that is a major part of resources.

But getting back to the roads, I remember when my dad, as the state road foreman, built the road from Natural Bridges to Hite. Art Chaffin had promoted the road with the Utah Industrial Development Commission. They were to come up with about $10,000 in cash on each side to build that road. My dad and his very meager crew were given the responsibility to build the road on this side. Art Chaffin got the contract as an independent to build the road from Hanksville down on the wash to Hite where they put in a ferry. I went out there with my dad and I helped him flag the road. There were no culverts in the road so he would have to go through all that timber from there to Fry Canyon and it was very difficult. For each wash, and there were a lot of them along that drainage, we had to find a solid rock crossing or a place where it would not wash out easily and then get an alignment from one wash to another.

They got to Fry Canyon where the canyon is so narrow you can jump across it, about 35 feet deep and about 35 feet wide at the bottom. They went to the mountain and cut some timber and made a bridge across there which saved about ten miles. They got on down to White Canyon and where the bridge goes now my dad had the idea if they could get some timbers and get the state to provide a little more money they could build a bridge across there because it is fairly narrow. They were not able to do that so from the point where you came around, North Point I believe it is, and you look across to Farley where the road went down and crossed White Canyon, it was about two miles across, but it took ten miles by the road. They did put in a bridge across White Canyon by the river, and Art Chaffin put the ferry in at Hite.

I remember when they were working on the road I used to go down and camp with my dad. Hubby Shumway, or Glen, as he is more generally known now, used to go down with us and we would get in Fry Canyon on a sand bar and with pitchforks fork those catfish out of there and have a big catfish fry. Art Chaffin used to row across the river and pick us up and take us over to his farm. He raised dates and figs and the best watermelons you ever tasted. Those are some of the things I remember in my teens. I think I was about 15 or 16.

Then I would hear my dad and Lynn Lyman and the other old-timers talk about how someday we would have a road across there. It was always kind of a dream. That was very important if you wanted to go to St. George or Cedar City. When I was pretty young our family would get in the pickup and of course I would sit in the back. We would carry a grub box and bedrolls and we went to Cedar City to visit my grandmother who was over there with her sister. We picked her up. I do not even remember where we went but it seemed like it took forever. To get there you had to go to Thistle and then back down. You could go down through Emery County and across Salina, but that was a dirt road kind of like what we had here. There were still stretches of dirt road between here and Moab. The other alternative: we could go to Cortez, down to Gallup, and across from Winslow, Holbrook, and Flagstaff and up across the Kaibab. If you were lucky you could get down across the reservation, but you never knew when you would make it.

I remember the bad winter of 1948. My truck was stranded in Monticello, so we decided to go to St. George. It took us a couple of days. We got stuck up Price Canyon and we had all kinds of trouble. We decided we were not going to go back that way, that we would come back through the reservation. Actually, at first we were going to Flagstaff but the radio said with the blizzards the roads were closed, so we decided to come up through the reservation. We got up to about Cow Springs and that road was just a ditch. It was drifted full of snow and we got stuck. So we turned around and headed the other way. We met the mail truck, and the driver said, "Oh you can make it. I'm going to Kayenta; follow me in and if you have trouble I'll hook the chain on." So we did, but pretty soon he could not pull us even with chains on his duals. So we just left the car there and we got in the back of that truck with the rest of the Navajos. We got into Kayenta, Arizona, about 8 or 9 o'clock that night and we were there for ten days. There were no phones so we could not let anyone know where we were.

When I got home my grandmother had passed away and I had not known about it.

Roads to me were very important, and I kept thinking about what these guys were saying, that someday we would have a road. After I started prospecting and saw how rough that country was, it just did not ever seem possible — building a road. I remember when they dedicated U-95, I think I was a junior in high school. Governor Maw, Bishop Rogers, and all the dignitaries were down there with the band from Loa and the high school band from Blanding. Some of the people were talking about maybe someday we would have that road paved. Somebody said maybe before 20 years and I thought, "Oh, impossible," and that was in 1946. We dedicated U-95; finally had it finished and paved in 1976. It was called the Bicentennial Highway, and it had been 30 years! So again, I really had an early exposure to the roads and the needs. I carried that with me driving over a lot of those roads and trying to make a living first hauling uranium and then going into the mining business. The way I got started is that I had a truck and I ran out of an ore haul. I had to have something to haul so Hubby Shumway and I went together and got a jackhammer, compressor, and a wheelbarrow. That is all you had to have then. You did not have to register with the Mining Safety Health Administration or get permits. I hate to think of anybody starting out from the very bottom like we did then. But I became even more aware of the need for roads.

My next real experience with roads and that dream that I had remembered some of the older people talking about — my dad, Lynn, and many other people — was back when I was in the service in the mid-'50s. I had never been on a boat in all my life. The first airplane I had ever been on I was 25, just before I went in the service. I drove a jeep from here down to Oljato to meet some people that I was involved with from Salt Lake to look at some drilling. They flew in in a Beachcraft from Salt Lake and left there at 7:30 and got in Oljato at 9:00 in the morning. I left Blanding at 4:00 in the morning to get to Oljato at 9:00 to meet them. That guy had to go back to Moab after some parts and he asked if I wanted to go with him and I said, "Sure, I've never been in an airplane in my life." So we took off, and 40 minutes from the time we had taken off we were in Moab. When I saw that country from the air for the first time, it did not look as big and formidable as it had.

Then I went into the service, and we lived in New Jersey. When I was going to school at Fort Monmouth, we used to go into New York City. The only high walls I had ever seen before were these rocks in the canyons. To go back there and see those buildings was quite a different experience. We would go into New York on weekends. Somebody suggested we take the Staten Island ferry. So we did and that is the first time I had ever been on any kind of a boat except the old rafts we used to nail together and float on dirt ponds outside of town. I thought that was wonderful. That was after the time that the Upper Colorado River Project had been authorized. I was reading in the paper, I do not remember what year it was now, something about a group — Lynn Lyman, Joe Lyman, and Lorin Hawkins, and I do not know who else — went out the old road to Halls Crossing. We knew Lake Powell was going to be there, and I think those fellows went out there to see if there was a possibility of getting a road through that country, along the old Mormon trail. I started thinking about that and for the first time I really believed that it might be feasible, that there would indeed be roads across southern Utah. I felt there ought to be a ferry across there, kind of like the Staten Island ferry rather then two dead-end roads. So that was kind of in the back of my mind.

I returned home from the service and became a little bit interested in the political system. Our assessed valuation was up and in my opinion we were making a mistake by lowering our mill levies instead of using the revenue while we had it to develop some of the basic resources such as transportation and roads, agriculture, tourism, and many of the other potentials we have. We were still a county whose state roads were

Goosenecks of the San Juan River, 1979. Photograph by G. B. Peterson, © 1983.

dirt roads or gravel even though at that time we had been carrying a mill levy of about 16 mills for county purposes. When we were poor we only had $3.8 million in assessed valuation and 16 mills brought in only about $50,000. Then we had a $132.8 million assessed valuation and we dropped the mill levy, because of pressure from the oil and mining companies, to 2.95 mills. I thought, "My land! We ought to maintain that mill levy. If we could pay it when we were poor we can certainly pay it for a few years, and we would have had an extra million and a half dollars." A million and a half dollars would have done a lot to get in some roads.

246

We have Natural Bridges, Hovenweep, the Goosenecks; we have a lot of scenic attractions that we talk about. Lynn Lyman would take people; Frank Wright would take people; but I will tell you it was extremely hard to get there. So we started really working on some roads, and I got interested and involved in the political system for those reasons, to develop those resources.

I do not want to appear in any way vain and I hope you will not take it that way. The goals and the things that I have felt strongly about were getting some paved roads in the county. Those goals were of course getting Utah Highway 95 and getting a road from Bluff to Mexican Water and getting a road from Bluff to Montezuma Creek. We really goofed up in that in the late '50s when we were so tunnel-visioned in Blanding and Monticello and the county that we literally prohibited the road coming from Cortez through McElmo, Bluff, Mexican Hat, and Monument Valley as part of the Navajo Trail. In fact, we made sure that we were not even going to build a·road to the oil field that would facilitate the road at the time. That is the reason we went to the bottom of White Mesa and across that drainage and back up on the MacCraken and then parallel to the road that went from the bottom of White Mesa to Bluff, having to drop off that hill and cover about twice as many miles as if we had gone from Bluff to Montezuma Creek. The reason that we did not want that road was because we were afraid that road was going to "bypass" Blanding and Monticello. On September 8, 1958, I believe it was, we got the governor of the state, Governor Clyde, and the road commission down here at a public meeting. In the meantime Colorado had already put the road down to McElmo to the state line on their state system and they were ready to construct it. We got our governor and our road commission to make a public promise and take official action that they would not meet Colorado at the state line with an oiled road. Immediately the Navajo Trail Association forgot that segment, and that is the reason that U.S. 160, now the Navajo Trail, skirts just around Utah and goes south of us.

That road today carries two and a half times the traffic in the summer months of even Interstate 70. I felt that was a mistake at the time. That was another reason for my interest.

But in order to develop our road system it had to be county and state. We needed U-95; we needed the road from Bluff to Mexican Water as part of the north-south main highway. Now we have a new U.S. number for the highway. We got the number a year ago and it covers the road from Malta, Montana, to Chambers, Arizona. It will develop into a major north-south highway for the national parks, monuments, forest areas, recreation areas, and all the mineral and energy resources in the area connecting with that single numbered highway. That was an important goal. The road from Montezuma Creek to Red Mesa is an important road. The road from Bluff to Montezuma Creek, the one we should have had 30 years ago, is now in process. We are working on the road from Aneth to Ismay as part of that route.

The county has just recently completed some more of the road across Cahone Mesa that provides not only school bus needs for children to get them to school but an access to Hovenweep National Monument and another direct link into the Cortez area. Those were parts of the road system that we felt were important for the overall transportation system. I took a lot of flak because of the Halls Crossing road because I had a personal interest out there. But we got that road built for a very low amount of county money, and in the deal we got the state to take it over as a state road. It has not cost the county anything since it came on the state system. If we would have ignored it and left it, the road would have cost the county much more. It was costing the county every day and every month because we had the responsibility of maintaining it, and as more people drove on it the costs increased. In getting that road built, and giving it to the state, we have spent less money at this point than we would if we had done nothing.

The road into Canyonlands was another county road. We made a deal on a cooperative agreement and helped to have the road upgraded to a paved surface; then we gave it to the state. The road from Bluff to Mexican Water is now a state highway. So we're getting rid of some county roads that always have been functional as state roads. The county had the maintenance responsibility for the road to the Natural Bridges National Monument. We got rid of that and the road to Goosenecks State Park which was a county road. We had the only area in the state where roads to state parks or national parks and monuments were county roads. So we got the state to take them from us too. We are going to get them to take Hovenweep, and we are going to give them Montezuma Creek to Red Mesa; they are already aware of that. It just takes a little time.

But U-95 really got going when Joe Lyman was the president of the chamber of commerce and called a meeting. He got officials from southern Utah counties together and mayors of the cities. They all had their priorities but they all agreed that U-95 was the first priority. They got the funding started in 1964 with the bridges, and it was finally completed in 1976. There are roads outside of our area we were involved in planning with the other southern Utah areas, like the Boulder Grove road which is a connection with our network. It is one of the most beautiful drives in the whole state of Utah. One of the things that makes it so beautiful is that it goes up to about 10,000 feet and you can see most of our county; that is where the beauty is.

We have some concrete plans now going to get a ferry established between Halls Crossing and Bullfrog to connect with the Burr Trail on the other side of the lake. That will open up all kinds of opportunities and potential there; including the possibility of a community area adjacent to Halls Crossing. We are working on the mechanics of that potential and also in agriculture. There could be about four thousand acres of irrigated farmland. Waters rise in the lake to within about three hundred feet, and Utah and San Juan County still have some unused water rights. It has the potential for a combination resort and agriculture community. I doubt if we

"Big Indian," Monument Valley, 1983. Photograph by G. B. Peterson, © 1983.

"Bear and Rabbit" and "Castle Rock," Monument Valley, 1983. Photograph by G. B. Peterson, © 1983.

Monument Valley, west edge of Sentinal Mesa, from left to right: "Stagecoach," "Bear and Rabbit," "Castle Rock," and "Big Indian," 1983. Photograph by G. B. Peterson, © 1983.

ever had more than 4,000 acres of adequately irrigated land in the whole county.

We did get some highway numbers. Not very many years ago we had no U.S. numbered highways south of Monticello. We now have U.S. 191 and U.S. 163, an alternate that will only go from Kayenta to the junction west of Bluff. But we have some ideas for the future. When we get the Bluff-to-Montezuma Creek road and the Aneth-to-Ismay road we hope to extend that number into Colorado, possibly to Telluride.

Now to reservations. Back until the late '60s we did not accept or assume any responsibility for building or maintaining the roads on the reservations. When we started moving in that direction we had some problems. There were people in our county that did not know whether we should because that was really considered to be the Bureau of Indian Affairs responsibility. But there had been an attorney general's ruling in 1951 that counties and the state had the same responsibilities to provide services and benefits for the Indian people as they did any other citizens. That is when they really started going to public schools. So all of a sudden we had the responsibility of educating these Indian children in the public schools. They could not get to school. All of the roads were dirt roads, and on the reservation they had never been maintained. The Bureau of Indian Affairs had virtually ignored the Utah part of the reservation. Those people were ignored by everyone.

The interesting thing is that when our assessed valuation went from $3.8 million to $132.8 million it was due almost entirely to oil and uranium. A lot of the uranium was produced on the reservation, and even though it was on the reservation it had the same formula for a tax base as it did off the reservation. The oil was virtually all on the reservation. So about 90 percent of our tax revenue, with which we were building libraries, recreation facilities, schools, and other amenities, were paid for with production of resources from the reservation. As far as I was concerned it was inconsistent. We should have spent monies to provide those same services, and in order to get those kids to school we had to. We still have a couple hundred miles of roads that are used as school bus roads but are dirt-covered trails. We have made some progress.

We now have about 500 miles of roads on the reservation. We had a problem of legality, from the state point of view, of spending B and C tax money on those roads unless they are controlled by the county. The minute we tried to get some jurisdictional authority, we were suspect to the Navajo tribe and their attorneys who thought we were trying to get something. Lynn Mitten, attorney for the tribe at that time, could not believe that San Juan County wanted to maintain and start improving those roads for anything but an ulterior motive. When we went down to try and get the legal work, he said, "What are you guys trying to pull on us?" He just simply could not believe that it was part of the services we were trying to provide to all areas of the county.

At any rate we have those roads and we have made a great deal of progress.

Some of the roads I have talked about across the reservation are terminal roads to help bring those kids in so those people can get an education and training so they can really be productive and get off the welfare system. Gary Shumway made the statement one time that Blanding is the only place in the world where we love the Lamanites and hate the Indians. Sometimes in the past I think we have only given lip service because we were not willing to give them a real opportunity. When I first came into the commission we had never had and still did not have one Indian employee. I think we had the idea that they could not do anything. From my mining experience on the reservation I have known some really good people. Dan Black, an Indian who was killed at the bridge at Mexican Hat in 1958, was one of the smartest people I ever met. He could not speak much English but he could run anything and fix it.

We got a program started with roads on the reservation. We had some old equipment that I was trying to get rid of to upgrade our county equipment and make it more efficient. We had a program come into the county for some of these Navajo people that wanted to work, that were on welfare. The only thing they lacked was communication skills and training skills. We gave them the best of the old equipment and got a supervisor, Teek Lyman, to train them to be qualified operators. With this old equipment they even learned to be mechanics. Today we have some Navajo Indian employees that have been with the county about 15 years. It is really a success. Those guys are some of the most skilled equipment operators in the whole state. They are all good. Take for example, Jimmy Grant. If he is not the best motor grader operator in the state of Utah, he is second. He is an artist. Those guys have pride in their skill and pride in accomplishment, and as far as their job responsibility and being on the job and not taking sick leave and not drinking, their average is as good as our Anglo average.

We have over 2,000 miles of county roads. A lot of those that I have not mentioned we have oiled. We oiled the Monument Valley-to-Oljato road which was a major school bus road. Until that new school is built there those kids are riding the bus up to 80 and 90 miles each way each day. At least most of the roads were oiled. We oiled miles of road out on Douglas Mesa. We have improved the roads along the Monument Valley-Tuba City route. We have improved the roads across from the Red Mesa to the Bluff-Mexican Hat road. A lot of the roads go from north to south to the river. They are still scattered, but we have made a lot of progress in improving those roads.

Now our funding for our roads comes from the state in what they call B and C money, C money going to cities and B money to counties. That money is allocated to the county on a formula from the revenue when we buy a license plate and pay registration. That revenue is collected statewide and allocated back to the counties and cities on a formula. If we have a collector road we get a portion from the gas tax. We finally got that all combined. We get an allocation of federal money that we have to match. We built the bridge at Hatch with what they call SOS money which meant Safety Off-road System. We built a new bridge at Verdure Creek with what they call bridge replacement money, and we are working to get that kind of funding on Montezuma Creek. The problem that we have had is that if there has never been a bridge it is not considered inadequate. At some of the national meetings I asked, "How, if you never had the money to build an inadequate bridge, is that more or less inadequate than a nonexistent bridge?" I never really got an answer to that part of the rules.

We have made an effort since 1967, a major effort, using your tax dollars to fund a very accelerated growth program. We spent capital improvement funds on some of these roads that should have been state roads, but the state would not pay for them unless we had a system. We have put in about a million dollars, and we have built about 14 million dollars of roads that are now state roads. We got 14 to 1 with that money. Those roads were built because the state had a greater need and a greater priority for them. Instead of the Bureau of Indian Affairs spending a little money and running a grader in our area once in a while, we have entered into a contract with them where they pay San Juan County and we do the maintenance, so we get a little extra revenue from them. We have an arrangement with the Utah Division of Indian Affairs where, in order to accelerate the development and improvement of those roads on the reservation beyond what the county can do by itself, if they recommend and approve a project, they pay 25 percent of the total cost of that project; that is another reason we have been able to accelerate the improvement and development of some of these roads.

The Navajo people are very desirous of a road connecting Navajo Mountain with Oljato and Monument Valley. It is a formidable task, but the only way we can get it is to plan it. It may take a while, but it is a desirable goal. We still have dreams of the old highway system in Canyonlands National Park to be developed as it was promised when they created the park. The plans included a loop road through the area back to Beef Basin, back across Salt Creek, back across Elk Ridge and what we call the Kigalia scenic way, and a connection with the causeway and down into Blanding. We still have a dream of improvement of the roads up over the mountain for a nice summer drive between here and Monticello and a connection from Monticello Lake intersecting the Canyonlands Road down by Indian Creek so we could have a better access from the San Juan County area instead of all the benefits going to Moab. The Park Service failure and reneging on their promises to develop the park the way they originally planned has deferred that, but I have met with Secretary Watt a couple of times and we are hopeful that we will get some changes in that.

The nature of the assessed valuation on our resources is very dangerous. It goes up and down like a yo-yo. Right now the assessed valuation for all of our homes, farms, ranches,

private lands, automobiles, livestock, machinery, and equipment — virtually everything real and stable that will be here
even if the oil wells and uranium mines are closed — is only
15 million dollars. The total revenue in our mill levies would
be about $320,000 or $330,000. We spend over a million
dollars a year just on the roads. With this special funding we
will spend $3 million on the Bluff-Mexican Hat road, but we
have been saving up, and the Utah Division of Indian Affairs
is furnishing three quarters of a million, but that still will not
build the entire road. They are very expensive. The problem
is maintaining what we have — recreation, schools, medical
facilities, and roads — when the revenue from the oil and gas
properties drops. Because of that we drafted legislation and
persuaded the state legislature to pass a law entitled the Tax
Stability and Trust Fund Act. The purpose of this law is to
allow counties to maintain their mill levy at the normal rate
when assessed values increase dramatically during the production of nonrenewable resources and to place such extra
revenue into a permanent trust fund so when the assessed
value declines interest earned from the trust fund will enable
the county to continue to support facilities and services that
were built during the impact of the growth. If we had had
the legal authority and foresight to have implemented a tax
stability and trust fund program in 1956, the county would
have a much lower mill levy now and in the future.

San Juan County has adopted a program for such a trust
fund which presently has about two million dollars. We had
hoped to build a greater fund before our assessed value again
tumbles, but it looks like our tax base will fall by about $40
million in 1983 from the 1982 level of $215 million.

The wealth is the land. There is no other source of
wealth except the land. I think sometimes in our nation,
especially in the urban areas in the East and maybe even
some of our urban areas in the West, there are people who
are one or two generations away from the land. They have
forgotten, if they ever knew, where wealth comes from. I was
to a meeting not long ago and Secretary of Interior Watt

talked about this very issue. He said, "Contrary to many of the Liberals in the East that think wealth is in banks and offices and in things like that — it is not. The wealth that comes from the land — raw material, resources, food, fiber, minerals, and energy — are the only things that make those offices and the wealth in those banks possible." We never should lose track of that. The only way we develop that wealth is with the intelligence and the planning of human beings, tools, and resources to make those things into usable items for people. That is really part of the standard or the quality of life. We have become so accustomed to the material things we enjoy and take for granted that we sometimes think that wealth is bad.

I recently completed a series of meetings as a member of the National Bureau of Land Management Advisory Council. Some of the very issues we talk about are whether we

River running through Piute Farm Rapids on the San Juan River before Lake Powell was formed. USHS Collections.

lock up a lot of land or whether we maintain a balance and utilize some of the resources of those lands. There is a need for a balance. Certainly we do not want to destroy our lands, but we have got to maintain the utilization of these resources. Transportation and water are the key elements. Human beings cannot live without water and they cannot live without food and they cannot live without fiber. Energy and technology make those things more available and make life easier. We also must have the ability to pay for them; we need jobs and businesses. Most of the roads in our area were built as the result of a basic need.

We have a beautiful country. It is a treasure of scenic wonders and minerals, of agricultural, recreational, historical, archaeological, and cultural resources. It is up to us to look ahead and plan for our future and the future of our children and grandchildren with the wisdom to balance the options and preserve our heritage and our ability to survive.

Roads and Resources of San Juan County

Kenneth R. Bailey

In my early memories of road developments in San Juan County, I recall the first road cut through the Comb Reef west of Blanding by contractors Whiting and Haymond with Jim Wardle their superintendent. Western Mine Supply Company, which I then owned, leased them a compressor and they started from the top with the cut through Comb Reef. Difficulties with fractures and slides made it desirable to come up from the bottom some 300 yards away. Whiting and Haymond said they would keep renting this compressor if I would deliver it to the bottom of the Comb. This made it necessary to take the compressor to Blanding, over Elk Mountain, through the Bears Ears, then across a road just brushed out with a cat to the bottom of the Comb, a major undertaking in itself.

About this same time my partner, E. J. Hall, and I furnished the compressors, steel, bits, dynamite, and supplies for Nick and Felix Murphy of Moab, Utah, to put in the first road off the rim of Dead Horse Point down the Shaeffer Trail.

Many roads in the county have been built by private and public financing to reach and extract the natural resources of San Juan County. Several are still being built for this purpose, and there is cooperation between agencies to build these roads to county road standards, after which the county takes over the maintenance.

In years past there has been a superhuman effort made to develop water, roads, and private property in San Juan County. The development of natural resources and the rise in assessed valuation is a good indication of the business and industrial activity in the county. It indicates the tax base available as a resource to provide the desired services. The assessed valuation from 1938 to 1982 reflects a tremendous increase and fluctuation.

1938	....	$ 1,282,961	
1954	....	3,879,071	
1960	....	132,839,639	Previous peak
1972	....	46,851,350	Decline
1982	....	213,375,509	Current all-time peak

Looking south from Deadhorse Point above the Colorado River toward the Blue Mountains. Photograph by G. B. Peterson, © 1983.

It would be well to note with the current all-time peak valuation of $213,375,509 that 90 percent of this valuation is assessed on mines, oil wells, and other natural resources. It would be very difficult to even provide the services of the courthouse without this natural resource tax base.

In reviewing past commissioners' minutes about budgets, on March 2, 1881, we note the total budget for schools was $900. On October 6, 1898, bonds in the amount of $4,000 were to be issued "for the purpose of paying off the indebtedness accrued and that will accrue in consequence of the increased expense to the county by the change from territorial to state government and other causes."

On December 28, 1929, the budget for state and county roads was $13,000, out of a total expenditure of $32,630. Two years later, on December 30, 1931, the budget for state and county roads was $7,500, out of a total expenditure of $24,875. Ten years later, on December 26, 1941, the budget for county roads was $500, out of a total expenditure of $7,500. By 1941 the state had taken over a number of roads.

The 1982 budget called for:

Collector and B. roads	$2,435,066
Capital improvement roads	2,000,000
County roads	816,300
Total on roads	$5,251,366

Many roads in the county are built on a cooperative basis. The largest current project, the road from Bluff to Montezuma Creek, is an example. The estimated cost for one structure, the grade, and drain is approximately $3,000,000. Of this amount, the Utah Division of Indian Affairs is contributing $750,000. The roads in San Juan County are really the lifeblood of our economy and survival.

PART SEVEN

Mining

Mining on the San Juan River at Mexican Hat, c. 1894. USHS Collections.

Uranium Mining on the Colorado Plateau

Gary L. Shumway

One day in the summer of 1898, John Wetherill led an archaeological expedition into a shallow cave in western San Juan County, Utah. There were no Indian ruins in the cave, and Wetherill, as the party's guide, had only stopped there for lunch to get out of the sun. However, once inside the cave, he saw something that momentarily made him forget the heat. In the cave wall was a petrified tree, surrounded by yellow stains, and, just outside the cave entrance was another petrified log whose carbonaceous material had been almost entirely replaced by vivid yellow, blue, black, and green minerals.

While the archaeologists prepared lunch, Wetherill dug into the soft ore with his pocket knife, then, satisfied that his discovery was worth the effort, built a rock monument by the log outside the cave entrance. Between two flat rocks near the base of the monument he placed a piece of paper on which he had written his claim to the minerals located there.

Wetherill never returned to the cave, nor did he record his claim. But he had fixed the location of his discovery indelibly in his mind. Forty-five years later, when he knew that his long, eventful career was closing, he described the cave with the yellow stains to a young friend, Preston Redd. Intrigued by Wetherill's account, Redd followed his directions to the cave in Red Canyon, found the outcrops, and soon uncovered the rich uranium deposits of the Blue Lizard Mine.[1]

Wetherill's interest in the petrified logs and associated minerals was not unusual on the central Colorado Plateau in

Placer mining on the San Juan River, 1894. USHS Collections.

1898. For a number of years, explorers, prospectors, cattle-men, and others had stumbled across mineralized "logs" and other outcroppings and had submitted samples for assaying in the hopes that they contained valuable metals.[2] Always in the past, the assays had shown only traces of gold, silver, or other important metals. However, as Wetherill left his home in Mancos, Colorado, that spring, the Colorado Plateau was abuzz with news that the riddle of the strange outcroppings had been solved and that there might be a market for the ore in the future. Some ore from one of the claims in western Colorado had been given to Charles Poulot, a graduate of the Paris School of Mines, who was doing technical work at the Cashin copper mine. When he was unable to complete the chemical analysis of this strange mineral, he had sent it to his professor, Charles Friedel, in Paris, who determined that it contained uranium and vanadium in a new mineral combina-tion which he named carnotite.

Perfectly timed with the identification of the Colorado Plateau ore was a demand for uranium and vanadium from a number of sources. Since 1871, small amounts of uranium oc-curring as pitchblende in the gold and silver mines of the Central City mining district of eastern Colorado had found a limited market in Europe. At first used mainly for pigments in dyes, inks, stained glass, and ceramics, after 1896 European scientific and technological interest greatly increased the de-mand for uranium. Of by far the greatest long-term impor-tance was the discovery by Antoine Henri Becquerel in 1896 that invisible rays emanated from uranium ore; a discovery that, among other things, led ultimately to nuclear fission. But, though scientific fascination with radioactivity and its im-plications created a limited market from the outset, of much more immediate economic importance was technological in-terest in both uranium and vanadium as ferro-alloys in making fine steel.

Active exploitation of carnotite began in the spring of 1898 when Gordon Kimball of Ouray, Colorado, obtained a lease on the Copper Prince claim, from which Poulot's sam-ples had come. By June, Kimball had mined ten tons of carno-tite, which contained 21.5 percent uranium and 15 percent

Raplee's placer mining works in Oil Basin, twenty-five miles west of Bluff, 1894. Special Collections, Marriott Library, University of Utah.

vanadium. By the next spring, local interest in the new industry was sufficient that when a cowhand named Tom Francis found some good deposits in McIntyre Canyon, San Miguel County, Colorado, he precipitated a local rush. By 1906, the known deposits of carnotite extended from Cold Creek, just south of Price, Utah, to Coal Creek, near Meeker, Colorado.[3]

The problems of an uncertain market, low ore prices, and the demand for only high grade ore kept the carnotite industry very unstable from 1898 through 1906. Between 1906 and 1909, carnotite production was limited almost entirely to that extracted by claim owners doing the required $100 worth of assessment work each year. Most of this was stored on the mine dumps against the day the miners felt would yet come when there would be a good market for their ore.

Beginning in 1910, the prospects for the miners and large companies alike appeared to be getting brighter as the demand for carnotite began to accelerate due to a new, exciting use for one of the elements it contained. Becquerel's discovery in 1896 that uranium would fog otherwise unexposed photographic plates set a number of scientists to exploring

Big Indian copper mill in Dry Valley. Photograph Copyright 1979 Steve Lacy Wild Bunch Photos.

the implications of uranium's radioactivity. Two of these scientists, Pierre Curie and his Polish wife, Marie Sklodowska Curie, soon concluded that pure uranium was much less radioactive than uranium ore, and in 1898 they proved the existence of a new, highly radioactive element in the ore, which they named radium.

Almost from the moment of its discovery, a number of the properties of this unstable element aroused scientific interest, and by 1910 medical researchers began to look hopefully at the effects of radiation on cells. Noting that young, rapidly dividing cells subjected to moderate radiation were killed while more mature cells were less drastically affected, they perceived that radium held promise for the treatment of cancer. By 1913 a number of medical researchers, including the prestigious Dr. Howard Atwood Kelly of Johns Hopkins University, had conducted substantial research with the limited amounts of radium salts available and were convinced that if greater amounts of more nearly pure radium were available, radium radiation would have major efficacy in the treatment of at least some types of cancer. Their findings, boomed by Bureau of Mines officials and other Progressives who were excited by the curative possibilities as well as alarmed by foreign buyers, led to a major interest in radium in the United States. For a time, there was even serious consideration in Congress given to bills that would prohibit the exportation of much radium and perhaps even nationalize the carnotite deposits. Only through the concerted effort of Standard Chemical Company, which by 1913 had obtained most of the known carnotite reserves and secured contracts to sell in Europe all of the radium it could produce at $120,000 per gram, were sufficient anti-socialistic, free enterprise sentiments martialed to defeat the proposed legislation.

Stung by opponents of the legislation who insisted that federal science was by its very nature inefficient, the Bureau of Mines officials and other Progressives turned to the National Radium Institute, formed as a cooperative arrangement between the Bureau of Mines, Dr. Kelly and other researchers, to demonstrate what could be accomplished through national planning. Between 1914 and 1917 the NRI produced seven grams of radium bromide at an announced cost of $37,000 per gram, an achievement that not only seemed to vindicate those who had faith in government science but also blunted the demand in Europe for Standard Chemical's and other radium companys' radium at $120,000 per gram.[4]

Between 1911 and 1922 there was a demand for carnotite not only for cancer treatment but for other scientific inquiry as well as for more mundane uses such as for making luminescent watch and instrument dials. However, in 1922, the already depressed domestic radium industry was dealt a death blow. The radium market was captured by Belgium with the opening of a huge new plant of the Union Miniere du Haut Katanga in Oolen, Belgium, which processed pitchblende, running as high as 80 percent uranium, from the massive deposits of the Luishwishi and Shinkolobwe mines of Katanga in the Belgian Congo.

The loss of the radium market resulted in a decade in which there was almost no large company exploitation of the carnotite deposits. A handful of independent miners and prospectors, satisfying the very limited market for uranium for ceramic colorants and radium for patent medicines, retained their hope in a prosperous carnotite industry while high-grading the richest parts of a few exposed deposits. Elsewhere, the tunnels caved in or filled with water or tumbleweeds. Prospectors allowed their claims to lapse by failing to do the annual assessment work, and mining and milling equipment was left to rust. On every mine dump, lower grade ore stacked to one side began to leach to a bright canary yellow as if to remind miners it was there should a brighter day come in the future.

The loss of the world radium market was as disorienting to the miners and prospectors of the Colorado Plateau as it was to the large radium companies. Long before 1923, most of these men had recognized the futility of trying to operate

their own claims and had sold them to one of the large concerns, accepting employment as miners or going out to prospect for new claims. Because their livelihood depended

*Unidentified uranium miners in southeastern Utah, 1918. USHS
Collections.*

on the ability of the large companies to sell carnotite, they shared with their employers the initial shock of the Union Miniere announcement, then the eventual realization that resistance was futile.

For a decade after 1924 there was almost no market for carnotite. Howard W. Balsley managed to keep his Yellow Circle claims in San Juan County, Utah, operating on a small scale during most of this time, as did J. W. Lewis, who had some good claims near Gateway, Colorado. But no other independent miners produced more than a few tons. The ore was sold to the United States Radium Company of Orange, New Jersey, and to other refining companies. Part of the refined radium was used in the manufacture of luminous paint and for a limited amount of research; however, much of it was sold to quacks who used it for medicaments such as radioactive water, salves, tonics, and other nostrums.[5] The purveyors of these remedies capitalized on the large amount of publicity given to the therapeutic potential of radium by the proponents of radium legislation and subsequently by the radium companies. At times raising false hopes for persons who had been informed by their doctor that they had diseases of a terminal nature, most preparations were designed for less vicious, if no more useful, purposes. These ranged from radioactive tonics to cure baldness to a glass bulb enclosing a rod smeared with radium paint which, according to the inventor, would, if suspended above one's bed, disperse "all thoughts and worry about work and troubles, and bring contentment, satisfaction and body comfort that soon results in peaceful, restful sleep."[6]

Neither Balsley nor Lewis was involved in these quack schemes. They delivered their ore to legitimate refining companies who found their own markets. However, it is doubtful that these two men or many of the other miners would have found anything too amiss in most of the medicaments advertised. The majority of the miners believed in radium cures, and some were patrons of the quack remedy business themselves, wearing sacks of high grade uranium around the neck to cure cancer of the throat and drinking bottles of water containing chunks of carnotite for the alleviation of rheumatism.[7]

This very limited market for carnotite had little impact on the fortunes of most miners, and the years between 1924 and 1934 represent the bleakest chapter in the history of the uranium industry. Nevertheless, this period was not devoid of bright spots. The very drabness permitted another springtime for the independent miners that would never have been possible otherwise. So disheartening was the outlook for the carnotite industry that the radium companies who had gathered in most of the known ore deposits permitted many of their claims to lapse. The companies, anticipating a burgeoning demand for radium, had built roads, blocked out reserves, and often even drifted to ore bodies before the sudden impact of Katanga uranium forced them to cease operations. As these claims became a part of the public domain once more, prospectors who had not lost their faith in the future of carnotite reclaimed them and thus found a greater reason to hope for a reinvigorated industry.

Also, despite the adversity of this decade, many of those individuals who were to provide leadership in the areas of ore production and prospecting became known during this time. The most important of these new leaders was Howard W. Balsley. Balsley came to Moab, Utah, in about 1912 as an employee of the National Forest Service, fell in love with the area, and decided to settle permanently. As a federal worker, he had a steady income that was considerably larger than most persons on the Colorado Plateau, and it was inevitable that he would be approached by prospectors who were willing to share whatever they found for a grubstake.

More out of consideration for the prospector than from a hope of becoming wealthy, Balsley agreed to grubstake several men. One of these was Charles Snell who, while out prospecting on Balsley's account, purportedly dreamed one night that he was in the Cane Springs area in northern San Juan County where he saw a yellow circle of carnotite in the

*Howard Balsley with truck used to haul uranium ore, c. 1917.
USHS Collections.*

white sandstone. Snell went to the area he claimed to have
seen in his dream, located the yellow circle, and discovered
a number of good outcrops in the vicinity. Through generosity to Snell and a number of other prospectors, Balsley became half owner in some good carnotite claims. He quit his
government job to develop these just in time to get in on the
loss of the radium market.

The next few years were the most trying of the more
than sixty years Balsley devoted to the carnotite industry. He
was inexperienced, had little working capital, and was hard
put to find enough of a market to stay in operation. Through
sheer determination, he survived the decade with his own interests while providing encouragement to the other miners.[8]

Balsley became a symbol of hope for the beleaguered
miners and prospectors of the Colorado Plateau. In addition
to buying their high grade, he listened to their problems, as-
sisted them in any way possible, and encouraged them to

retain their claims and look for a better future. He was honest in his dealings with the miners: his assays were correct, he paid top prices for both the uranium and vanadium content of the ore, and he paid promptly and fairly. If he had any fault it was in being so sympathetic to the plight of the miners and so generous with his own resources that he failed to pursue the kind of policies that most "good businessmen" would have recommended. When the government halted the sale of uranium in 1943, Balsley had little more wealth or property than many of the other independent miners.

Of importance in another facet of the carnotite industry were the Shumway brothers. In 1910 Peter M. and Mary Johnson Shumway had moved their family of twelve children to Blanding, Utah. While the oldest son, Peter, moved to Moab, staked some of the first carnotite claims in that area, and married a woman he met in one of the carnotite camps, the rest of the brothers remained in Blanding, eked a precarious livelihood from the soil as small farmers, cattlemen, and gold miners, and began to raise large families of their own. Only occasionally did they visit their older brother who had become so involved in the carnotite industry.

In the spring of 1931 Thomas A. Jones, a neighbor of Arah E. Shumway, brought a piece of yellow ore to him, stating that his sheepherder, Benito Sanchez, had found an outcropping of it in Cottonwood Canyon and wondered if it might be gold. Shumway immediately recognized the ore as carnotite and so informed his neighbor, indicating that if it were a good enough deposit there might be a market for it in the future. Jones was not interested in the discovery, and Sanchez was only interested to the extent of offering to tell where he had obtained the ore for an interest in a claim staked there. However, Shumway was quite curious about this sample of carnotite, found so far from any other known discovery. After advising his brother Harris of the sheepherder's find, these two men walked into the area described by Sanchez. Although their initial attempt was unsuccessful, they returned to the area and found that there were outcrops of carnotite up and down Cottonwood Canyon.

Two more of the Shumway brothers, Seth and Lee, became interested in the report of Arah and Harris, and between March 20 and May 26, 1931, the four located and recorded thirty-seven claims. These claims were to be fairly important for the deposits of ore they contained, with the group still producing more than fifty-eight years later. They were also to contribute to the economic growth of the area by providing employment to miners, truckers, mill employees, and others. More important, however, was the introduction of the younger Shumways to the carnotite industry which these discoveries provided. During the next two decades, besides being active in ore production, the Shumways would more than match the rest of the miner-prospectors combined in the location of previously undiscovered claims in southeastern Utah.[9]

The Shumway brothers related their experience of mining the very rich ore from their Lonesome claim. This claim had been discovered west of Cottonwood Canyon by Lee and Harris Shumway in 1932 when they saw the vivid yellow outcrop while prospecting on the other side of a gulch. After Balsley began buying ore, Seth and Arah Shumway mined and shipped the ore from two high-grade trees that comprised the principal deposit on the claim. Because of the oxidized state of the ore, it was possible simply to scoop out the yellow powder with a shovel and place it in sacks, blasting being necessary only to strip off the overburden when it was no longer possible to reach the ore with a shovel. After several pickup truck loads of these sacks of ore had been shipped to Balsley, he sent an assay, informing the Shumways that the entire lot ran over 20 percent in uranium.

As remembered by participants two decades later, these were simple, tranquil years. An occasional pickup load of sacks of high grade brought enough revenue to supply those things that must be purchased. Most of those mining at that time also kept pigs, chickens, a vegetable garden, and an orchard containing apple, pear, peach, cherry, apricot, and plum trees, with the fruit and vegetables eaten fresh or canned for winter use. The national forests surrounding the mines teemed with deer, which became a standard part of the miner's diet, in season or out. But if this combination of farming, mining, and poaching provided a subsistence for the miner and his family, it did not bring real prosperity. Nor did it provide the kind of community standing that the miners and their families wished for. Despite what in retrospect seems to have been an idyllic life of pastoral simplicity, the miners continued to hope for an opportunity to do more than sell an occasional few sacks of high grade.

Late in 1936 it began to appear that the miners' long wait for prosperity might soon end. In response to a slight rise in the price of vanadium, a number of small companies began making plans to refurbish the small mills built before 1923 or to build new ones that would concentrate vanadium. Between 1936 and 1941 several small companies did begin

Fry cabin, 1980. Crampton Collection, Marriott Library, University of Utah.

operations, thus providing a limited market for miners' carnotite as well as encouraging prospecting by purchasing claims.

However, miners' hopes that this activity would bring prosperity were ill-founded. Despite the persistence of the small companies as well as the miners, none of the mills proved successful. In part, this was attributable to the same factors that had made small mills uneconomic in the past: lack of experience, inefficient processes, the high cost of transporting chemicals and other supplies, and the fact that the margin of profit was not very great even under optimum conditions. More important was the fact that the milling companies were attacked by two large companies who considered the vanadium industry as their personal domain and who controlled much of the carnotite reserve.

The details of the steps taken by the Union Carbide and Carbon Company and the Vanadium Corporation of America to control the production and sales of vanadium from carnotite during this time cannot be fully told here. In essence, Union Carbide's subsidiary, the United States Vanadium Company, in the late 1920s took over most of the mines once owned by Standard Chemical Company and through the next two decades added other properties. After some years of concentrating on production from its Peruvian Minasragra mine, the Vanadium Corporation of America during the early 1930s began to consider vanadium production from its own Colorado Plateau properties, the core of which were the Maggie C. and other Long Park properties earlier developed by the Bureau of Mines under the National Radium Institute agreement. Before the VCA could begin local production, Union Carbide offered an arrangement whereby its subsidiary, United States Vanadium Corporation, would mine vanadium which it would then sell to VCA who would remain in control of ferro-vanadium sales. This complicated agreement met a variety of needs, not only of the VCA but also of the USVC and other Union Carbide subsidiaries as well. Though their activities would eventually lead them into a quagmire of antitrust litigation, for more than a decade the USVC and the VCA controlled the vanadium industry on the Colorado Plateau.

The determination of these two companies to beat down competition, especially after 1936 when worldwide demand for steel led to the formation of a number of small companies, compelled the USVC and VCA to ever more high-handed actions. Then, in May of 1942, the USVC received a superb opportunity to control the vanadium industry when it was designated as the government agent of the wartime Metals Reserve Company with the responsibility of bringing about unlimited production of vanadium for the war effort.

Although instructed specifically to stimulate independent production, the USVC officials, now government agents, shared only with VCA the fact that it had been empowered to pay up to 50¢ per pound for vanadium, and the two companies agreed between them to limit to 31¢ per pound the amount paid for almost all vanadium besides that produced by themselves.

The rise in price for vanadium from 21¢ per pound, which the two companies had previously offered (having established this as their cost for mining ore from their own larger, easily accessible and relatively high-grade deposits), proved to be a substantial stimulus for independent miners, despite the collusion of the two large companies. When to this increase were added such government mandated inducements as haulage allowances for remote deposits, development assistance, loans for purchase of equipment, acceptance of low-grade ore, and the construction of additional mills, independent miners responded with considerable enthusiasm.

Despite the reluctance of the two large companies to endanger their hold on the Colorado Plateau by truly encouraging independent activity, the federally sponsored Metals Reserve Company was highly successful in fostering production from independent miners' claims. For most carnotite miners, the Great Depression did not begin in 1929; it had begun at least in 1923, and it lasted until 1942. To be promised a market for all of the ore they could produce seemed like a dream come true, and the miners responded enthusiastically.

Most of the outcrops had long since been high-graded, and few miners had possessed either the foresight or the money to drill their claims and block out reserves. Furthermore, either the USVC or the VCA had purchased most claims that promised to be commercially exploitable. Nevertheless, the independent miners contributed almost 40 percent of the total domestic vanadium production during the Metals Reserve period.[10] In addition, as lessees, they accounted for most of the domestic production credited to the VCA and part of USVC's. Total domestic vanadium production, which in 1941 had been 2,513,051 pounds, rose to 4,439,130 pounds in 1942, then to 9,975,878 in 1943, before dropping to 3,527,054 pounds when the Metals Reserve program ended at the end of February in 1944.[11]

By the close of 1943, the miners had been successful in providing vanadium for any foreseeable wartime need, and when the USVC requested that the Metals Reserve program be discontinued, the government complied, terminating all contracts as of February 29, 1944.[12]

In February 1944 the independent miners of the Colorado Plateau faced a future that had not looked so dismal since the radium crash of the 1920s. The mines, earlier gutted of high grade ore, were now almost entirely devoid of known reserves of even low-grade carnotite. Additionally, in less than two years the miners had supplied enough vanadium to last the nation for years to come, even considering the greater demands of the war. There seemed to be little hope that there would be a market for vanadium beyond that which could be supplied by the two large companies. Furthermore, in 1943 the government had unaccountably forbidden the sale of uranium, even in small quantities for ceramic colorants. Looking at their depleted reserves and recognizing the futility of attempting to market carnotite even if they had some to sell, miners became convinced that the day they had waited for so long had come and gone again. Throughout the Colorado Plateau, the miners ceased to work their claims, sold their equipment, locked up their powder magazines, and began to look for other work.

Even prospecting, which miners had fallen back on in the past, seemed to offer no hope. In San Juan County, Utah, where most of the new discoveries were being made, claim locations had numbered 151 in 1942 and 71 in 1943; in 1944 there were 4.[13] In a day in which even the federal government was offering its carnotite mills for sale for almost nothing, the faith the miners had exhibited in the future of carnotite seemed to taunt them. They recalled the many times their wives had pleaded with them to settle down to a respectable job, even a WPA project, and begin to provide for their families as other men in the area did. They recalled the tears of their children who had been forced to go to school in shabby clothes and had been ridiculed because they had fathers who "didn't work, but just spent their time camping out in the hills." They had consoled their wives and children by telling them, for the hundredth time, that some day carnotite would be worth more than gold, and they would have a nice home, nice clothes, and would be proud of their father. But they had been wrong, they now realized bitterly.

Most of the people of the United States endured the inconveniences occasioned by World War II knowing that the end of war would bring an end to austerity. For the carnotite miners, the end of the war would simply mean exchanging one kind of austerity, shared voluntarily by most of the nation, for another, more personal kind. While the rest of the nation bought new cars, refrigerators, electric stoves, clothes, meat, sugar, and gasoline, they would simply return to the other kind of austerity they had always known, in which the inequities of their life compared with their neighbors' were so noticeable. And now the miners could not even have the hope of a bright day in the future to sustain them. They had no way of knowing that the federal government had for some time been feverishly engaged in a project that would trigger a carnotite boom greater than their wildest dreams. They learned the truth on August 6, 1945, when President Truman announced that after years of intensive effort in the Manhattan Project, the United States had dropped an atomic bomb on Hiroshima.

The beginning of the atomic age in August 1945, however, did not mean immediate prosperity for the beleaguered Colorado Plateau miners. In 1946 the U.S. Congress passed an Atomic Energy Act which created the Atomic Energy Commission and gave the commission control over the domestic uranium market. As the AEC stewardship began in January 1947, miners, anticipating a federally sponsored industry with ore worth $5.00 a pound and purchased at government mills, waited for the commission to circulate ore purchasing agreements. Instead, the AEC on April 12, announced that it had negotiated a contract for by-product uranium with VCA, and that company would purchase uranium on a schedule beginning at 35¢ a pound for 0.20 percent ore, with a top price of $1.10 per pound of uranium in ore assaying 2 percent or better.[14]

Despite miners' strong complaints, 1947 passed without any marked improvement in ore-purchasing policy although the AEC did announce that the government had decided to retain the Monticello, Utah, mill instead of selling it to the VCA as earlier reported and that higher prices for ore were being contemplated.[15] In April 1948 the AEC announced that it would pay $1.50 a pound for uranium in ore averaging over 0.20 percent and 31¢ a pound for vanadium averaging over 2 percent, if brought to the Monticello, Utah, mill.[16]

This program offered decidedly higher prices than those of the previous year and had the additional advantage of dealing directly with the AEC instead of with one of the two large companies. Nevertheless, the miners were still restive. Before they could begin production, they explained, they would have to search for new deposits of ore and go to the expense of reopening their mines which had not been worked since 1944.[17] Sympathetically, the AEC added a 50-cent per pound bonus on uranium, to be used strictly for the development of the mines, and agreed to pay the expense of hauling the ore to the mills. The AEC also announced its intention to purchase the Durango mill and have it ready for production by early 1949.[18]

The government's favorable new ore-purchasing policy touched off a flurry of activity on the Plateau. By mid-June miners were establishing mining camps, building and repairing roads, buying new equipment, and doing the "dead work" necessary to find new ore deposits. At the same time, prospectors were actively staking claims for the first time since 1943.[19]

Prospectors' enthusiasm for the new AEC policy was apparent from the record of claims staked in San Juan County, Utah. From August 1, 1943, to December 31, 1947, only 94 claims had been filed. However, from January through September of 1948, 292 uranium claims were staked in that county alone.

Despite their enthusiastic response to the new AEC policy, the miners and prospectors soon learned that the day of jubilee had not come. Assuming that the new policy would mean a return to the Metals Reserve prosperity of the early '40s, miners throughout the Plateau looked forward to the July 12 opening of the sampling plant at Monticello. When the date came, however, the AEC ordered a one-week delay because the sampling facilities were not ready. On July 19 the Monticello mill opened and 800 tons of ore poured in from throughout the region. After working for two days and processing sixty tons of ore, the sampling plant broke down. Several new attempts were made to crush the ore for sampling, but the available machinery could not process the flood of ore.[20]

Miners, comparing the cost of exploratory work, road building, machinery, mine renovation, and supplies with the amount paid by the AEC for the little ore that had been processed, rapidly became disillusioned. By the end of September even Fendoll Sitton, who owned some of the richest, most extensive ore bodies belonging to independent miners, declared that he was going to sell his equipment and lay off his men.[21] He advised others to do the same. Miners were soon exclaiming that the AEC had been given $800,000,000 to spend in 1948 and seemed to have plenty of money for everything except the purchase of domestic uranium.

Satisfied that a small annual yield was all that could be expected at a reasonable cost, the AEC, between 1948 and 1951, pursued a policy of encouraging production from mines that could produce larger amounts at a low cost, while offering little encouragement to owners of small ore bodies.[22] This AEC policy left almost no one happy on the Colorado Plateau. Even those who did have mines that could be exploited under the existing price schedule were haunted by the fear that they would deplete their ore bodies in a market that offered very little profit, only to see the AEC raise the prices considerably in order to get the uranium from the smaller producers.

Although the AEC policy of fostering only low-cost operations continued until 1951, the most discouraging period for the miners came in late 1948 and 1949. Low prices for ore and poor marketing conditions caused most miners to work unenthusiastically or cease production entirely. After the hope they had felt in mid-1948, the subsequent despair was felt even more keenly.

However, by late 1950 the AEC was ready to make another reappraisal of the Colorado Plateau operation. With the Soviet Union now able to produce nuclear weapons, and with the United States at war with the Communist powers in Korea, there was a greatly heightened demand for a nuclear weapons stockpile. At the same time, the reserves of the Shinkolobwe mine were getting low, and the known Canadian reserves were almost exhausted. Furthermore, as early as 1949 officials began to realize that the original estimates of the domestic reserve were far too low, just as the producers were insisting. During 1949 and 1950 a large number of new deposits were discovered, and the reserves on claims previously filed were found to be much greater than had been thought. It was also apparent that only the periphery of most favorable areas had been explored. Finally, John K. Gustafson, who had guided the ore procurement policy since the beginning of the Manhattan Project, retired in 1950, and his successor, Jesse C. Johnson, proved to be much less committed to a small, low-cost domestic industry.[23]

In January 1951, 150 members of the Uranium Ore Producers Association petitioned the Atomic Energy Commission, asking for higher ore prices, larger development and haulage allowances, and increased government drilling and other benefits. The AEC responded by announcing that, effective March 1, 1951, the government would purchase all of the ore the miners could produce at $3.50 a pound for uranium running over 0.20 percent and 31¢ a pound for vanadium.[24]

With this announcement came the promise of prosperity to the Colorado Plateau. For fifty years miners had dreamed of this day as they filled their ore sacks with high-grade and shipped them to France or Germany via Galveston, as they went to work in the mining camps of Standard Chemical Company, as they sold their high-grade to the ever-encouraging Howard Balsley, as they worked their lease from the USVC or the VCA, or as they waited those last five years, each month confident that the wait would soon be over. It was over. And, as if to compensate for the half-century of waiting, the AEC on June 29 declared that persons who found new deposits would be paid an additional $3.50 a pound for up to 10,000 pounds of uranium mined from each property.[25]

Even before the promulgation of the 1951 program, mining and prospecting activity had begun to pick up. Ore production, which had decreased in 1948 and 1949 to 115 tons of uranium oxide, shot up in 1950 to 320 tons.[26] Moreover, since early 1948, prospectors had been active throughout the Plateau, driven by the hope of finding a bonanza that would be exploitable under the existing price circular and by the belief that the AEC would soon improve its prices.

However, this mining and prospecting activity was tame compared with the enthusiasm shown after the spring of 1951. By vastly increasing the number of mines that could be operated profitably and the amount of profit that could be made from each mine, AEC policies sent miners to work with an enthusiasm they had not shown even during World War II. The result was a rapid increase in ore production, with the 1951 total of 630 tons representing almost a 100 percent increase over 1950. Also, the very favorable price schedule and the $35,000 bonus offered for ore mined from a new deposit prompted prospectors to take to the canyons and mesas of the Colorado Plateau in a search for more outcroppings.

With the old prospectors, who had dreamed of this day all of their lives, went a new generation of prospectors. Some were young men who benefitted from the things they had learned while accompanying their fathers. Others were farmers, ranchers, and merchants from the Plateau who previously had ridiculed the miners' faith in uranium's future but now put their acquaintance with the area to practical use. Most

Head frame, shops, and hoist building in the Big Indian District. USHS Collections.

were strangers to the Plateau who brought their Geiger counters and geological training to compensate for their ignorance of the terrain. From the combined efforts of these men came soaring uranium production beginning in 1954. As they came to record their claims in the county courthouses during 1951 and 1952, the Colorado Plateau began to hum with an excitement that it had never known before. All that was needed to trigger a boom of major proportions was for one of the prospectors to strike a bonanza.

On the western slope of the Lisbon Anticline in northeastern San Juan County, Utah, a series of small outcroppings of uranium occurred in the Shinarump formation. These had been discovered in 1916, but recurrent attempts to mine them had failed even though many of the prospectors of the region had at one time or another staked claims there. In May of 1948, Dan Hayes, Jim Bentley, and W. Y. Brewer located twelve claims along these outcroppings and during the next few years mined a small amount of ore. One day in March 1951 a young petroleum geologist who had lost his job with one of the major oil companies visited these Big Buck claims, where Hayes was working at the time. After looking at the very definite anticlinal structure of the terrain behind the outcroppings, he asked if Hayes would mind if he staked some claims behind the Big Buck group. Upon receiving Hayes's good natured assent, the prospector located fifteen claims, giving them such names as Linda Mujer, Besame Mucho, Te Querio [sic], Mujer Sin Verguenza, and Mi Vida. The young geologist's name was Charles Augustus Steen.

The next year and a half was a time of many frustrations for Steen. He was as optimistic as prospectors usually are. However, he did not have a job and he had a family to support. After many discouragements he decided to gamble all he had on an attempt to strike ore on his claims in the Lisbon district. He obtained a dilapidated core drilling rig which he moved to a canyon that cut down through the Wingate formation on his Mi Vida claim. By thus lessening the distance he would have to drill, he hoped to reach the Shinarump formation before the rig broke down completely.

From the beginning the project was rife with discouragement. Steen's wife and children were living in a tar-paper-covered shack with a meager supply of food and clothing. Nor were conditions promising at the Mi Vida. The rig, never in good condition, broke down, was repaired, then broke down again. Attempts to obtain parts and supplies from local mining supply outlets were met with a polite but firm rejection. Finally, Steen accepted money from his mother who mortgaged her home in Texas. Sinking the last money that he could hope to borrow into one final attempt to reach the Shinarump formation, Steen patched up his rig and began drilling once more. Then suddenly all of his hopes collapsed. Still several feet above the level at which he could hope to encounter ore, the diamond bit used to cut through the rock spun off the drill pipe and was left in the bottom of the hole. With no money to either fish the bit from the hole or to drill a new hole, Steen realized that his dream of finding uranium was ended. He now was faced with the necessity of going to his tar-paper shack and informing his wife and family that this venture, like others in his life, had ended in failure.

Almost as an afterthought, Steen removed some of the rock cores from the core barrel of the drill pipe and tossed them in his jeep. After arriving in town he stopped at a service station where a friend was testing with a Geiger counter some rocks that his son had found while prospecting. Placing one of his own cores near the probe of the counter, Steen watched in disbelief as his unpretentious gray core "pegged" the needle of the counter, even in its lowest range. Before the drilling rig had broken down completely, he had drilled into the top of fourteen feet of a very rich uraninite-type ore in a deposit so extensive that it passed beyond the limits of the Mi Vida onto the Big Buck claims.

Finding little difficulty now in getting capital to finance a drift to his ore, Steen began operations in the fall of 1952 and reached his ore the next February. By September of that year he had already mined over a million dollars worth of ore from the Mi Vida, and the roads to all of the mills in the area were packed with Utex company trucks going to and from his mine.[27]

The news of Steen's bonanza reverberated through the canyons and mesas of the Colorado Plateau and burst upon the national consciousness. As newspaper and magazine articles detailed this saga of a prospector who climbed from abject poverty to dazzling wealth, the effect was predictable. For months, people throughout the nation had heard fantastic rumors of the fortune waiting for them on the Colorado Plateau and of the number of persons who were already taking advantage of this opportunity. Joe Cooper and Fletcher Brunson, they heard, had paid $1,000 for a claim in a remote portion of San Juan County, Utah, and since discovered ore bodies so large that they were turning down offers of $10,000,000 for their mine. The Shumway brothers, after twenty years of successful prospecting, continued to make new discoveries in areas hitherto unsuspected and to find a good market for their claims. Fendoll Sitton, who paid $200,000 for some of the Shumway claims in western San Juan County got the AEC to drill them and on the first claim blocked out deposits containing several million dollars worth of uranium.

While many people were able to come to the region and actively search, a far greater number preferred to remain at their secure jobs and merely sink their savings into the new El Dorado. The willingness of many thousands of such people to invest their savings in the uranium industry greatly influenced the nature of the uranium rush that flourished with such intensity between 1953 and 1956. At the outset this market for claims kept prospectors actively staking claims with even a very small outcrop of ore, which could be sold for at least $1,000. Even before the supply had been exhausted, investors had begun clamoring for any that were located in a favorable area where there was a possibility that through drilling (which the investor hoped he could get the AEC to finance), another Mi Vida would be discovered. Soon, most of the areas that were considered favorable for the discovery of uranium were claimed.

Few of the miners who formed companies in late 1953 and early 1954 expected a rush to their doors for their stock. If they could just raise operating capital, they would feel repaid for their efforts. However, in their simple aspirations, they failed to consider the extent of speculative fever and the ability of certain promoters to stampede investors their way.

A promoter named Jay Walters moved to Salt Lake City shortly after the news of Steen's strike broke in 1953. Sensing the possibility of interesting the public in uranium stocks, he bought a few claims and early in 1954 formed the Uranium Oil and Trading Company, capitalized at 3,000,000 one-cent shares. Finding the established brokerage firms reluctant to handle his stock, Walters enlisted the aid of a young agent named Jack Coombs. Coombs received permission from a friend, Frank Whitney, to peddle stock in the latter's coffee shop and the first week sold $10,000 worth of stock. With this promising beginning, Walters formed another company, Alladin Uranium, and promptly sold $43,000 worth of stock. Even more encouraging, within a few weeks after opening, both stock issues had closed and the market price of each had gone up at least 500 percent. Coombs and Whitney both left their post in the coffee shop, established their own investment firms, and prepared for the stock boom Walters anticipated.[28]

The rush was not long coming. By May the demand for uranium issues far outstripped the capacity of brokers to service the requests of customers. Daily sales soared from a manageable 200,000 shares in March to 7,000,000 shares in May. Between February and June 1954 speculative interest in the penny stock market was fanned to white-hot intensity by the continued announcements of bonanza uranium discoveries, the well-publicized success of some of the first companies who had offered stock, and the almost universal success of uranium stock offerings. Some of the hysteria subsided early in June, but uranium stocks continued to move very well for another year.

Federal Uranium, with claims near Steen's Mi Vida, had begun its stock offering in January 1954 at a cent a share. By late May the bid price was over 20 cents. Lisbon Uranium, also having claims in the general vicinity of Mi Vida, opened its stock offering at 20 cents. It instantly jumped to 35 cents, then 80 cents, and one month later was at $2.25. Standard Uranium, also claiming property on the Lisbon Anticline, opened its public offering at $1.25 per share in May 1954. On the first day all 1,430,000 shares were sold.

The demand for uranium stocks was so brisk that few investors took time to study the soundness of the stock they were buying. The company prospectus outlining property owned, development plans, remuneration of officers, and other details was seldom read carefully even if it was honestly presented. Furthermore, as the intensity of the boom began to affect all involved, the companies became increasingly embroiled in the speculative spirit of the times.

For about eighteen months uranium stocks sold actively, if somewhat erratically. There was little basis for the price most of these issues obtained beyond the fact that investors, caught up in the fever of the rush, were willing to pay ever higher prices. With no dividends and few bonanza discoveries the stocks could not be sustained in their inflated state. By mid-1955 they had begun to fall. Many continued to be offered for years to come, but their fascination diminished quickly. By the end of 1956 stocks that had once sold for 30¢ were going for one-half cent per share, and shortly thereafter most of the companies quietly ceased to exist.

Few of the penny stock companies survived the fall of 1955, but after the orgy was over they became the scapegoats. However, it was not the miner, given the title of company president in return for contributing his producing property, who garnered the stock profits. In fact, to a much greater degree than is usually the case, the risk capital was funneled into the expensive search for uranium, precisely as it had been intended. That portion siphoned off went almost entirely to the promoters, who exhibited remarkable ability in extracting a maximum profit from a minimal investment. By purchasing stock before the public offering, running up the price by carefully placed rumors, and then selling at peak profits, a few of the promoters were charged with fraud. However, as one writer put it, "most got away with nothing

Oil drilling rig in Lisbon Valley, c. 1962. USHS Collections.

more punishing than money for their escapades."[29]

The decline of the stock market was just one symptom of the ebb in popular enthusiasm for uranium. By the end of 1956 there was little question that the rush was over. However, for the miners the boom in the uranium industry was not over. The mining boom, dating from the favorable ore purchasing policy of 1951, had preceded the uranium rush and did not, in fact, diminish appreciably for another decade. The wild, ecstatic days of the rush were simply the adolescent years of the uranium industry. As they ended, the industry became what one writer characterized as "a tough, mature business where the survivors are those big enough to find and mine enough high-cost ore to come out ahead."[30] Some of these companies were survivors of the uranium stock market crash: Standard, Federal, Lisbon, and Atlas. But most of them were the large mining and oil companies of the United States such as Phillips Petroleum, National Lead and Zinc, New Park Mining, the Texas Company, New Jersey Zinc, Homestake Mining, Anaconda Copper, Humble Oil, Getty Oil, Kerr-McGee, and others who now saw an advantage to entering the uranium business. These companies expended millions of dollars to find, mine and mill what was often high-cost ore. At the same time, they profited from AEC milling contracts that provided for amortization of facilities within five years and a guaranteed market for all concentrates produced at a price originally designed to encourage production.[31]

The AEC decision to continue the purchase of uranium even after the nation's strategic needs were met resulted from a fundamental shift in emphasis from military needs to a broad peacetime application of atomic energy for electrical power generation. If the generation of nuclear power by private industry was to come about, the AEC realized, the federal government would have to subsidize the uranium industry until the demand for nuclear fuel from private sources ended the need for government support. In May 1956 the AEC confirmed its commitment to the industry by guaranteeing its ore procurement program until at least 1966.³²

By deciding to push the development of peacetime nuclear energy the AEC provided a striking example of the federal government's power to make long-range plans for the benefit of the nation. No individual utility company could have funded such a mammoth, long-range, risky venture. If nuclear generation of electricity was to become a reality, at least before the near exhaustion of the world reserves of fossil fuels, it would have to be initiated by public rather than private enterprise.

In committing itself to support the uranium industry until private enterprise could create its own market, the AEC put its prestige on the line for what was at best a risky gamble. The commission estimated that the private market would develop between 1965 and 1970, but there was no way to be certain. Much depended upon the utility companies' willingness to participate in the development of the technology necessary to make nuclear energy competitive with fossil fuels for the generation of electricity. There was a possibility that nuclear energy might not become competitive for many years.

At a time when many experts were scoffing at its estimates as being far too optimistic, the AEC in 1962 projected that by 1980 the United States would have nuclear plants capable of generating 40,000,000 kilowatts of electricity. As early as 1964 these estimates began to appear too conservative, and in 1966 they were increased to 80,000-110,000 MWE. At the close of 1968 they were revised upward again with experts in the industry projecting a capacity of at least 150,000-170,000 MWE for 1980.³³

The coming of age of the nuclear power industry had a marked effect on the domestic uranium industry. Instead of tottering on the edge of extinction, it showed more vigor in the late 1960s than it had during the feverish days of the mid-1950s. For, despite reserves that once seemed inexhaustible, it was apparent by 1966 that there was not enough uranium to supply the projected fuel needs of plants until 1980.[34] The result was a mining boom of unprecedented dimensions. In 1967 and 1968 alone, uranium companies acquired mineral rights to over sixteen million acres of federal, state, railroad, Indian, and other lands.[35] Drilling and other exploratory work also reached a new high. In the peak boom year of 1957 companies had drilled 9.2 million feet. The 1968 total was more than double that figure.[36] Even the uranium stock market, once looked upon as a colorful, one-time spree, returned with part of its former allure.[37]

As has happened so many times before in the history of the uranium industry, however, the great promise of sustained prosperity once again proved illusory. For a few heady years there was a great demand for all of the uranium that could be produced. So great was the demand throughout the world and so limited the known reserves that there was even a concerted effort to establish a uranium cartel committed to pegging uranium at a price of $40 per pound.

But if uranium producers in the Intermountain states were satisfied with their role and utility companies were grateful for nuclear energy in a day of skyrocketing costs for increasingly scarce fossil fuels, there were others in the nation who did not feel so comfortable with nuclear energy. Some Americans were genuinely concerned about the generation of fissionable materials that might fall into the hands of irresponsible individuals, the real danger of a nuclear accident that could expose large populations to radiation, and the nagging question of how safely to dispose of the mounting accumulations of very dangerous nuclear waste. These fears were fed in March 1979 when one of Metropolitan Edison Company's Three Mile Island turbines shut itself down. The Pennsylvania plant's operators became concerned about assuring that coolant not overfill the reactor. In so doing, they overrode the plant's core cooling safety functions, despite insistent system warnings, allowing the core to melt and release low-grade radiation into the air. Not one person was hurt when almost everything that could go wrong did at a sizeable nuclear power reactor in an urban area of the eastern United States. This fact might have been reassuring to a nation that had been fed an almost constant antinuclear diet by the media. Instead, this accident became the symbol of nuclear disaster.

Persistent, substantial construction cost overruns, caused partly by ever-stricter federal safety requirements, rising and sometimes raging environmentalist opposition to specific nuclear facilities, and the growing problem of the disposition of nuclear waste have led most utility companies to seek other means for generating electricity in the United States. At least temporarily the predicted shortages of uranium have instead become a glut. At a moment when huge new reserves of high-grade uranium have been located in northern Arizona, southern Utah, and in the old carnotite area, and Energy Fuels Company has constructed a large, highly efficient mill at Blanding, the domestic uranium industry seems headed for the greatest slump since the mid-1940s.

There may come a day when the dumps of a thousand mines will have washed to the San Juan and out to sea and the portals will have filled with tumbleweeds. On the other hand, there have been other bleak times in the history of the uranium industry, and the day may quickly come when compressors and blasting powder once again compete with the pervasive quiet of a summer day on the Colorado Plateau. If it never happens again, few can really begrudge its demise, for a generation of independent miners who had waited and prayed for their ship to come in lived to see it safely home, and another generation enjoyed the prosperity it brought.

NOTES

[1]Interview with Preston V. Redd, Blanding, Utah, January 1, 1964. A typed transcript of the tape recording of this interview is available in the California State University, Fullerton, Oral History Collection, and in Special Collections, Clark Library, Brigham Young University, Provo, Utah. A search of San Juan County, Fee and Entry Records, County Courthouse, Monticello, for the period from 1896 through 1906 showed that Wetherill failed to record his claim. However, Redd found the discovery monument with a claim paper inside when he followed Wetherill's directions to the claim in 1943.

[2]Howard W. Balsley, Address given before the Moab, Utah, Rock, Gem, and Mineral Society, May 12, 1960, p. 8 (copy in author's possession); Kathleen Bruyn,

Uranium Country (Boulder: University of Colorado Press, 1955), p. 99; "Uranium," *Salt Lake Mining Review,* February 23, 1914, p. 15; David Lavender, *One Man's West* (Garden City, New York: Doubleday, 1956), pp. 304-5.

[3]U.S. Geological Survey, *Mineral Resources of the United States, 1901* (Washington, D.C., 1902), p. 270; J. M. Boutwell, "Vanadium and Uranium in South-eastern Utah," *U.S. Geological Survey Bulletin 260* (Washington, D.C., 1905), pp. 200-210; Don Sorensen, "Wonder Mineral: Utah's Uranium," *Utah Historical Quarterly* 31 (Summer 1963): 282-83; *Mineral Resources of the United States, 1906,* p. 526; Richard B. Moore and Karl L. Kithil, "A Preliminary Report on Uranium, Radium, and Vanadium," *U.S. Bureau of Mines, Bulletin 70* (Washington, D.C., 1913), pp. 9-29; Herman Heck and William G. Haldane, "Study of Uranium and Vanadium Belts, Southern Colorado," *Colorado State Bureau of Mines Report, 1905-6* (Denver, 1906).

[4] For a much more extensive account of this important facet of uranium industry history, with source citations, see the author's Ph.D. dissertation, "A History of the Uranium Industry on the Colorado Plateau" (University of Southern California, 1970) pp. 11-79.

[5]Roy Gibbons, "Wanted: Old Time Radiation Victims," *Science Digest* 46 (September 1959): 532-37; *Mineral Resources of the United States, 1926,* pp. 265-68.

[6]*Mineral Resources of the United States, 1926,* p. 268.

[7]Interviews with Howard Balsley, Pete and Hattie Dalton Shumway, and Seth Shumway. Typed transcripts of the interviews with Balsley and Pete and Hattie Shumway are located in the California State, Fullerton, Oral History Collection and in Special Collections, BYU.

[8]Interview with Balsley; *San Juan Record* (Monticello, Utah), September 6, 1934, p. 1.

[9]Interviews with Pete and Hattie Dalton Shumway, Arah, Seth, Harris and Lee Shumway; San Juan County, Fee and Entry Records, "Book R," pp. 505-36; *Minerals Yearbook, 1932-33,* p. 329. Typed transcripts of the interviews with Shumway, located in the California State, Fullerton, Oral History Collection and in Special Collections, BYU.

[10]Blaire Burwell, "Chart of Carnotite Production, 1936-48," MS in Burwell papers; *Minerals Yearbook, 1943,* p. 663.

[11]*Minerals Yearbook, 1942,* p. 665; *Minerals Yearbook, 1943,* p. 663, *Minerals Yearbook, 1945,* pp. 649-50.

[12]*Nisley* v. *Union Carbide,* pp. 1369, 2153, 2777. For a much more detailed account of the collusion between the two large companies and the Metals Reserve period see Shumway, "A History of the Uranium Industry," pp. 92-138.

[13]San Juan County, Fee and Entry Records, "Book R-1," pp. 356-480.

[14]*Times Independent* (Moab, Utah), May 1, 1947, p. 1; June 26, 1947, p. 1; *Minerals Yearbook, 1947,* p. 1206.

[15]*Times Independent,* August 21, 1947, p. 1; January 1, 1948, p. 1.

[16]Jesse C. Johnson, "AEC's Uranium Procurement — Domestic and Foreign," remarks prepared for delivery before the Wyoming Mining Association, Riverton, Wyoming, April 17, 1959, pp. 4-5; *Nisley* v. *Union Carbide,* p. 1813; *Deseret News,* March 10, 1948, p. 6; *Engineering and Mining Journal,* May 1948, p. 108; Grand Junction Office, AEC, "Chronology of AEC Domestic Uranium Raw Materials Program," p. 1.

[17]AEC "Chronology," p. 1; *Times Independent,* September 30, 1948, p. 1.

[18]*Times Independent,* May 13, 1948, p. 1; June 3, 1948, p. 1.

[19]*Times Independent,* May 20, 1948, p. 1; June 17, 1948, p. 1.

[20]*Times Independent,* July 1 , 1948, p. 1; July 29, 1948, p. 1; September 30, 1948, p. 1.

[21]*Times Independent,* September 30, 1948, p. 1.

[22]*Times Independent*, December 29, 1949, p. 1; February 16, 1950, p. 1.

[23]John K. Gustafson, "Uranium Resources," *Scientific Monthly* 69 (August 1949): 115-20; *Minerals Yearbook, 1950*, pp. 1257-58; Harold B. Meyers, "The Great Uranium Glut," *Fortune*, February 1964, p. 159.

[24]Grand Junction Office, AEC, Press Release No. 10, February 28, 1951.

[25]Atomic Energy Commission, "Domestic Uranium Program Circular 6," p. 1.

[26]Robert D. Nininger, "World Production and Reserves of Uranium," Address before the 12th Annual Minerals Symposium of the American Institute of Mining, Metallurgical, and Petroleum Engineers, Moab, Utah, June 23, 1967, figure 4.

[27]*Engineering and Mining Journal*, September 1953, p. 72, Perrin Stryker, "The Great Uranium Rush," *Fortune*, August 1954, pp. 89-93, 1 8; Bruyn, *Uranium Country*, pp. 117-20; *Salt Lake Tribune*, January 25, 1953, p. E-1; *Deseret News*, February 13, 1953, p. B-1; *Salt Lake Tribune*, July 29, 1953, p. 21; *Times Independent*, August 13, 1953, p. 1, August 20, 1953, p. 1; Thomas E. Gillingham, "Uranium," *Mining Congress Journal* (February 1954): 116-17; Charles A. Steen et al., "Uranium Mining Operations of the Utex Exploration Company in the Big Indian District, San Juan County, Utah," U.S. Bureau of Mines, *Information Circular 7669* (Washington, D.C., 1953), pp. 1-4.

[28]"Pennies for Uranium," *Time*, April 5, 1954, pp. 89-90; interview with Trent Parker, Salt Lake City, Utah, May 9, 1964.

[29]Meyers, "The Great Uranium Glut," p. 110.

[30]"Coming of the Giants," *Time*, May 26, 1956, p. 90.

[31]Meyers, "The Great Uranium Glut," p. 159.

[32]Allan E. Jones, "Address before the Ninth Annual Minerals Symposium Uranium Section," Moab, Utah, May 22, 1964, p. 2 (copy in author's possession); "AEC Announces New Uranium Procurement Program and Extension of Initial Production Bonus," AEC, Press Release No. 150, May 24, 1956.

[33]Elton A. Youngberg, "The Present Uranium Situation," paper read before the Wyoming Mining Association, Riverton, Wyoming, May 13, 1967, p. 3; Glenn T. Seaborg, "The Nuclear Industry — 1968 and Beyond," Financial Forum on Nuclear Energy, New York, October 30, 1968, pp. 4-5.

[34]"The Future of Nuclear Fuel," *Magazine of Wall Street*, March 1967, pp. 24-27, 43.

[35]Allan E. Jones, "The Regional Uranium Picture," paper read before the Wyoming Governor's Conference on Uranium, Casper, Wyoming, November 1, 1968, p. 3 (copy in author's possession).

[36]*San Juan Record*, February 27, 1969, p. 12.

[37]Harold B. Meyers, "Another Big Whirl for Uranium," *Fortune*, April 1968, pp. 128-31. One miner, who sold his claims to a large company for $100,000 and 250,000 shares of stock in mid-1968 saw the stock shoot up almost 1,000 percent within a few months, increasing his paper assets over two million dollars. Interview with Devar Shumway, June 28, 1969.

Uranium Mining in San Juan

Hanson L. Bayles

My first involvement with uranium was in the early 1950s. I hauled ore from the Posey mine in Red Canyon. We hauled it in two-ton trucks and averaged about seven and one-half to eight tons of ore a load. The road was dirt all the way, going from the northwest part of Blanding through Big Canyon, Brushy Basin, Cottonwood, then over the Elk Mountain through the Bears Ears and on to Grand Flat. We took bedrolls with us because we never knew how long the trip would take. It usually took about eighteen hours from Blanding to the mine and back. Today we can take a large diesel semi out to Red Canyon and haul twenty-five to thirty tons in six hours.

I also hauled from Cottonwood to Durango, Colorado. Devar Shumway and Lark Washburn would take the truck out to Cottonwood and load it, usually with a wheelbarrow or horse and cart. I would take their pickup out about noon and take the load of ore to Durango.

I later hauled from the Whirlwind mine. To get there we would go to Bluff through Monument Valley into Arizona, then back to Oljato Trading Post, then north to the San Juan River. We would climb up on a mesa, then back the truck down the other side on the edge of a ledge to the mine. The road was so steep that we could haul just part of a load at a time. We would take the truck back off the mesa, dump the load on the ledge, then go back and get another small load. We would then shovel enough ore on the truck for a full load. We hauled this ore to Monticello and Durango.

Uranium mine in southeastern Utah, 1918. USHS Collections.

At this time the way across the San Juan River at Mexican Hat was over the old swinging bridge. If we were driving
one of the larger trucks some of the ore had to be dumped

in a bin on the other side of the river. The truck would then cross the bridge and dump the rest of the ore in a bin on this side, then go back across, load the truck out of the bin on the other side, cross the bridge, and load the ore on this side. The road south of Blanding was dirt or gravel all the way. This trip would take from eighteen to twenty-four hours — sometimes longer depending on the problems encountered. Sometimes the creeks would be flooded, or the sand was so deep we would get stuck.

My first mining experience was in Cottonwood in the Morrison formation where the ore could be anywhere. Sometimes it was overhead or to the side of the drift or under the drift. Usually, if there is a trash pile in the mine, ore is found along the edge of it.

The miners used to mine with wheelbarrows or mine cars on metal rails. Later, they started using horses and carts. They would make a mine cart which consisted of a metal bed with a hinged endgate mounted on a frame with rubber tires. It had two pipes sticking out in front so a horse could be put between them. The horse was then able to pull and turn the ore cart, which held a thousand to fifteen hundred pounds of ore. The ore was shoveled into the cart by hand.

I later worked in the Shinarump formation. It is quite different from the Morrison. The Shinarump formation sits on top of the Meonkopi formation which is a red shell-looking rock. Usually the ore is found right on top of the Meonkopi. Also in the Shinarump are what we call "mud banks" of a clay-looking type of rock that is quite dangerous if it is in the top of the drift because it falls easily. Quite often ore is found along the side of the mud banks.

Through the years the methods of mining have changed. A shuttle car was starting to be built which had a diesel motor and was safe to use in the mine. At first the ore was shoveled into it with shovels. Later front-end loaders were used. Today the shuttle cars can haul ten tons or more, and the loaders usually are rubber tired and are easy to operate.

The first four-ton shuttle car I know of cost less than

$5,000. Today shuttle cars are over $30,000. Loaders used to cost $10,000; now they are over $80,000. Jackhammers or air drills at first cost $250; now they cost $3,500. Dynamite was $6 a box and now it is $50 to $60 a box.

Ammonium nitrate is now being used as an explosive when mixed with diesel. There is also an explosive that is called detaprime. It is about an inch and a half long and looks like a small red hose with the end bent over. A detonating cap can be pushed into the end of the detaprime and is used as a primer to set off the charge.

Dynamite was used to set off the ammonium nitrate, using one stick to each hole that was drilled in the rock. Miners sometimes got what we called a "powder head," which is a severe headache, when they handled dynamite if they were not careful.

After the ore was brought from the mine it was put into wooden bins or metal bins, then the trucks would pull under the bins to load. Today the ore is piled on the ground and loaded with front-end loaders.

At the present time the uranium market is depressed, and because of this not many mines are in operation. It will be interesting to see the changes that will take place when the market opens again.

Brief History of Montezuma Creek

Don Kemner

I left California with a welding machine, a fourteen-foot trailer, and a light plant for electric power and arrived in Montezuma Creek on December 31, 1957. I was assured a job by Shell Oil Company on their lease work, building tank batteries and shipping lines for future oil development. On locating at the "water wheel," as it was called, I was grabbed by Superior Oil Company and did not get to work for Shell until later years.

In the late 1950s it took at least five hours to go from the Aneth oil fields on the south side of the San Juan River to Shiprock, New Mexico. It took as long to go to Cortez, Colorado, from the north side. There were no roads, only trails. Very few automobiles were driven by the natives of the region. Sheep was their livelihood. The women of the Navajo tribe would hide until the "Anglo" was gone. No liquor was allowed on the reservation, and they would take it away from anyone caught with it. Punishment was severe enough so that you were barred forever from the reservation if you got out of turn.

Oil shipping and gas lines for El Paso Natural and Four Corners pipeline were next in order. The El Paso plant was built about 1961. These tank batteries were tied in to the main lines and oil began to find its way to the outside world via pipelines instead of tank trucks. Oil wells were never developed unless they had a potential of five hundred barrels per day. It was not uncommon to have a well produce three thousand barrels a day. Gas was flared all over the basin just as is being done on the north slope today. The United States Geological Survey put a stop to this waste after the El Paso natural gas plant was built.

Soon after production from the field leveled off at a high peak, engineers decided that the fields should be water-flooded even though almost all wells were still flowing a vast amount of oil.

Water-flooding killed the gas pressure which brought the oil to the surface, and almost overnight the production of the field dropped to a fraction of what it was before. Salt water plagued the companies, causing leaks in pipelines and corroding everything it touched. When mixed with natural gas the salt water formed hydrogen sulphide which was highly corrosive.

About this time the whole country was filled with government vehicles, and the tribe began to come into its own.

Lunch break on an oil drilling rig in Glen Canyon. USHS Collections.

Pumping unit in the White Mesa oil field. USHS Collections.

Navajos were employed and trained to build homes, irrigate, and work at gainful employment. In some cases they were trained and employed by the oil companies. Clinics were set up. Home training, cooking, and other crafts were taught to the Navajo women. Children of that era graduated from schools, then colleges or vo-ed centers. Government-sponsored schools were set up all over the reservation. El Paso Natural Gas Company built the elementary school being used now and sold it to the school district for the sum of $1.00. The bridge was completed joining the north side with the south side of the river. Merrit Carter, one of the old-timers, and his wife were caught in a flash flood while bringing books to the center of learning and many of them were soaked on delivery.

There are few old-timers left in this community. The women saw to that. They gave their men the alternative of quitting and going elsewhere or they would leave anyway. Some did not even wait for that. They left, period.

Merrit Carter, Marvin Miller, and I are the oldest old-timers. We have seen Montezuma Creek grow from hogans, construction camps, temporary air strips, dirt trails and uncontrolled washes, and rivers to a community in the making.

Our only civic organization is the Montezuma Creek Lions Club. It has organized community participation and interest to provide a park, community building, high school, swimming pool, walkways for students, outdoor lighting, telephone service, tree planting, and a police substation. The Lions Club has promoted better public highways and bridges, cooperation with the Navajo police, and a true community spirit between whites and Indians.

Our county commissioners deserve a big share of this credit although in many cases it was like moving a mountain to get them started.

PART EIGHT

Education

Bluff school. USHS Collections.

A Sense of Dedication: Schoolteachers of San Juan County

Jessie L. Embry

During the 1940s Zenos L. Black, the superintendent of schools in San Juan often found it difficult to hire teachers for the county schools. He recalls that one time he went to Cortez, Colorado, to try to talk a woman in returning to the classroom. She explained that her health would not permit her to teach again but she had a daughter who had just graduated from high school who would like to be a teacher. Black decided to hire the daughter and took her to an isolated community twelve miles from the highway. She taught the first part of the year and then returned home for the Christmas holidays. When she returned to open the school again, the road to the community was blocked with twelve or fourteen inches of snow. With the consent of her parents, the girl gathered all of her belongings together and hiked the twelve miles into the school. As a result of this hike, she developed pneumonia. When her parents found out about her illness, they took her to the hospital. While she was recovering, her mother taught at the school, Superintendent Black adds, "If you can beat that for dedication! I dare you to do it because you just can't."[1]

This story is not an isolated incident of the devotion that the teachers in San Juan County had to their profession before the uranium and oil booms. The men and women who came to the area to teach had to contend with isolated conditions, low salaries, few teaching materials, and inadequate schoolhouses. Despite these problems, they stayed and added a great deal to the communities in the county. Their history is an important part of the settlement of San Juan County and a good example of the development of education in the state of Utah.

The first problem facing the school boards and administrators in San Juan County, as well as other rural areas of the state, during the early years was how to obtain qualified teachers. There were no educational facilities in the county to train the local residents to be teachers, and it was expensive to send them away to school. It was difficult to lure trained teachers away from the Wasatch Front. At the turn of the century, the school trustees hired most of the teachers by correspondence and gambled on what type of teacher would show up in town.[2] As transportation improved, the superintendents traveled north to talk to the graduates of the normal schools and to advertise their openings with the teacher agencies.[3]

San Juan Cooperative Company building in Bluff. Photograph Copyright 1979 Steve Lacy Wild Bunch Photos.

Convincing the teachers to come south to teach was sometimes difficult, but the superintendents were usually able to find a few teachers, either directly at the normal schools or at the agencies, who were willing to make the move. Superintendent H. Lloyd Hansen interviewed Reta Bartell at the University of Utah.[4] Elizabeth Price was also hired by Mr. Hansen, who often used agencies like the Yorgenson Teachers Agency and the Robinson Teachers Agency in Salt Lake City to find teachers. Elizabeth Price recalled her momentous visit to the latter:

> As I went in, there was a superintendent talking to Miss Robinson. He told her what he wanted for his teacher in Blanding. It was just exactly what I had. When he got to me, . . . he said, "What do you teach?" I had been listening to their conversation, so I told him everything I had. He said, "I will take her."

Even though later he found out that she was married, and married women were not usually hired to teach at that time, Mr. Hansen gave her a job and offered her a blank contract if she would return the next year.[5]

The young women the superintendents hired to teach in San Juan County had a variety of qualifications. Most of them had been to normal schools either at the University of Utah or Brigham Young University. Until the 1920s they were only required to have one year of schooling beyond high school. In 1926 the law was changed, and they were required to attend two years of normal school.[6] Ada Palmer, who went to Grand County first to teach, said that she decided to be a teacher because "It only took one year to be certified, but at the end of the year, they raised the standards to two years. I had to go back and take the second year."[7]

In the 1920s it was difficult to get teachers to go to the outlying counties, so many times the superintendents hired women who had not met the state requirements. Mabel Redd started at BYU and then had to quit school for a time because she ran out of money. She taught at Wallsburg in Wasatch County for a year before returning to complete her schooling and then going to San Juan to teach.[8] Josephine Roberts went to BYU and then the University of Utah but did not complete the requirements at either school. She said, "In those days it was hard to get teachers here in San Juan County. No one wanted to come down here and teach school. I was not very well qualified scholastically, but they were short of teachers. They were willing to take me." J. B. Harris hired her to teach at La Sal.[9]

During the 1930s, though, jobs were harder to find. Gladys Stephenson recalled that only four people from her normal class at BYU in 1931 received contracts to teach. She continued in school because she had a part-time job at the university. In 1936 she was hired to teach in the one-room schools east of Monticello.[10]

The trained schoolteachers accepted the offers to teach in San Juan County for a variety of reasons. Reta Bartell recalled, "I had always had an interest in rural life. City living didn't appeal to me. I had been interviewed by superintendents from around Salt Lake City, but I was familiar with those places. I guess partly I was looking for adventure."[11] Helen Redd, however, was not sure where she was going. She said, "Since I had been raised within a block of the railroad all my life, I had refused a contract to go to Kamas, Utah, because it was off the railroad." She did not realize at the time that by accepting a contract in San Juan County she would be much farther from the railroad.[12] Marie Redd came to San Juan County to escape an art position that she had been offered in American Fork which she did not feel qualified to accept. "Also," she said, "I wanted to get away and see a little more of Utah, so I applied down there at San Juan and I got the position. When I met Brother Albert R. Lyman and got better acquainted with him, he said, 'I don't think you came down here by chance.'"[13]

Teachers who were hired in Salt Lake and Provo had a long way to travel before they arrived at their classrooms. Helen Redd recalled that first trip: "When we got to Thompson the conductor told us that was where we were to get off the train to go to Moab and then Monticello. I was

just about to turn around and go back." She had been on the
train all day, and it was another three hours' drive to Moab.
The next morning they got up early and set out for Monticello. She recalled:

> The roads were not surfaced and were just cut trails here and
> there. On the way to Monticello, the truck driver told us every
> disaster that had happened on the road. He told us what would
> happen if it was raining when we got to a certain point. We
> would have to stay there by this wash because even with a team
> we wouldn't be able to ford it. By the time I got to Monticello
> I was really homesick, blue and scared.[14]

Alverda Carson did not get a contract to teach until October, so she was willing to teach wherever she could find
a job. When she got on the train with a friend, the conductor
asked, "Did you girls bring your six-shooter?" and added that
they were going to wild country. The train did not reach
Thompson until midnight. The stationkeeper let them spend
the night there. The conductor had scared the women so
badly that they carefully put their purses under their pillows
and locked the door. When they woke up, however, their
purses were on the floor. The next morning they met the bus
drivers who were taking them to San Juan County, and the
drivers greeted them with, "Good morning, schoolmarms."
They told them that the teachers were the only young
women that ever rode down with them. All the way to Monticello, the drivers told them how destitute the area was.
They said that the people ate groundhogs, there were no
bathrooms, and they would have to take baths in a tin tub
with only a quilt around them for privacy. Mrs. Carson was
not shocked; she had done all those things. But Norma Fall
had lived only in Provo, and when she heard all these stories,
she was ready to turn back.[15]

Marie Redd and Elizabeth Price had similar experiences
the first time they came to southeastern Utah. Mrs. Redd recalled, "We got on the train in Provo and came to Thompson
and got off the train late in the evening. We came to Blanding
in a little Ford car and the roads were terrible. It seemed like
we were going to the end of the earth."[16] Mrs. Price, who

came later, still found travel difficult. She recounted:

> When we got home there was a contract for me to teach in
> Blanding. My husband said, "You can't go down there . . . . I will
> just take you down there to show you what kind of a forsaken
> place it is." We started out and we got as far as Moab. The car
> heated and we had a lot of problems. He said, "I am glad I got
> that out of your head." I said, "You have not; I am going."[17]

The teachers were lucky if once they arrived in San Juan
County they could stay in Monticello or Blanding, even
though they were small towns compared to the cities that
they had come from. Other teachers were sent out to teach
in the one-room schools in areas that were very remote.
Helen Redd explained, "Because we were a day late getting
to Monticello, our superintendent, Lloyd Hansen, said, 'I'm
sorry; I have filled the positions here, but we have two
schools in the district and I'll have to put you girls out there.'
That was almost the finish for me but I thought about it and
decided I did have a little pride left and I couldn't go back
to my family or friends and admit I was a failure." Since
Helen had more baggage then her friend, she was taken to
Ucola, seventeen miles out instead of the school thirty-five
miles away. "On the way to Ucola he explained a two- or
three-hundred foot wall there had been built by an escaped
inmate from the state mental hospital and that he had escaped twice since then."[18]

Alverda Carson's first teaching position was at Cedar
Point, and she recalls the trip out to that small community.
Superintendent Hansen took her to the school and she re-
members weaving back and forth between the trees until she
was sure that they had lost all sense of direction. Getting to
Cedar Point was not an easy trip since they had to go into
Colorado and then backtrack into Utah to go around the can-
yons and arrive in town.[19]

Once the teachers arrived in the communities there
were often new surprises. One time Superintendent Hansen
took a teacher out to one of the schools to begin the term.
He discovered when he arrived that the citizens did not want
the teacher that he had selected for them. A number of them

met him when he arrived in town "and gathered around the car when it stopped. A surly spokesman for the group warned Mr. Hansen that if he stepped from the car he would shoot him. Unruffled by this threat, Mr. Hansen calmly stepped out of the car and said, 'I don't believe that you will shoot.'" After talking with the people for awhile, Mr. Hansen left and the teacher stayed.[20]

One of the first surprises, especially in the rural areas, was the schoolhouse. Alverda Carson went with the superintendent to see the school immediately after arriving in Cedar Point. She recalled later, "Seeing it I thought, 'surely that can't be the schoolhouse where I am to teach. My eyes are playing tricks on me. Surely I am not back in the early 1800s.' It looked more like a barn than a house." Alverda found that the inside appearance was as discouraging as the outside. "It was very hard to push the door open. The rough lumber served for outside and inside. . . . There was not any ceiling to it, just rafters which let in the sun, rain and snow in some places. (There was) just a cook stove to heat up this large room."[21] Helen Redd had similar problems at Ucola. "When the wind blew, it would just blow right through the building and all the papers would go too."[22]

The living arrangements were sometimes a surprise also. The schoolteachers who remained in Monticello and Blanding usually boarded with a family in the area or lived in a home with other women who were also teaching in the schools. Reta Bartell remembered that Superintendent Hansen had arranged for a place for her to stay with "Aunt Emma Wood" who was a widow in Monticello.[23] There were three other schoolteachers who also lived at Aunt Emma's. Marie Redd lived in "what we called the little rock house" in Blanding with three schoolteachers. They rented the home from "Uncle Wayne Redd," who thought it was his duty to not only give the teachers a place to live but also to show them a good time. Mrs. Redd remembers that one time he took them on a sleigh ride during the noon hour. "He whirled the sleigh around as fast as it could. That little . . . sleigh flew into the air and onto the ground with us luckily on top just as the bell rang."[24]

The teachers who went out into the country to teach also usually boarded with a family. Sometimes the homes were very small and there was not any extra room for the teacher. Occasionally there was strain between the teachers and the family. Alverda Carson disliked the family and the house that she was to live in at Cedar Point and was delighted when someone offered her a dilapidated log cabin to live in; at least there she could be by herself.[25] Living with a family could be delightful, however, if the family and the teacher got along, and most of the teachers enjoyed living with the families and being a part of the community by sharing the parents' homes.

Sometimes the nearest families lived quite a distance from the school, and the teachers had to walk. Helen Redd walked a mile and a half to the school in Ucola.[26] Clement Johnson recalled that when the teachers lived at his home, sometimes the snow was so deep that they had to drag a log behind a horse for the mile and a half to the school so the teacher would have a trail.[27]

The school board felt that the towns should provide a place near the school where the teachers could live.[28] In the 1930s when Gladys Stephenson went to Cedar Point, the superintendent told her she could live with the Carters a mile and a half from the school or she could rent a small log cabin about a block away from the school. She decided to stay in the log cabin.[29] By 1941, however, housing was not that close in Cedar Point, and the school board threatened to close the school unless the citizens provided a home near the school for the teacher.[30] By 1946 the board minutes reported that there now was a dwelling for the teacher.[31]

Whether the teacher was in the isolated community, though, or in the larger towns, those were lonely times for a young girl who had just graduated from normal school and who might have never been so far away from home for such a long time. Marie Redd in Blanding remembered, "I could see so far and I was lonesome. At Christmas and Thanksgiving we couldn't go home."[32] Helen Redd added, "Life wasn't always easy here and lots of things I was used to were hard to get along without. I could hear the old engine whistle in my mind when I was out there teaching and that would make me feel so homesick."[33]

Dorothy Adams, who worked as a teacher supervisor, said that many of the teachers were so lonely that "the biggest service I did in my supervising was just listening to them. A teacher who is isolated has nothing — no social life, except her children." Since quite often she roomed with the families, she could not discuss her problems there or she "would have the whole community on her neck. So she would get bottled up with problems that were really not too important," and she just needed to express them to a willing listener.[34]

Sometimes when there was no one to listen, the loneliness was too much for the young teachers, and they left in the middle of the year. Mabel Redd explained that she taught all the grades in La Sal depending on what teachers came and how long they stayed. "Many, many times they would stay two or three months and they would get lonesome and quit. . . . I don't know how many times I finished the school year because the teachers were sometimes not qualified or because they were just lonely and didn't want to stay there."[35]

The teacher turnover was a concern around the turn of the century. The superintendents attempted to hire local people who usually remained in the area longer. Those who came from the outside often stayed only one or two years.[36] The turnover was still a problem in the 1930s. The local people usually stayed in the classrooms for a number of years, but every year about twenty of the approximately thirty teachers were newcomers to the schools.[37]

Loneliness was not the only reason for the turnover; San Juan was a very poor county and the teachers' salaries were especially low. According to J. B. Harris, the first teachers in the area were paid in farm produce, and around the turn of the century, twenty-five years later, $50 a month was a good starting salary for a woman.[38] In 1908 the salaries ranged from $45 to $100 a month.[39] J. B. Harris recalled the year they were paying him $100 a month as the principal at the school in Bluff: "After we'd been going a week or two they decided to put in a third teacher. They talked a girl down and told her they could pay her only sixty dollars. The other girl was getting about seventy-five. I went to the treasurer of the school board and said, 'You give the new teacher ten dollars out of my check.'"[40]

Salaries remained low in San Juan County. Ada Palmer explained that she went to teach in Grand County in the 1920s for $105 a month: "The railroad went through Grand County so they had more funds than they had in San Juan County. A teacher who began teaching in San Juan was only paid sixty dollars a month at the time, and San Juan County really had a difficult time in making ends meet."[41]

In 1925 the school board established a salary schedule.

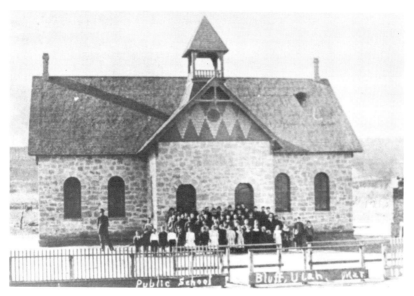

Bluff schoolhouse, 1896. Photograph Copyright 1979 Steve Lacy Wild Bunch Photos.

318

Those with one year of college after high school would receive $85 a month; two years of normal school, $95 a month; three years of college, $110 a month; and a bachelor's degree, $130 a month.[42] Reta Bartell explained that with those salaries it was difficult to get into trouble. "By the time you paid $40 for your board and room, $8.50 for tithing; and three dollars a pair for three pairs of silk stockings, you didn't have much pin money left to spend."[43] Helen Redd explained that she paid $30 for board and room out of her $85 a month. Ada Palmer said that it cost no less than $25 for a woman's dress.[44]

During times of economic or other problems, these small salaries were reduced even further. During the flu epidemic of 1918, the school board decided that teachers would be paid in full for the first month of the quarantine and as much as possible after that for the time lost. A statement of this policy was given to the teachers, and if they could not accept it, they were asked to resign.[45] During the depression of the 1930s, the school year was shortened and then the teachers were not given a raise. When the money was not available, they were required to wait for their pay. In 1933 the school board reported that the taxpayers had suggested that the teachers' salaries be cut and the board agreed. All those making $100 or less a month were cut $4 a month. Those making between $125 and $175 a month received 10 percent less, and the superintendent who made over $175 a month received a 15 percent cut.[46] After those cuts, salaries continued to increase a little bit each year during the 1930s and 1940s.[47]

Even with the improved salaries, teachers' pay was still low in San Juan County. When Lars Anderson wrote a master's thesis on education in the county in 1952, he reported that while the beginning salary of $2,600 a year for a teacher holding a bachelor's degree compared well with the state average, the $3,350 maximum for those holding that degree was low. He added that the rapid turnover also kept most of the salaries in the lower brackets.

Despite these problems, however, many people stayed in the area because of the congenial atmosphere and because the women teachers married and continued to teach.[48]

Even in the earlier days the friendly surroundings helped the teachers adjust to the county and helped them stay in the communities. Reta Bartell remembered that "the people were sincere and friendly. They welcomed us, gave us jobs in the community and helped us to 'fit in.'"[49] Superintendent Zenos Black remembered hiring a teacher for Horsehead who just knocked on his door and announced that she had come to teach there. Later he asked a member of the school board what the people thought of Mrs. Reese and was told, "Oh, they think that she is just one of the most wonderful things that ever happened to our community."[50]

The teachers were usually respected by the students as well, although sometimes the students liked to play pranks on them. John Rogers remembered that when he was young in Bluff the boys tied the bell gong one Halloween so it would not ring. "The teacher was quite surprised when he went to ring the bell for school and it wouldn't ring. Some of the boys were watching about a block away to see what he did."[51] Alfred Frost recalled that they gave the teacher a really hard time at La Sal. All eight grades were in one room, and "while she was teaching the other grades, we were supposed to study, but it seems like we did more throwing things around, talking and sneaking around than anything else. We were just raising hell. I will tell you that those teachers really earned their money in a place like that."[52]

Teachers usually had ways of dealing with these problems. Luella Rogers said that J. B. Harris threatened, "You kids shut up or I will tie your hair together and hang you over these rafters."[53] Hazel Loomis recalled that she kicked a "great big Mexican, as big as a man" and much bigger than she out of class in Monticello, and when he tried to return, she chased him with a broom. "I bet if I had caught him, I would have really hurt him," she recalled.[54] When Zenos Black went to visit the school in Cedar Point, he discovered the young teacher had a willow on her desk and jokingly told her, "I see you have the board of education here on your desk." She replied, "Yes, and I use it too."[55]

Gladys Stephensen, who taught at that same Cedar Point school twenty years earlier, explained how she dealt with pranks. "The students loved to do little things like get little lizards and put them in your desk." When she knew the students had been out catching lizards, she told them to get the lizard out of her desk and they did it. "It is just a matter of being a friend with them as well as being their teacher."[56]

On the whole the teachers and their students had a good relationship, and many people looked back with fond memories of what their teachers taught them. Mary Lyman Reeve remembered that Louise Elliott Redd "made a real issue of getting to school on time" and taught the children how to draw spheres in arithmetic. She also convinced the children that they wanted to study. Mrs. Reeve said that no one dared go to a party without having their lessons done. During the week, the children would go home and do their chores and then come back and study together.[57] Other students have fond memories of the things that they learned from their teachers.

Many of the women who came as teachers stayed in San Juan County not as teachers but as wives and mothers. They fell in love with one of the local young men, married, and set up their homes. When the teachers arrived, the superintendent warned them about getting involved with the local cowboys and ranchers. Gladys Stephenson said that when she went to teach in Cedar Point in the 1930s she was told, "Just don't find some of these boys down there that can be really nice and get seriously involved." Mrs. Stephenson added that she had no problem and was just good friends with the young men in Cedar Point.[58] Helen Redd said, however, that the warnings were worthwhile and added:

We had been told all of these stories about the people that you mustn't go with . . . . I can see as I grow older those stories were a real favor to us girls. The girl that came with me married a fellow from Cedar Point before the school year was up. In our contracts it said if we married during the year we forfeited our last month of wages and would not be rehired. She fell for this boy, married him and lost her wages. She left him quite soon after.[59]

Mrs. Redd took this warning not as a sign that she should avoid all the young men of San Juan County. She should just be careful whom she dated. She met John Redd at a dance in the outlying communities and then again at the teachers' institute in October or November just after she arrived in southeastern Utah. They went together for about a year; she finished her year of teaching but did not sign a new contract, and they were married the following November.[60]

There were other young schoolteachers who also met their husbands while they were teaching. Marie Redd remembered that she had dated A. J. while they were both attending BYU, but she got better acquainted with him while she was teaching in Blanding.[61] Josephine Roberts met her husband

Blanding church and Relief Society hall which also served as a school. Photograph Copyright 1979 Steve Lacy Wild Bunch Photos.

while she was teaching at La Sal and he was working as principal of the same school.[62] Reta Bartell also met Kenneth Bailey at one of the dances. When she did not see him for a month, she wondered what had happened. Later she learned that he had been out on the range. When he returned he came to see her. He took all the teachers who were living at one house to a show, but one of them said when they got back that she knew Ken liked Reta the best because he put her boots on for her first.[63]

Mabel Redd also met her husband while she was teaching. She recalled:

> Joe wasn't in town when I first went there, and his Uncle Parley picked me out for Joe. He kept telling me, "Now don't get going with any of these boys because Joe's coming home pretty soon." I was all ready not to like Joe before we began. One day after school we went to Uncle Parley's store where Joe was working. Uncle Parley called out, "Here's the girl I've been telling you about, Joe." Joe and I was both so embarrassed that neither one of us said hardly anything. The first time I went with him at all was when we were walking up to the Post Office after dinner to mail some letters and we met Joe as he was riding on a black horse called Satan. He stopped to talk with us, and pretty soon he lifted me on to his horse, and we went for a ride. That was the beginning of our courtship.[64]

As Helen Redd explained, the teachers' contracts stated that once they married they would have to quit teaching. Although some married women such as Elizabeth Price were hired to teach and some like Josephine Roberts continued to teach after they were married, most of the time only single women were teachers. Many of these former teachers, however, were "drafted" back to the schoolroom in one way or another during World War II. During the war there was an extreme shortage of teachers because many of the women teachers had left to work in war-related industry and the young men teachers had been drafted into the armed services. It was even harder to convince young women to come to rural Utah to teach when there was such a great demand for them in cities.[65] According to Reta Bartell, "Women teachers considered this as 'the falling off place at the end of the world.'"[66] Dorothy Adams added, "Teachers were almost impossible to get at that time; everyone was working for the war effort. . . ."[67]

Mrs. Adams, who had married during the 1930s and quit teaching, returned to the classroom. She explained, "All during the war years, I taught wherever they needed me."[68] Reta Bartell did some substitute teaching, and "then in 1945 Superintendent Zenos L. Black drafted me back into the schoolroom where I taught the third grade."[69] Ada Palmer, who had taught in Grand County, also returned to the classroom.[70] Although Helen Redd did not formally teach in the classroom, she helped the students at the high school with music.[71]

Superintendent Black complimented these women when he said:

> The salvation of our schools in San Juan County were these good women who had trained to be teachers, getting what we call a two-year normal certificate and who had married, settled down in our community and were raising families. We immediately went after them to come in and teach. Many of them were reluctant, but in order to help out the community and the school situation, they would get up early in the morning, take care of their families, and then come and teach school. Then they would go back and do the work that they would supposedly do all day long, in just a few hours . . . . They sacrificed and loaned themselves to the school effort. I just take my hat off to those people.[72]

When the war ended some of these teachers, such as Ada Palmer, quit teaching once again. She said the return to the classroom was "only temporary because I didn't have my degree and I couldn't go back to school at that time."[73] Others, like Reta Bartell, continued to teach and attended summer school for recertification. She eventually received her B.S. degree so that she met the state requirement for teachers.[74] According to Gary L. Shumway, these women were the best teachers in the county when he was going to school.[75]

Whether these women who came to San Juan County to teach and then got married returned to the classroom during

World War II or not, they added a great deal to the cultural development of San Juan County. They became involved in community activities and helped improve the towns where they lived. They also raised families where they stressed the value of education. They had a lasting and a continuing effect on the area. Even those who stayed only one or two years, like Elizabeth Price, helped expand the horizons of the young people in San Juan County. Similarly, local teachers who were already committed to the community included the classroom as part of their sphere of influence. All these teachers dedicated much of their lives to education in San Juan County.

NOTES

[1]Zenos Black Oral History, interview by Gary L. Shumway, 1981, p. 24, LDS Family Oral History Project, Charles Redd Center for Western Studies, Oral History Program, Manuscript Division, Harold B. Lee Library, Brigham Young University, Provo, Utah.

[2]Lars Anderson, "A History of Education in San Juan School District" (Master's thesis, University of Utah, 1952), p. 27.

[3]San Juan County School District Board Meetings, July 9, 1942, p. 385, San Juan County School District Office, Monticello, Utah; Utah State Annual School Report, 1936, p. 81.

[4]Reta Bartell Oral History, interview by Jessie L. Embry, 1973, p.5, Southeastern Utah Oral History Project, Charles Redd Center for Western Studies. Hereinafter referred to as Southeastern Utah Oral History Project.

[5]Elizabeth Price Oral History, interview by Jessie L. Embry, 1973, p. 18, Southeastern Utah Oral History Project.

[6]Utah State Annual School Report, 1926, pp. 19-20.

[7]Ada Palmer Oral History, interview by Jessie L. Embry, 1973, p. 2, Southeastern Utah Oral History Project.

[8]Mabel Redd Oral History, interview by Gregory Maynard, 1973, p. 1, Charles Redd Oral History Project, Charles Redd Center for Western Studies. Hereinafter referred to as Charles Redd Oral History Project.

[9]Josephine Redd Roberts Oral History, interview by Gregory Maynard, 1973, p. 2, Charles Redd Oral History Project.

[10]Gladys Hook Stephenson Oral History, interview by Jessie L. Embry, 1980, tape in process, County School Legacy Oral History Project, Utah State Historical Society, Salt Lake City, Utah. Hereinafter referred to as County School Legacy Oral History Project.

[11]Bartell, p. 6.

[12]Helen Redd Oral History, interview by Jessie L. Embry, 1973, pp. 2-3, Southeastern Utah Oral History Project.

[13]Marie Ekins Redd Oral History, interview by Jessie L. Embry, 1973, p. 7, Southeastern Utah Oral History Project.

[14]Helen Redd, pp. 2-3.

[15]Alverda Carson Oral History, interview by Jessie L. Embry, 1973, tape in process,

County School Legacy Oral History Project.

[16]Marie Ekins Redd, p. 7.

[17]Price, p. 18.

[18]Helen Redd, p. 3.

[19]Carson, tape in process.

[20]Anderson, p. 6.

[21]Alverda Carson, personal history, copy in possession of author and the Utah State Historical Society.

[22]Helen Redd, p. 6.

[23]Bartell, p. 5.

[24]Marie Ekins Redd, p. 5.

[25]Carson, tape in process.

[26]Helen Redd, p. 4.

[27]Clement Johnson Oral History, interview by Richardson Swanson, 1973, p. 3, Southeastern Utah Oral History Project.

[28]San Juan County School District Minutes, September 4, 1941, p. 312.

[29]Stephenson, tape in process.

[30]San Juan County School District Minutes, September 4, 1941, p. 312.

[31]Ibid., September 3, 1946, p. 344.

[32]Marie Ekins Redd, p. 8.

[33]Helen Redd, p. 6.

[34]Dorothy Adams Oral History, interview by Richard Swanson, 1973, pp. 19-20, Southeastern Utah Oral History Project.

[35]Mabel Redd, p. 12.

[36]Anderson, 29, 34.

[37]See lists of school teachers in San Juan County District Minutes, January 21, 1933, p. 214; March 30, 1934, p. 219; April 27, 1935, p. 225; April 24, 1936, p. 241; April 27, 1937, p. 252; April 22, 1938, p. 272; April 4, 1939, pp. 294-295; April 2, 1946, p. 341.

[38]Anderson, p. 15.

[39]Utah State Annual School Reports, 1908, p. 359.

[40]Anderson, p. 38.

[41]Palmer, p. 4.

[42]Anderson, p. 59.

[43]Jessie L. Embry "Schoolmarms of San Juan County," p. 6 (copy in possession of author and at the Utah State Historical Society).

[44]Helen Redd, p. 4; Palmer, p. 11.

[45]Anderson, p. 58.

[46]San Juan School District Minutes, March 28, 1932, p. 211; Anderson p. 57.

[47]See salary schedules in San Juan County School District Minutes, January 21, 1933, p. 214; March 30, 1934, p. 219; April 27, 1935, p. 225; April 24, 1936, p. 241; April 27, 1937, p. 252; April 22, 1938, p. 272; April 4, 1939, pp. 294-295; April 2, 1946, p. 341. The high, low, and average salaries for these years were as follows:

1933	high	$120 per month	1937	high	$1620 per year
	low	$ 60 per month		low	$ 800 per year
	average	$ 81 per month		average	$ 970 per year
1934	high	$135 per month	1938	high	$1680 per year
	low	$ 75 per month		low	$ 804 per year
	average	$ 93 per month		average	$ 983 per year
1935	high	$150 per month	1939	high	$1700 per year
	low	$ 85 per month		low	$ 840 per year
	average	$ 95 per month		average	$ 964 per year

1936	high	$1530 per year	1946	high	$2600 per year
	low	$ 765 per year		low	$1300 per year
	average	$ 869 per year		average	$1595 per year

[48]Anderson, pp. 116-117.

[49]Bartell, p. 6.

[50]Black, p. 25.

[51]John Rogers Oral History, interview by Jessie L. Embry, 1973, p. 38, Southeastern Utah Oral History Project.

[52]C. Alfred Frost Oral History, interview by John F. Bluth, 1973, p. 12, Southeastern Utah Oral History Project.

[53]Luella Rogers Oral History, interview by Gary L. Shumway, 1973, p. 51, Southeastern Utah Oral History Project.

[54]Hazel Loomis Oral History, interview by Richard Swanson, 1973, p. 7, Southeastern Utah Oral History Project.

[55]Black, pp. 23-24.

[56]Stephenson, tape in process.

[57]Anderson, pp. 17-18.

[58]Stephenson, tape in process.

[59]Helen Redd, p. 13.

[60]Ibid., p. 19.

[61]Marie Ekins Redd, p. 8.

[62]Roberts, p. 2.

[63]Embry, pp. 7-8.

[64]Mabel Redd, p. 2.

[65]Black, pp. 21, 75.

[66]Bartell, pp. 10-11.

[67]Adams, p. 8.

[68]Ibid.

[69]Bartell, pp. 10-11.

[70]Palmer, p. 4.

[71]Helen Redd, pp. 20-21.

[72]Black, pp. 75-76.

[73]Palmer, p. 4.

[74]Bartell, pp. 10-11.

[75]Black, pp. 75-76.

San Juan County Schools

Reta Bartell

My first experience with one-room schools came in the fall of 1956 when I became elementary supervisor in San Juan School District. I brought to the job thirteen years of teaching experience, so I had a fairly good understanding of an elementary school curriculum. Besides being the largest school district in the state, San Juan was one of the poorest. For years a good part of the money spent on education in the district came from the State Equalization Fund. But none of this prepared me for the eleven one-room schools I was given to supervise, in addition to the larger schools at Monticello and Blanding. These eleven schools were scattered all over the district: La Sal and La Sal Creek in the far north; West Summit; East Summit; Cedar Point and Eastland between Monticello and the Colorado State line to the east; Aneth to the far south across the San Juan River at Montezuma Creek; Bluff and Mexican Hat in the southwest; and Fry Canyon and Hide Out, over fifty miles west of Blanding.

The typical one-room school was a small, lonely building, off by itself, way out in the "sticks" and badly in need of paint. Inside were a dozen desks of different sizes, a teacher's desk, and several shelves attached to the wall. On the shelves stood a teacher's roll book and an assortment of basic reading, arithmetic, spelling, and language texts, most of them outdated and worn. One shelf held expendable supplies — notebooks, ruled paper, pencils, crayons, and a three-inch stack of colored construction paper. A stand by the door held a grey enamel wash dish and a galvanized bucket for drinking water. In the bucket was a battered dipper. Beside the big pot-bellied stove stood a coal or wood bucket, empty.

It was the teacher's job to build her own fire after taking out the ashes. This was done early enough to thaw out the room and the drinking water before the children arrived. She swept her own floor and did the housekeeping chores. Her "homework" consisted of scheduling the necessary basic subjects to be taught to about eleven children in eight grades each day. Enrollment could fluctuate from seven to twenty-six students. She had attendance and progress records to keep. She had no breaks in the day. Lunch was brought from home and eaten at school. She was responsible for playground duty at recess every morning and afternoon, so she played ball and pop-the-whip with the kids. She kept the outdoor privy disinfected with powdered lime. She furnished Kleenex for running noses and Band-Aids for skinned knees.

I saw some of the best education take place in our one-room schools. Dedicated teachers like Joan Saunders, Mamie Massatto, and Hazel Sobers who, besides teaching children to read, write, and do arithmetic, taught them to live cooperatively together, to respect one another, to be honest, to laugh and have fun, and to assume some responsibility for their own learning.

I also saw some of the worst teaching. I always moved a little chair beside a child who was reading and had him read to me. One day the child read to the bottom of the page. Ending in the middle of a sentence, he slapped the book shut and put it in his desk. I asked, "Aren't you going to finish the story?" He said, "Teacher said to read two pages and that's two pages." I asked, "But don't you want to know how the story ends? What happens?" His look told me enough. Needless to say, I had a conference with the teacher after school, and reading in that classroom changed. That is what I was there for, to help teachers improve their teaching skills. I understood how the teacher was pressed for time. A blanket reading assignment of two pages may make sense if it is the last two pages of a story and you want a child to have the satisfaction of finding out, by himself, how the story ends, so he can tell you. But not otherwise. . . .

*School children playing softball in Bluff, 1983. Photograph by
G. B. Peterson,* © *1983.*

I thoroughly enjoyed my visits to the one-room schools. My car was always loaded with books and supplies that were desperately needed. The boxes of library books which I circulated from Monticello Elementary School Library assured my welcome.

This is contrasted with what took place in the district after the uranium and oil booms when, within just a few years, the assessed valuation of San Juan County shot up from 3 million to 153 million dollars. We became known as the "Rags to Riches School System."

As money became available, an extensive building program extended over the whole district. New, modern schools demanded by increased enrollment were built at La Sal, Monticello, Blanding, Bluff, Montezuma Creek, and Mexican Hat. Large, spacious classrooms with wall-to-wall carpeting were equipped with flexible furniture that could be moved by the students themselves. Shelves and cupboards held basic and supplementary instructional material, learning aides, flash cards, basic texts, workbooks, reading laboratories, programmed reading workbooks, filmstrips and projectors, picture files, puzzles, math and phonic games, supplementary readers, and a wealth of library books. There were sinks with running hot and cold water, art easels, art supplies, and all kinds of physical fitness equipment.

Teachers were encouraged to innovate. Some buildings had open classrooms, large spaces that could be converted into several small areas by pulling partitions out of the walls. New programs such as team-teaching and flexible scheduling were tried. The affluence brought about consolidation of schools in the county. Rural children were bused to the larger centers, and the day of the one-room school came to an end. But I learned that "things" do not make a child learn. The teacher is still the key person in the classroom.

In the early 1960s we recognized a serious problem in the schools at Blanding and those south. The enrollment of Indian children in these schools ran from 30 to 98 percent, and most of them did not speak a word of English. We knew that the teachers would have to teach English as a second language. After a thorough investigation of available programs we decided to invest in material that was being researched and published in Albuquerque, New Mexico. I spent a month of the summer vacation at the Southwest Cooperative Educational Laboratory in Albuquerque, becoming acquainted with and learning to use the material we had agreed to buy for the next school year. In order to participate in the program we had to agree to use the teaching material under close supervision, send feedback reports to them on a set time schedule to evaluate the program's effectiveness, and continually educate our teachers in the proper use of the material.

This was the most thrilling experience I ever had in the classroom. I held a first-generation institute with fifteen teachers from the Blanding, Montezuma Creek, Bluff, and Mexican Hat schools for a week before school started that fall. They were teachers of Head Start and kindergarten children. We set up a learning center at the Park Terrace School. We placed five Indian children who knew no English on little chairs facing a teacher. The teacher used realia in her hands, such as a ball. She taught full sentences, conversational English, about the realia. For example: "This is a ball. Catch the ball," — fitting the action to the words. We used a TV camera to record each teacher's performance. The other teachers wrote their critique of the performance. Then the film was replayed, and the teacher made her own critique. A discussion followed, bringing out the important points of the lesson. At first teachers were hesitant about criticism, but they soon overcame it because you feel all right about being criticized if you know you can have a turn to criticize the others. During the week each teacher had numerous times to teach before the camera and to evaluate her and everyone else's performance. Later in the year I held second- and third-generation institutes with the same teachers. Each flip-chart lesson built progressively on the lessons which had gone before. We used this program for six years, going with the child from kindergarten through fifth grade. I have seen Indian children come into our schools not knowing a word of English and with this kind of instruction for thirty minutes a day be initiating conversation in English in three weeks. It was simply unbelievable!

Other kinds of help were given to these children. One summer we took all third-grade Indian children from the Blanding schools to Salt Lake City to visit the zoo, the train station to see a train come in and leave, the airport to watch the big planes land and take off, and the State Capitol. They saw the city at night. On the way home one little boy said to the teacher, "I'm not going to tell my parents what I saw. They wouldn't believe me!"

I was so pleased to see this article in the *San Juan Record* recently:

> Whitehorse High School Students Earn Nineteen Literary Awards
>
> With ardent teacher encouragement, many students nervously submitted poetry and short stories to several literary publications and contests this year.
>
> Bursting on the national magazine scene is Norma Jean Blackhorse. Her poem, "A Bridge Between" was purchased by the

Indian Students, 1973. Photograph by Ken Hochfeld, USHS Collections.

334

Christian Board of Publications to be printed in their national periodical "Alive" in January of 1984.

Gloria Todachinnie took fourth with "Missing You." Fifth was reeled in by Rose Clah with "Friends." Seventh place was taken by Sharon Lee's "The Little Girl."

The prestigious Southwest High School Creative Writing Awards Contest from New Mexico State University received 876 entries from 56 schools. Two Whitehorse High students — Gloria Todachinnie and Ella Jay — received honorable mention.

All in all, Whitehorse students are lengthening their stride academically and stepping out into the world of published authors.

I like to think that some of these students were exposed to our classes in English as a second language when they were in the elementary school at Montezuma Creek. One never knows how far-reaching are the seeds one sows.

Education in San Juan County

Zenos L. Black

I grew up in Blanding and went to school there for twelve years, graduating from high school in the spring of 1925. I graduated from the University of Utah in the spring of 1930 with a degree of Bachelor of Science and a teaching certificate. I taught in Idaho for twelve years, then came to Monticello as principal and teacher of the school which contained grades one through twelve. It was when World War II was in full swing.

Many of the young male teachers of the state had been called into the military service, and both male and female teachers had abandoned the teaching service to work in the war industry where salaries were much higher than in the teaching field. Consequently, there was an extreme shortage of teachers. Our distance from the populated areas made it worse for us because the teachers who were left preferred the larger schools. As I recall, that first year, 1942-43, we started out with a teaching staff of six teachers for grades one through eight and two teachers plus myself for grades nine through twelve. I taught five classes and did the work of principal in my spare time. Every teacher was loaded to the hilt. Several of the classes exceeded forty pupils and none of them, with the exception of home economics, had less than thirty. The teachers were dedicated and not afraid to work hard, and we managed to have a pretty good year. We did get some relief during the year in the high school. At Christmas time, a young lady, who had taught there the year before, came to visit some of her friends and the superintendent got her to come into the school and finish out the year.

In June of 1943 I was appointed superintendent of the San Juan School District. Needless to say, I was overwhelmed. There were so many things to do and so little time to do them. There was no secretary, so I had to do all the chores of the office, all my own correspondence, keep the records, make all the orders for equipment, books, and supplies, etc. I did not know where to begin or what to do. Finally I learned a very positive lesson. I told myself, "You can do only one thing at a time. Choose one thing, do it, then choose another thing and do it. Keep doing this and soon the picture will change." That is what I did, and after a few weeks things began to look better.

During those early years, the two biggest problems concerning the operation of the schools were: first, to staff the schools with the very best teachers that it was possible to get; and second, to get enough money to operate the program. Miss Embry has talked about the problems involved in getting teachers to come here for the meager salaries, $60 to $90 per month, we were able to pay. I can verify this from personal experience. I have interviewed hundreds of prospective teachers all over the state of Utah and parts of Colorado and my success rate has been poor. I have met with young men and young women, prospects for teachers, many of them, only to be told "no" when they found out where San Juan was located and what the salary would be. I made one trip with Lloyd Hansen, the former superintendent, to recruit teachers. He told me that he had very little success signing teachers until August. By that time, the other school districts, especially in the populated areas, were about filled up with teachers. Candidates without a job, being afraid they might not find anything better, were willing to talk with him. You might think that to be a poor way of recruiting and that all we would get would be the poorer teachers. Not necessarily so. Yes, as I was going through the schools in Blanding, we had some poor teachers, but we also had some of the best teachers who ever set foot in a classroom. After I started recruiting, we had a few poor teachers, but we also had many many good ones, teachers who were dedicated and placed their pupils above all else and gave them their all. Our pupils received a good basic education and those who went on to college measured well above the average students of the city schools.

During the war years and for several years following the close of the war, we had to rely heavily on local people to staff our schools. Fortunately for our children and our schools, quite a few of the young girls, normal school graduates who had come to the district to teach, met, fell in love with, and married local boys. They settled down here and raised families. I appealed to these ladies publicly and privately to come into the schools and make a contribution to the welfare of the children of the communities. Many of them responded positively and came in for a few years. Some of them remained in the schools after the teacher shortage, returned to college during the summers, and qualified for teaching certificates. We also had two or three men who left their work and came in to help with the teaching. We could not have carried on without these men and women. With them, our schools and our children were blessed. One of these young ladies, Reta Paige, came to Monticello about 1924. After a year or two, she married Ken Bailey and settled in Monticello to make her home with her husband. During the teacher crisis, I contacted her to come and help in the schools. She declined as she thought she was needed more with her family than with the schools. I told her that if she changed her mind, to contact me. After a year or two, she came and said she was ready. We put her to teaching the third grade in Monticello. While I was superintendent of schools, I made it a policy to visit every school at least once a month and to visit and observe every teacher at work two or three times each year. After visiting Reta several times over a period of years and watching her work, I was impressed with her ability and her personality. When I had a vacancy for an elementary supervisor for the district, Reta was my choice. She was an excellent supervisor. She had the personality that attracted teachers to her and made them her friends. Through her hard work and zeal, the many teaching aids she had at her fingertips, and a keen knowledge of teaching methods, she was able to be of great assistance to the one-room teachers as well as those in the town schools. If teachers were hesitant as to how to proceed with their class, she could step in and demonstrate for them, or she could sit and observe them and then counsel with them on their strengths and how they could improve. She was one of the best.

Financing the schools in the county was difficult. The only state aid received was based on $25 per school-age child as of October each year. Every October, each school district in the state had to enumerate every child in that district and make a report to the state office before receiving the money. It was difficult to enumerate the children in San Juan who lived on the Indian reservation, because their homes were so scattered, and in many instances no roads went to the hogans. Lloyd Hansen, while he was superintendent, had taken it upon himself to enumerate the Indian children. Over the years he had made many friends among the Indian people and was able to get a pretty good enumeration. I wondered what I would do, then I thought, "These are war years and there is sugar rationing. Each family has to sign up with a government agency and list all their children before they can receive sugar stamps." All I needed to do was to locate those agencies and get permission to copy their records. I spent about three days looking up the agencies and getting the information. Needless to say, our district received more state aid that year than ever before because the count of the children was more complete. A few years later, the state legislature changed the formula for state aid, so the enumeration became less important.

After uranium was discovered in San Juan the valuation of the property of the county began to increase and we had a little more money to work with. In 1943 the valuation of

Monticello Boy Scouts in 1973 Pioneer Days Parade. Photograph by Ken Hochfeld, USHS Collections.

the county was just over 3 million dollars. After the big oil field was discovered in the Aneth area, along with the uranium ore in the county, the valuation rose to a high of 134 million dollars. In a few short years, San Juan School District had risen from the poorest school district per capita to the richest. This was a new feeling and a new experience for the school board and for the superintendent. We were practical, however, and did not resort to unnecessary spending. We were able to raise our teachers' salary schedule so that it was the highest in the state on the base, though not as high as some on the upper end. We were able to bid for the most qualified teachers and to get some of them. We still had the problem of location, however. Many prospective teachers said, "It's too far away."

When new people began to move into the district, we needed more school buildings. Some of our existing buildings were getting old and needed to be replaced, and some of them needed additions. We were able to accomplish all this without going into debt and by keeping the tax mill levy at a minimum. New buildings constructed during this time included Monticello High, Monticello Elementary, Blanding Elementary, Albert R. Lyman Elementary, San Juan High, Montezuma Elementary, Bluff Elementary, Mexican Hat Elementary, and La Sal Elementary. At the time I retired as superintendent of schools there was only one building still in use which was standing when I started. I was happy that all this had been accomplished with very little burden on the tax payers. I found out, however, that even though money helps, it does not solve all the problems.

One of the problems we faced during the 1940s and 1950s was the consolidation of schools. It was a very difficult task. San Juan School District, geographically, is the largest school district in the United States. Although most of the people lived in the towns of Blanding and Monticello, others lived at their mines, dry farms, ranches, and other areas quite some distance from the towns. Roads were mostly dirt and often built over rough terrain. Travel was hazardous and sometimes impossible. The policy was if there were six school children in an area, we would try to make a school available to them. From the late 1930s through the 1950s, we operated one- or two-room schools at Old La Sal, La Sal, Lockerby, Ginger Hill, Bug Point, Cedar Point, Horsehead, Eastland, Frye Canyon, White Canyon, South Montezuma, Blanding Indian, Bluff, St. Christophers, Mexican Hat, Ucolo, East Summit Point No. 1, East Summit Point No. 2, West Summit Point No. 1, West Summit Point No. 2, the north rim of White Canyon, and White Canyon. Some of these schools did not exist more than a year or two. People would leave the area and there would be no children for the school.

We had some very interesting experiences at these one- and two-room schools. If a family lived two and one-half miles from school, we would reimburse the parents a few dollars per month to help with expenses of getting their children to school. A certain father, a widower, living fifteen miles from a school, brought his two sons, about eleven and thirteen years old. He parked a sheep camp, a small lumber room on wheels, and left his sons there to go to school. Things seemed to go well until Thanksgiving when the superintendent received word from the teacher that the two boys were in trouble and he should come out and investigate. The superintendent arrived at the school and the boys were turned over to him immediately. The boys had broken into the cellar of one of the farmers in the neighborhood and had taken two or three bottles of fruit. Upon investigation, the superintendent found that the only food that the boys had in their sheep camp was a little bag of flour. Those poor kids were half-starved and, being too proud to beg, had helped themselves to something the farmer had plenty of. Their father, for some reason, had failed to check on the needs of the boys, and they became too hungry for their endurance. Needless to say, the boys were not referred to the sheriff. Other arrangements were made for them.

About eight o'clock one evening, a week after the school season opened, a knock came on my door. I went to the door, opened ·it, and there stood a little lady, five feet two inches tall, weighing about one hundred ten pounds. I greeted her and she said, "Are you Superintendent Black?" I told her I was and asked what I could do for her. "I came to teach your Horsehead School," was her response. A few days before, I had written a note to the *Deseret News* explaining that there were two or three of our schools not opening because I could not get anyone to teach them. The paper had written a little news item. Mrs. Reese, the little lady, had read the article. She had been a teacher and thought it was a tragedy for those children not to have a school. She decided to try and help. I was a little skeptical. After all, if she was a teacher, why had she not obtained a job in the city area where she lived. She indicated that she had not intended to teach, but when she read the newspaper article, she decided she would like to try it. The next morning I took Mrs. Reese out to Horsehead, helped her find a place to board with one of the families and then turned over the school to her, not without some misgivings. I did not have an elementary supervisor to work with her so decided I would give her a week or two to get started, then visit her to see how she was doing. It was three weeks later before I was able to get back to Horsehead. As I opened the door and walked into the classroom I wanted to turn around, leave the room, and cry. The pupils were up out of their seats, some of them in small groups talking and laughing, there was lots of noise. It was disturbing to one used to a quiet classroom. Things seemed to be in great disorder. Fortunately, I controlled my feelings, greeted Mrs. Reese, and asked her to continue and I would observe for awhile. As I waited and watched, I began to see things which I had not noticed at the beginning. Mrs. Reese was conducting recitation class with one group, two or three groups of children were discussing their lessons together and exchanging ideas, and three or four pupils were studying individually. As time went on and my insight improved, I found an orderly classroom, every pupil assigned and every pupil participating. Yes, it was noisy, but not disorderly. I left the school two or three hours later having learned a good lesson, "Things are not always what they seem to be at first glance." Three weeks later, I asked one of the school board members, who happened to live in the Horsehead area, how the people liked Mrs. Reese. He said, "We think she is the best thing that ever happened to us."

I had the experience of moving a school across the Colorado River. The Garfield School District had been holding a school at Hite, a little community near the mouth of White Canyon located in San Juan across the river and up the river about two miles. Some of our White Canyon pupils had been going to the Hite School. It became known to the Garfield superintendent and to me that only two of the pupils were Garfield students and eight of them were San Juan students. The Garfield superintendent wanted San Juan to take over the operation of the school because it was so remote from his headquarters and most of the pupils were from our district. It was not feasible for us to operate a school in another district, so we decided to move the school to the little community of White Canyon. The White Canyon community had a one-room lumber building which the people used as a community center, and we received permission to use it for the school year. I made arrangements with one of the board members to use his truck; and he and I, along with our wives, proceeded to travel the long, twisting, and dangerous road to White Canyon, a distance of over ninety miles. We drove to the Hite Ferry, ferried the truck across the Colorado River, and proceeded to the Hite school. We loaded the school desks, equipment, and available books and supplies, then proceeded back to the ferry and across the river. It was a little scary, but we made it without any trouble. We set up the classroom in the White Canyon building and got one of the local ladies, Janet Blake, to teach the school. It was an interesting year for the two Hite children who crossed the waters of the Colorado River in a motor boat twice a day, with their father.

Most teachers are dedicated and willing to give their best and then some more for their pupils. I was looking for a teacher for our West Summit Point school. I heard about a woman in Colorado on a dry farm, who was a good teacher. I found out where the farm was and went to see her. She could not take the school, but she had an eighteen-year-old daughter who had just graduated from high school. She wanted to go to college, but money was short and her mother said she might take the school. I talked with her and we decided to give it a trial. I visited her two or three times during the fall and early winter. She lived in a little one-room shack just back of the schoolhouse. There was no electricity, no water except what she pumped by hand out of a well. Her shack was heated by an old kitchen coal and wood range. Her furniture consisted of a bunk bed and a chair and table. The schoolhouse was a one-room frame building heated with a pot-bellied stove. There was one door in the building, a wooden floor, and four or five windows on the south side which were the only source of light. She was her own janitor and had to build the fire each morning and keep it going during the day. She carried her own coal and wood and swept her own floors. The conditions were primitive. And her closest neighbor was at least a mile away. I visited her several times during the fall and early winter. Each time, she seemed to be bright, cheerful, and happy and the children seemed to be doing well. Christmas time came and she went home to spend Christmas with her family. A day or two before school was to start, the first of January, there was a heavy snow storm. The storm blocked the road to Summit Point with ten to fourteen inches of snow. A less dedicated person would have waited a week or so until the roads were cleared. This young lady, however, took the attitude that if the school calendar said the schools were to open Monday, January 2, then her school would open on Monday, January 2. The day before school was to open, her parents took her to the Summit Point road turn-off, and she proceeded to walk to the Summit Point School through twelve inches of snow, a distance of fourteen miles. She was exhausted when she reached the school, but her school opened on time. At the end of the week, she developed a serious case of pneumonia brought on by her exposure and exhaustion and had to be taken to the Cortez hospital. Normally the school would have closed, but not this one. Her mother went to the school and taught until the girl was able to return. I learned then where and how the young girl had developed her great sense of responsibility, dependability, and dedication.

Consolidation was difficult because of bad roads and long distances. When a school was established in an area, the people felt more of a community spirit; and to take away their school, in their minds, would destroy the community. In time roads were improved. In 1945 I talked with the people of the little community of Ucolo about closing their school and busing their children to Monticello where they could have better schooling. Their reaction was decidedly negative because of danger to their children, long days for their children, including bus riding time, and the breaking up of the community when the school was gone. I told them that this was only a suggestion and that we would not close the school without their consent. However, I pointed out, that it would continue to be very difficult to obtain a good teacher for Ucolo, and the time might come when no teacher was available. On the other hand, the children could be assured of good schooling in the Monticello schools. I told them that according to their decision, we would continue to operate the school to the best of our ability. During this meeting, I remembered what David Gourley, the assistant superintendent of schools for the state of Utah, had told me soon after I accepted the position of superintendent of schools for San Juan School District. He said, "Superintendent, you will find many things that need to be done and many things that need to be changed. Take your time. Don't rush into anything involving changes before the people are ready. It is much easier when the people are ready to move with you."

Roads were improved and school busing became safer, so in 1947 I requested that the school board allow me to order two school buses. The consent was given and the buses ordered. At our August school board meeting, a delegation from the Ucolo area came to meet with the board. I did not know what their problem was, so I was surprised when they presented a petition, signed by all the parents of the area, requesting that the school board send a bus to Ucolo to bus their children to Monticello for the coming school year. And so the San Juan School District entered into the realm of school busing service, not by coercion of the people, not by persuasion of the people, but by the request of the people. As roads improved and people found that there were advantages to school busing, more buses were added, more of the one-room schools were closed and consolidation moved along smoothly.

One-room schools were needed in our school district before traveling became easy. The conditions under which the children went to school were meager and primitive. Supplies

Footbridge across the San Juan River used by Navajo children to reach school buses, 1973. Photograph by Ken Hochfeld, USHS Collections.

and books were limited, and too often teachers were untrained. However, the product of these schools, the pupils, was usually good. I am personally acquainted with community leaders, successful businessmen, professional men and women, who got their start in our one-room schools. These kinds of schools, for the most part, are no longer needed, but they served their patrons well during their time.

Another important story is that of education for the Indian children residing in San Juan. By treaty, made when the Indians were placed on the reservations, the U.S. Government was to take the responsibility of educating the Indian children living on the reservations. The government has not done a very good job of living up to the treaty. Some day schools and some dormitory schools were established, but not nearly enough. Only a small part of the children were being reached. One little two-room dormitory school was established in San Juan County at the Aneth Trading Post. This school could accommodate a maximum of forty pupils. There were several hundred other Indian children on the reservation who had no access to any school. The public school officials did not feel that it was their responsibility and, for the most part, did nothing for these children. Some of the Indian families gradually migrated from the reservation to other parts of our county, principally in the Blanding and Bluff areas. No effort was made to keep these children out of school; at the same time no effort was made to get them in school. The Indian parents often moved from place to place and did not see the need of their children attending school. During the 1930s, an effort was made to make it possible for the children of the families of the Ute Tribe to go to school in Blanding. The families were on the move most of the time so the government provided a dormitory for the children, and the school officials accepted the children in the schools. This plan was carried on for two or three years and provided for twenty or thirty children. It was not successful and the program was abandoned. The dormitory was expensive, the Ute children did not get along very well in school, they kept running away and were truant from school, and the parents did not cooperate. However, those children who attended school learned to speak English and have been an aid in teaching their children and urging them to go to school.

The real breakthrough for the education of the Indian children did not come until the 1950s. Albert R. Lyman, a true champion for Indian education, came to me several times and wanted me to push for a dormitory in Blanding to house Indian children where they could be kept clean, properly fed, and cared for. They would then attend the Blanding schools. I did not agree with this plan. My opinion was that children are much better off living with their parents. They needed the parental influence and love which they could not get in a dormitory. Also, I would hear talk among people of the community that they did not want the Indian children in their schools. They felt that the Indian children would cause discipline, scholarship, and pupil morale to deteriorate. I recalled what David Gourley had told me about not making changes until the people were ready.

In the late 1950s Albert R. Lyman, his wife, and a few other interested Blanding citizens, built a two-room schoolhouse on the west rim of Westwater Canyon. There were twelve or fifteen Indian camps within two or three miles of the schoolhouse. Mr. Lyman and his wife proceeded to open and conduct a school for the Indian children of that area. They had fair success with their project but because of their age it was quite hard for them to get to the school so they got two or three Blanding men to move the building to Blanding in the northwest part of town. Lyman and his wife conducted the school in the new location for another year with an enrollment of about fifteen pupils and an average daily attendance of about eight. At the end of that school year, George Hurst, president of the school board, and I thought that the school should be taken over by the school district and operated as one of our schools. The rest of the board members agreed. We operated this school for two or three years as an Indian school, and then I suggested to the board that we close this school and integrate the pupils into our regular school grades. It was agreeable with the board members, and so we made the change with little opposition.

About this time, St. Chrisopher's Mission, near Bluff, was conducting a one-room school for the Indian children in the immediate area of the Mission. With the approval of the Mission, we incorporated that school into our system, operated it for two or three years, then took the children to Bluff to our regular school.

Financially we were in good shape. We could take on these extra responsibilities without difficulty. Within a few years of the integration of these two Indian schools with our regular schools, school busing was accepted by our people as a way of life. We established bus routes wherever there were children to come to school, provided roads were available and in fair to good condition. We built a new school building for elementary students at Montezuma Creek, our first venture with buildings on the reservation, and bused the high school students to Blanding. We sent buses to Mexican Hat and Monument Valley to bring children to school. The San Juan School District was finally involved in the education of all school age children who lived in the district. This took many years but was finally accomplished with very little opposition from our people. When I left office, the school district still had two problems to solve for the benefit and convenience of the Indian people and the education of their children. High school students in the Montezuma Creek area rode the bus forty to fifty miles each way, and the Monument Valley high school students rode as many as seventy miles one way. These children would leave home before daylight and get home after dark, a high price to pay for their education. Since I retired, the district has constructed White Horse High School at Montezuma Creek and is in the process of building a combination elementary and high school in Monument Valley. This should go a long way toward shortening the long bus trips, because every child will have a school not too far away from home.

I enjoyed my twenty four years as administrative superintendent of San Juan School District and the opportunity to contribute my efforts and my philosophy and to see the amazing growth and development of education in San Juan.